*Desis Divided*

# Desis Divided

*The Political Lives of South Asian Americans*

Sangay K. Mishra

*University of Minnesota Press*
*Minneapolis*
*London*

Published by the University of Minnesota Press
111 Third Avenue South, Suite 290
Minneapolis, MN 55401-2520
http://www.upress.umn.edu

Library of Congress Cataloging-in-Publication Data

Mishra, Sangay K., author.
    Desis divided : the political lives of South Asian Americans / Sangay K. Mishra.
    Includes bibliographical references and index.
    ISBN 978-0-8166-8115-0 (hc)—ISBN 978-0-8166-8116-7 (pb)
    1. South Asian Americans—Politics and government. 2. South Asian Americans—Cultural assimilation. 3. South Asian Americans—Ethnic identity. 4. Transnationalism—Political aspects—United States. 5. United States—Emigration and immigration—Political aspects. 6. South Asia—Emigration and immigration—Political aspects. I. Title.
    E184.S69M57 2015
    305.8914'073—dc23                     2015019113

Printed in the United States of America on acid-free paper

The University of Minnesota is an equal-opportunity educator and employer.

21 20 19 18 17 16     10 9 8 7 6 5 4 3 2 1

# Contents

# Abbreviations

| | |
|---|---|
| AABEA | American Association of Bangladeshi Engineers and Architects |
| AAHOA | Asian American Hotel Owners Association |
| AALDEF | Asian American Legal Defense and Educational Fund |
| AAPI | American Association of Physicians of Indian Origin |
| AFMI | American Federation of Muslims of Indian Origin |
| AHAD | American Hindus against Defamation |
| AIA | Associations of Indians in America |
| AIANA | Association for Indian Americans of North America |
| AIPAC | American Israel Public Affairs Committee |
| AOPP | Association of Pakistani Professionals |
| APPNA | Association of Physicians of Pakistani Descent of North America |
| APSENA | Association of Pakistani Scientists and Engineers of North America |
| AWACKS | Airborne Early Warning Surveillance Systems |
| BJP | Bharatiya Janata Party |
| BPO | Business Processing Outsourcing |
| CAAV | Coalition Against Anti-Asian Violence |
| CAG | Coalition Against Genocide |
| CAIR | Council on American-Islamic Relations |
| COPAA | Council of Pakistani American Affairs |
| COPO | Council of Peoples Organization |
| CSFH | Campaign to Stop Funding Hate |
| DOJ | Department of Justice |
| DRUM | Desis Rising Up and Moving |
| DWC | Domestic Workers Committee |
| DWU | Domestic Workers United |
| FHA | Federation of Hindu Associations |
| FIACONA | Federation of Indian American Christian Organizations of North America |

| | |
|---|---|
| FOBANA | Federation of Bangladeshi Associations in North America |
| FOIL | Forum of Indian Leftists and Forum for Inqalabi Leftists |
| HAF | Hindu American Foundation |
| HAPAC | Hindu American Political Action Committee |
| HLC | High Level Committee |
| HSC | Hindu Students Council |
| HSS | Hindu Swayamsewak Sangh |
| IAFPE | Indian American Forum for Political Education |
| IAMC | Indian American Muslim Council |
| IASLC | Indian American Security Leadership Council |
| ICE | Immigration and Customs Enforcement |
| IDRF | India Development and Relief Fund |
| INA | Immigration and Nationality Act |
| IRCA | Immigration Reform and Control Act |
| IT | Information Technology |
| IWW | Industrial Workers of the World |
| LATWA | Los Angeles Taxi Workers Association |
| LAX | Los Angeles International Airport |
| LDC | Lease Drivers Coalition |
| MPAC | Muslim Public Affairs Council |
| NAAS | National Asian American Survey |
| NCPA | National Council of Pakistani Americans |
| NCSAO | National Coalition of South Asian Organizations |
| NELP | National Employment Labor Project |
| NFIA | National Federation of Indian Americans |
| NPT | Nuclear Nonproliferation Treaty |
| NRI | Non-Resident Indian |
| NSEERS | National Security Entry-Exit Registration System |
| NYCWU | New York Construction Workers United |
| NYPD | New York City Police Department |
| NYTWA | New York Taxi Workers Alliance |
| OCI | Overseas Citizen of India |
| PAKPAC | Pakistani American Public Affairs Committee |
| PBD | Pravasi Bharatiya Divas |
| PCHA | Pacific Coast Hindi Association |
| PENTTBOM | Pentagon Twin Tower Bombing Investigation |
| PIO | Person of Indian Origin |

| | |
|---|---|
| PNAAPS | Pilot Study of the National Asian American Political Survey |
| ROC | Restaurant Opportunities Centers United |
| RSS | Rashtriya Swayamsevak Sangh |
| SAALT | South Asian Americans Leading Together |
| SAAVY | South Asian American Voting Youth |
| SABA | South Asian Bar Association |
| SAJA | South Asian Journalists Association |
| SALDEF | Sikh American Legal Defense and Education Fund |
| SALGA | South Asian Lesbian and Gay Association |
| SAN | South Asian Network |
| SAPHA | South Asian Public Health Association |
| SAYA | South Asian Youth Association |
| TANA | Telugu Association of North America |
| TIE | The Indus Entrepreneurs |
| USCIRF | United States Commission on International Religious Freedom |
| USINPAC | U.S.–India Political Action Committee |
| VHP | Vishwa Hindu Parishad |
| VHPA | Vishwa Hindu Parishad of America |

# Situating Desis in U.S. Ethnoracial Politics

On September 27, 2014, the iconic Madison Square Garden in New York City—the home of the New York Knicks and New York Rangers—was occupied by an estimated crowd of 18,000 Indian Americans who were excitedly awaiting the newly elected prime minister of India, Narendra Bhai Modi, to arrive. Among the crowd were Democratic senators from New Jersey, Bob Menendez and Cory Booker; the senior Democratic senator from New York, Chuck Schumer; the Democratic senator from Indiana, Joe Donnelly; the Indian American Republican governor of South Carolina, Nikki Haley; and dozens of members of Congress from both sides of the aisle. The names of these elected officials were called out as they walked up to the stage one after the other to wave at the crowd. They were courting both their constituents and possible financial supporters even as they were developing connections with the new political establishment in India. With these elected officials on the stage, the scene was set for Modi, who walked into the arena to the frantic chant of "Modi," "Modi," to deliver a rousing speech in Hindi from a revolving stage. Narendra Modi's recent election as prime minister of India led to the rescinding of his travel ban to the United States, which had been imposed by the State Department in 2005 because of his alleged role in large-scale violence against Muslims as the chief minister of Gujarat (a province in western India). A crowd of several hundred Indian Americans was protesting outside the venue, pointing to his role in the violence against Muslims and Christians in India. Indian television channels were beaming live all across India Modi's rousing reception at Madison Square Garden, and this was being lapped up by people back home. The event in New York City was reflective of the growing political visibility of Indian Americans in the United States that brought a number of prominent U.S. elected officials to what appeared like a Modi victory rally. This increasing importance of Indian Americans was most astutely grasped by Narendra Modi, who used this event to successfully enhance his own popularity in

India as well as the United States. The event thereby embodied the positionality of Indian Americans as a powerful transnational force wielding influence in both countries, even as one could glimpse in it evidence of political differences between Indian Americans—between those inside and outside the Madison Square Garden.

Another 2014 event, considered to be an important milestone for the Indian American community, was the opening of an exhibition on Indian Americans at the Smithsonian Institution in Washington, D.C. The early impetus for the exhibition is attributed to president Bill Clinton's Executive Order 13125, signed in 1999, creating the White House Initiative on Asian Americans and Pacific Islanders, which included the Smithsonian in its broad mandate "to improve the quality of life of Asian Americans . . . through increased participation in Federal programs" (Srinivasan 2014). The exhibition, titled "Beyond Bollywood: Indian Americans Shape the Nation," was an explicit attempt to capture the multifaceted and complex history of Indian Americans and underline their contributions to the United States. Displaying diverse stories of members of the Indian American community—from railroad and farm workers in the nineteenth and twentieth centuries who were denied the right to citizenship to spelling bee champions, H-1B visa professionals, taxi drivers, and Silicon Valley entrepreneurs in the contemporary period—the exhibition was an attempt to create a narrative of Indian American contributions by going beyond stereotypes and clichés. Even as the exhibition won praise for celebrating the place of the Indian American community within the larger American society, it also evoked criticism that other South Asian communities—Pakistani, Bangladeshi, Sri Lankan, and others—were made invisible in its storytelling (Kalita 2014).

Some wondered whether an exhibition about Desi Americans or South Asian Americans that could bring their shared culture, languages, and racial experiences in the United States together was even possible. This exhibit was identified as a parochial and hegemonic approach by an Indian American community that does not want to be inclusive and tends to marginalize the experiences of other South Asian communities. Critics also drew attention to internal fissures, arguing that LGBT experiences as well as the issue of caste within the Indian American community were not addressed adequately (Lal 2014). The exhibition has undoubtedly created a complex story of Indian Americans, but the process of curating

Indian American identity and subsequent reactions to the exhibition underline the fact that such visibility may privilege an identity that is in reality more complex and contested both in terms of larger shared histories of South Asians as well as the cleavages within the community. This book engages precisely with these cleavages and contestations to analyze the political mobilization and participation patterns that have emerged from the community, both in the context of their attempts for inclusion in U.S. political structures as well as their continued engagement with the home countries. Moreover, *Desis Divided* situates the story of South Asian American political incorporation in the larger history of immigrant and minority political inclusion in the United States.

## South Asian Americans and the New Waves of Immigration

Early waves of migration to the United States, dominated primarily by European immigrants, gave way to migrants from Asia, Latin America, Africa, and the Caribbean, and their numbers increased sharply after a less restrictive immigration system was introduced in 1965. These waves have shaped the scholarship on immigrant political inclusion and adaptation and enhanced our understanding of the ways in which immigrant communities entered the U.S. political process and organized themselves to gain representation and influence.

The early corpus of scholarship on political inclusion of immigrants was largely focused on European immigrants, the overwhelming majority of whom joined the lower rungs of the socioeconomic ladder and worked their way up, leading to some important insights into the political and social inclusion of immigrant communities. A subsequent focus on Latino, Asian, African, and Caribbean groups emphasized the centrality of racial hierarchy in understanding immigrant political participation, making an important addition to the early scholarship on immigrant social and political inclusion. The post-1965 waves of nonwhite immigration, however, have also created communities that have significant segments of highly educated and skilled professionals and successful entrepreneurs alongside low-income immigrants and refugees. Because of their middle-class and affluent socioeconomic profiles, combined with nonwhite racial status, these groups do not completely fit the analytical frameworks that have been used to understand the political inclusion of many of the earlier immigrant communities. The history of these new immigrants underlines the need for a distinct theoretical framework that addresses the specificities of these communities. South Asian immigrants, along with a number of other Asian American communities, provide a perfect case for such an analysis, which would add an important layer to the existing scholarship on immigrant political adaptation. One of the largest Asian American groups, with a highly diverse socioeconomic profile, South Asian Americans have acquired importance not only due to their presence in different walks of U.S. society but also because of their fast growth. Since 2013 India has become the second largest source of immigrants to the United States after China, followed by Mexico. Scholars of migration are anticipating a long-term transition in the demographics of U.S. immigration (Chishti and Hipsman 2015). Given their rapid growth, an analysis of South Asian American political mobilization and inclusion, both in the context of U.S. politics as well as the transnational sphere, thus provides important insights into immigrant political incorporation that challenge some long-held assumptions.

South Asian Americans have traditionally not been too visible in the sphere of U.S. politics, despite being a group with a significant number of successful professionals and entrepreneurs having relatively high levels of social and economic capital. However, the successful elections of two U.S. governors of Indian American origin—Bobby Jindal of Louisiana and Nikki Haley of South Carolina in 2007 and 2010, respectively—turned a spotlight on South Asian American communities and their involvement with U.S. politics. The electoral successes of these two politicians of Indian American descent has triggered conversations on how deftly political aspirants from South Asian communities are negotiating the terrain of American politics. A political mobilization and aspiration of a completely different kind is revealed by the emergence of Bhairavi Desai, a woman labor leader of Indian descent, who leads the New York Taxi Workers Alliance. The group, composed of a large number of South Asian taxi drivers, has become one of the most important unions among immigrant labor and has provided an impetus for organizing taxi drivers across the nation.

Still another instance is the election of Kshama Sawant, an immigrant from India who came to the United States for graduate school, to the Seattle City Council as a Socialist candidate in 2013, following her involvement with the Occupy movement. Furthermore, the victory of Pramila Jaypal, an immigrant rights and racial justice activist, for a State Senate seat in 2014 from the Seattle area amplifies the progressive voices in mainstream politics that have emerged from the community. South Asian communities have also witnessed political interventions by groups such as South Asian Americans Leading Together (SAALT), Sikh American Legal Defense Fund (SALDEF), Sikh Coalition, and the Council of American Islamic Relations (CAIR), among others, to counter increased incidents of racial targeting and hostility against South Asians in the post-9/11 period. These disparate examples of South Asians' involvement in the U.S. political sphere represent the complex political contours of an emergent and increasingly visible community and underline the challenges of studying the political participation, inclusion, and representation of a relatively understudied group.

The complexity of analyzing the political inclusion of a group such as South Asians is reflected in the elections of Nikki Haley and Bobby Jindal and their link to South Asian American ethnic politics. Haley and Jindal, both conservative Republican governors, were born and brought up in the United States in Sikh and Hindu families, respectively, and converted to Christianity at different points in their lives. The political trajectories of these two Indian American politicians are shaped by conservative Republican ideologies that dominate much of the Southern states from where they have been elected. Their political strategies have been predicated on appealing to conservative white Christian voters, and their electoral campaigns have deliberately deemphasized racial and religious difference by foregrounding their Christian religious faith. Scholars and analysts have termed this approach a "deracialized" strategy—an approach that avoids bringing up racial issues in campaigns to have a wider appeal. The larger analysis of South Asian American political lives undertaken in this book contextualizes such instances of "political successes" and "breakthroughs" for South Asian candidates in the electoral arena and what they mean for South Asian American political inclusion. In particular, the book situates these and similar examples in the broader political incorporation trajectory of South Asians, a group that has voted overwhelmingly Democratic in the recent years. In fact, the percentage of South Asians voting for the Democratic Party in recent elections has been highest among all Asian American groups (Wong et al. 2011).

## Desis: 7-Elevens, Taxis, and Microsoft

South Asians, also known as *Desis*, are one of the fastest growing segments of the minority population in the United States, and they constitute one of the largest groups of the Asian American population.[1] *Desi* is a colloquial term in multiple South Asian languages that most likely originated from the word *Desh*, which means "country," or "homeland." The term is increasingly being used by diasporic South Asians to describe people with a common ancestry in South Asia, and has a special appeal among different South Asian communities because it goes beyond national identities such as Indian, Pakistani, and Bangladeshi.

While the history of South Asians in the United States goes back to the migration of peasants, peddlers, and seamen in the late nineteenth and early twentieth centuries, it was the post-1965 phase of immigration from the region that radically changed the nature of the community. Post-1965 immigrants include highly skilled professionals such as physicians, engineers, Silicon Valley entrepreneurs, scientists, and software professionals employed in multinational corporations such as Microsoft, Google, Intel, and Facebook. Given the changing socioeconomic profile of the community, a racialized framework of the "model" minority, which promoted the discourse of an underclass "problem" minority (African Americans) created by a culture of deviance and dependence in contrast to hard-working and successful minorities (Asian Americans), became a widely deployed way to explain the relative success of South Asian immigrants (Prashad 2000; Das Gupta 2006).

Even as these affluent South Asian Americans began to define the public image of the community, different modes of migration, such as the family reunification provision, diversity visa, agricultural worker provision, refugee visa, as well as undocumented migration, have brought working-class and low-income segments of South Asians to the United States in significant numbers. The middle-class and affluent segments of the community thus exist alongside a sizable number of working-class and low-income people. The socioeconomic diversity within the community has only intensified in recent years, with the continuing inflow of working-class populations from different South Asian countries (Prashad 1998; Mathew 2005; Das Gupta 2006). Indian, Pakistani, Bangladeshi, Nepalese, Sri Lankan, Bhutanese, and other South Asian immigrants have thus been joining the ranks of taxi drivers, restaurant and construction workers, gas station attendants, retail workers employed in stores such as 7-Eleven and Dunkin' Donuts, street vendors, and other working-class occupations. For instance, approximately 20 percent of cab drivers in New York City are South Asians, and a growing number of construction workers and street vendors come from this community.[2] The fast-changing nature of South Asian communities is reflected in the emergence of varied kinds of organizations within the community, an issue that will be discussed at length in chapter 4.

The internal differentiations among South Asians along the lines of education, income, and occupation are accompanied by religious, linguistic, caste, gender, sexuality, and country-of-origin-based differences. The successive waves of South Asian immigration have produced an extremely diverse community, and immigrants from different backgrounds with varied resources have adapted and settled in different strata of American society. For every engineer, doctor, and software professional in the community who most likely joins the middle or upper class, there are domestic workers, gas station attendants, taxi drivers, and construction workers who negotiate the social and economic realities of the United States very differently. The nation of origin has also shaped the ethnic and professional associations created by South Asian Americans and the ways in which they negotiate their identity and place in U.S. society. Identity formation along the lines of nation of origin—India, Pakistan, and Bangladesh, among others—is an important part of how immigrants define themselves, and the broader panethnic South Asian identity is in constant negotiation with these other identities, which are more well established. South Asians also belong to diverse religious faiths, including Hinduism, Islam, Sikhism, Christianity, Buddhism, Zorastrianism, and Jainism, among others. In fact, religious affiliations have played an increasingly important role in community formation, and they have shaped the ways in which South Asians have identified and mobilized themselves in the United States as well as engaged with the political process in their home countries. Religious identities such as Hinduism, Islam, Sikhism, and Christianity bring different challenges in terms of acceptance, recognition, racialization, adaptation, and group mobilization. Being a Muslim or Sikh American is a distinct experience in the United States today in comparison to being a Hindu American. For instance, the racialization of South Asians, Arabs, and Muslims in the post-9/11 period, discussed in chapter 3, foregrounded the intersection of race, religion, and nation of origin in constructing identities that were rendered "suspicious."

The South Asian communities today differ widely from those of the early twentieth century, when they were predominantly male. Women now constitute a sizable part of the South Asian American community. Foreign-born South Asian women have come to the United States in different capacities as students, professionals, domestic workers, and as dependents on male earners. South Asian women have negotiated their roles in a male-dominated community while facing the racial and sexual hierarchies of U.S. society as well as restrictions imposed by the immigration laws.[3] In addition, the emergence of queer South Asian American organizations has brought the issue of sexuality to the fore and underlined the silences and tensions within the community over the question of sexuality (Das Gupta 2006). The issue of caste discrimination has also acquired importance in South Asian communities with the recent increase in the number of immigrants who belong to oppressed castes or who were traditionally considered untouchable in the caste system.

Given such diversity, existing frameworks for studying minority political mobilization and incorporation, particularly the ones that have emerged from the scholarship on ethnic and racial minorities in the United States, do not provide adequate conceptual tools to understand the political socialization, mobilization, and inclusion of groups such as South Asian. The dominant theories privilege a group mobilization approach that emphasizes a unifying racial or ethnic identity that could appeal to all segments of the group. This book argues that the political mobilization and inclusion of South Asian communities in the United States is deeply tied to internal group distinctions, and the precise nature of ethnic mobilization could be better explained by foregrounding these important cleavages within the group. Furthermore, the book points to the importance of religion as a distinct category to analyze group racialization as well as mobilizations to contest racialization and gain recognition. This has important implications for analyzing groups such as South Asians, since religion has historically been an important element through which the group has been racialized.

The concept of *political incorporation,* a term that has been employed in multiple ways in the context of minority political participation scholarship, is used in this study to analyze political mobilization and inclusion of South Asian Americans. The conceptual framework of political incorporation has often been used to study a new immigrant group's entry, participation, mobilization, and representation in the political process. Broadly defined, political incorporation is a process through which new groups begin to engage with politics—through a process of defining themselves as a group and identifying common interests—and eventually achieve representation and influence in government (Browning, Marshall, and Tabb 2003; Rogers 2006; Hochschild and Mollenkopf 2009a). The scholarship on immigrant and minority political incorporation, which will be discussed at greater length in chapter 2, has been shaped primarily by two approaches that have emerged from the classic group experiences of European immigrants to the United States and of African Americans. The pluralist or assimilation model, based on the European immigrant experiences, underscores the relative openness of the political process and predicts a bumpy but complete inclusion of contemporary nonwhite immigrants in mainstream political institutions (Dahl 1961; Portes and Rumbaut 1996; Alba and Nee 1997). In contrast, the minority group or racialization model underscores the barriers to political inclusion faced by African Americans as the paradigmatic case of obstacle to minority incorporation. The model predicts that new nonwhite immigrants will also reproduce the experiences of African American political incorporation that include partial, halting, and incomplete inclusion; heavy reliance on racial or group identity; and grassroots mobilization (Hero 1992; Dawson 1994; Takaki 1998; Kim and Lee 2001; Tate 1994; Pinderhughes 1987).

These two models thus have contrasting predictions about the extent and pace of inclusion of contemporary nonwhite immigrants. However, both emphasize the central importance of a unified ethnic and/or racial mobilization for group political incorporation. In case of the minority group model, racial mobilization is an enduring feature, whereas the pluralist model considers ethnic mobilization only as temporary, until the group becomes a part of the mainstream economic and political process. Nevertheless, both agree that a unified ethnoracial mobilization is the way through which minorities initially achieve some level of political efficacy leading to a greater incorporation.[4]

South Asians are characterized, as noted earlier, by a combination of relative affluence, nonwhite status, and internal diversity along the lines of class, religion, nation of origin, gender, sexuality, and language, among others. The profile of South Asians neither matches the other racial minorities—except some Asian American groups—nor the associated expectations about their political incorporation. Given the economic and educational resources commanded by a significant segment of South Asians, there has been an expectation that they will more easily become a part of the mainstream political process and their level of political participation will be fairly high. The empirical evidence, however, presents a different picture: not only is the rate of political participation among South Asians rather low, but, like other nonwhite groups, they too encounter multiple obstacles to becoming a part of the mainstream political process. An alternative theory predicts that South Asians, because of their nonwhite status and continued experiences of racial discrimination, will mobilize and enter into the political process based primarily on a shared ethnoracial identity—Indian/Pakistani/Bangladeshi Americans or South Asian Americans—like other minority groups. This mobilization was expected to accelerate in light of the intensity of discrimination against South Asians in the post-9/11 period. However, the evidence does not find substantial support for grassroots mobilizing among South Asians to collectively challenge the growing racial hostility to the group or increased unified panethnic mobilization to influence the political arena. The findings suggest that the dominant response to racialization was along the lines of religious identity, and distinct mobilization patterns developed that reflected the exclusive ways in which different religious groups responded to the post-9/11 racial targeting.

The central question explored in this book is the nature and extent of ethnoracial mobilization leading to political incorporation of South Asian Americans and the manner in which it intersects with internal distinctions along multiple lines underscored earlier. To understand South Asian political incorporation, I propose a new framework that gives analytical prominence to internal group distinctions such as class, religion, nation of origin, language, gender, sexuality, and other differentiations while explaining group mobilization. I argue that the political representation, inclusion, and mobilization of South Asians cannot be analyzed without foregrounding the internal group distinctions that either *limit the possibilities* of a broader ethnoracial mobilization or produce one that is confined to particular segments of the community. This framework proposes to investigate ethnoracial mobilization from a perspective that is cognizant of the cleavages within the group. In each of the chapters, I trace the intricate way in which ethnoracial identity interacts with one or more kinds of internal cleavages to limit the possibilities of a broader group mobilization. Consequently, the framework emerging from the political incorporation experiences of South Asians highlights the reliance on selective elite mobilization—ethnoracial identity used to mobilize a narrow elite segment—in contrast to identity-based broader mobilization inclusive of the larger group, as suggested by the dominant models. The American Association of Physicians of Indian Origin (AAPI), Association of Physicians of Pakistani Descent of North America (APPNA), and the Indus Entrepreneurs (TIE) are examples of such organizations that are focused on mobilizing co-ethnics from a narrow stratum of the community. This approach also underlines the possibilities of cross-racial alliances and organizations that bring together people from different ethnoracial communities who are similarly situated in terms of their class and occupational status. Examples of low-income and working-class organizations such as New York Taxi Workers' Alliance (NYTWA), Restaurant Opportunities Centers (ROC) United, and Domestic Workers United (DWU) demonstrate that the nature of mobilization of low-income workers within South Asian communities is inextricably linked to their placing within these organizations that work toward producing multiracial mobilizations.

Religious identities have shaped the mobilization patterns within South Asian communities in particular ways that intersect with larger ethnoracial identity, indicating the importance of religious affiliation in producing certain mobilizations and limiting others. For instance, the mobilization patterns and organization building within the Sikh American community in recent years, speaking to specific Sikh experiences, illustrate the possible ways in which religious identity becomes an important axis of mobilization within the Indian American community. Moreover, the post-9/11 period witnessed how religious identities enabled as well as disabled broader South Asian mobilization against racial targeting. The new framework thereby suggests the limits of a unified ethnoracial mobilization approach among immigrant and minority groups in American politics and demonstrates the particular ways in which such mobilizations are specific to particular segments of the group without necessarily creating grounds for a broader group mobilization. This framework, however, does not completely preclude the possibilities of particular situations and junctures when a broader ethnoracial mobilization unifying the larger segments of the group can be achieved. The framework proposed here does not seek to replace the ethnoracial category as an important axis for mobilization, it rather suggests that ethnoracial mobilization is deeply contingent on different internal distinctions, and a closer analysis reveals the specificities of such mobilizations. The larger goal of this study is to reconsider ethnoracial solidarity as *the* most important means to overcome the social and political marginalization of immigrant and minority communities in U.S. politics. *Desis Divided* suggests that the differentiated nature of ethnoracial mobilizing, contingent on internal cleavages, makes the task of group social and political incorporation more challenging and demands more situated and specific analysis of inclusion and exclusion that different segments of South Asian Americans encounter.

## Methodology and Sites of Study

The book uses a predominantly qualitative approach, alongside some quantitative analysis, to understand South Asian American political incorporation. The findings rest on sixty in-depth interviews conducted with "key informants" and regular community members in the South Asian American community, including leaders and activists of Indian, Pakistani, and Bangladeshi descent in the Los Angeles and New York metropolitan areas. The interviews took place between March 2006 and April 2007, with some follow-up interviews in 2010. Approximately half of the interviewees were activists associated with South Asian organizations, and the others were regular community members. The rationale behind dividing the sample between activists and the regular members was to understand the perspective of both those who were involved in organizing and those who responded on the basis of their own individual experiences. The sample of community activists was chosen from a comprehensive list of South Asian organizations, created with the assistance of these groups, in the New York and Los Angeles area. While drawing the sample of activist/leaders, attention was paid to ensure that it represented different segments of the South Asian population in terms of nation of origin, religion, profession, class, gender, and generation. The sample of regular community members was obtained using the snowball method because of the difficulties of using random sampling in a smaller and dispersed population. Despite using the snowball method, the selection process was designed to take into account educational, class, gender, and generational diversity within the community.

Each interview lasted between forty-five and ninety minutes, and the interview questionnaire consisted of a range of questions related to the broader issues concerning political participation of South Asians in U.S. politics. A significant part of the interview was focused on racial discrimination faced by South Asians, with a special emphasis on the post-9/11 period. In addition, questions related to transnational engagements formed an important part of the questionnaire.

The qualitative data are supplemented with national data from quantitative surveys and the U.S. Census. The quantitative component of the book relies on the data from the 2000–2001 Pilot Study of the National Asian American Political Survey (PNAAPS) and the 2008 National Asian American Survey (NAAS). These two surveys provide more general data on political participation patterns of South Asians in the United States and their transnational engagements. It is important to note that, despite the study's attempt to focus equally on Indian, Pakistani, and Bangladeshi immigrants, the analysis draws a lot more from the existing literature on Indian Americans, and hence the analysis is lopsided in favor of this group. This is partly due to the fact that Indian Americans constitute more than 80 percent of the South Asian American population, but it is also a reflection of the shortcomings of South Asian American studies in terms of not producing enough scholarship on Pakistani, Bangladeshi, and other smaller South Asian communities.

This study is not a traditional comparison between New York and Los Angeles. These two locations have instead been used as illustrations of the two most important settlement areas for South Asians, having long histories and a sizable number of community organizations. The number of Asian Indians in Los Angeles County is 77,683, and the corresponding figure for New York City is 204,410 (U.S. Census Bureau 2009–2011). The New York metropolitan area has the highest number of Indian Americans, whereas the Los Angeles metropolitan area comes after the Chicago and Washington, D.C., metropolitan areas. Both New York and Los Angeles also have a significant number of Pakistani and Bangladeshi immigrants, albeit many fewer than Indian immigrants. In fact, the New York metropolitan area has the highest numbers of Pakistani and Bangladeshi immigrants. The numbers of Pakistani and Bangladeshi immigrants in New York City are 41,945 and 44,948, respectively (U.S. Census Bureau 2009–2011). Los Angeles County has 9,775 Pakistanis and 4,001 Bangladeshis, a relatively smaller number in comparison to New York City. Community activists, however, dispute the low numbers of Pakistanis and Bangladeshis and point to the possible undercounting of these two groups since these categories are not available as choices on Census forms.

It is important to point out here that South Asians are generally dispersed, even within these two large geographical units, and there are very few cities or electoral districts with large South Asian population concentrations. The reason for this pattern of settlement lies primarily in the trajectory of South Asian immigration in the United States, as discussed earlier, which has been generally driven by professional immigrants who settled in both urban and suburban areas in a scattered manner. However, New York City has seen a greater neighborhood concentration of South Asian Americans, and there are efforts underway to support redistricting efforts in Queens that will bring South Asians in the same assembly and city council districts to enhance their electoral representation (Kramer 2011). Alluding to this demographic reality, South Asian community leaders have pointed out the important difference between South Asian immigrants and other Asian immigrants who are far more concentrated. This demographic characteristic of South Asians—the lack of population density—has important implications for their political representation and incorporation that we will explore further.

South Asians in these two locations, despite having a dispersed settlement pattern, have developed commercial areas catering specifically to the community. These sites have become important avenues for constructing, maintaining, and performing ethnic identities in cities such as Los Angeles, New York, and Chicago (Shukla 2003). Artesia in Cerritos County, Los Angeles, and Jackson Heights in Queens, New York, are prime examples of commercial areas that are major centers serving South Asian communities. These areas have not only provided commercial opportunities and services for the community, but have also helped create a sense of community. They additionally reflect the demographic shifts that the South Asian communities have experienced. For example, Jackson Heights—dominated earlier by Indian shops with a sprinkling of Pakistani and Bangladeshi establishments—has seen a surge in Bangladeshi and Nepalese populations. The increased Bangladeshi presence in New York City is now evident in the appearance of many Bangladeshi food, grocery, and other establishments in the Jackson Heights area. Similar changes are also evident in the Los Angeles area, where the Bangladeshi community won important symbolic recognition by getting a smaller part of "Korea town," which has a sizable population of Bangladeshis, named "little Bangladesh" (Abdulrahim 2010). New York City and Los Angeles have both well-settled and newly arrived Indian, Pakistani, and Bangladeshi immigrants who belong to nation-of-origin-based associations as well as broader South Asian organizations. These two locations thus provide ideal settings for studying the political participation and mobilization patterns of South Asian Americans.

## Existing Scholarship and Organization of the Book

Early scholarship on post-1965 South Asian Americans focused heavily on developing a critique of the racialized discourse of the "model minority," which was produced in the context of a community that was dominated by stories of immigrant talent and the success of its highly educated and skilled professionals (Prashad 2000; Visweswaran 1997; Bhattacharjee 1992). The subsequent turn was to analyze the politics produced by marginalized segments of the community that questioned the stories of success and the model minority myth (Das Gupta 2006; Mathew 2005; Varghese 2006). These two distinct yet related streams of scholarship on South Asians are reflective of the growing schisms and differing realities. However, there has not been any attempt to systematically analyze how these schisms and diversity shape political mobilization patterns of South Asian Americans. In other words, how does a common identity of Indian/Pakistani/Bangladeshi American or South Asian American gloss over or negotiate the aspirations and mobilizations of specific socioeconomic groups that have distinct aspirations despite sharing a broader ethnic identity? The received wisdom in political science, sociology, and ethnic studies has been that a unified ethnoracial mobilization is an important prerequisite for minority and immigrant political empowerment and incorporation. *Desis Divided*, however, *foregrounds* the internal distinctions within the South Asian American community to understand the trajectory of their political incorporation in the United States, proposing a framework that gives centrality to the cleavages within the community that shape and limit a unified ethnoracial mobilization.

In chapter 1, I recount the social and political history of South Asians in the United States and explore their history of racial exclusion, political activism, and transnationalism in the early twentieth century. I analyze the significant changes in immigration patterns of the groups after the 1965 immigration reforms that led to a dramatic transformation of their socioeconomic profile. The chapter traces the formation of Indian, Pakistani, and Bangladeshi communities by identifying the internal differentiations within these groups. I conclude by situating South Asians in the larger context of the major Asian American immigrant communities to underscore some common trajectories and suggest that the framework developed in this book in the context of South Asians is potentially relevant for other Asian American groups as well.

In chapter 2, I discuss theories of minority and immigrant political incorporation, with a focus on new immigrant groups. The chapter begins by discussing the genealogy of the concept of political incorporation to identify a broad working framework that is equally attentive to the process as well as the outcome of incorporation. The discussion of the two dominant theories of political incorporation—the pluralist and minority group theories—underlines the broad theoretical import of these models for new immigrant groups and notes that both emphasize the centrality of ethnoracial identity-based mobilization for political incorporation. The chapter further analyzes theories emerging from scholarship on Latino, Caribbean, and Asian American groups, which have added important insights to the dominant theories. The chapter concludes by underlining the need for interrogating a political incorporation framework based on the notion of a unified ethnoracial mobilization.

In chapter 3, I use the case of racial targeting of South Asians in the post-9/11 period and their reactions to the targeting to illustrate the importance of internal distinctions such as religion in shaping the fractured political response to intensified discrimination. In the days and months following September 11, 2001, South Asians in the United States were lumped together and racialized as threatening outsiders. The lumping together of all South Asians existed alongside a more differentiated targeting based on particular religious identities such as Hindu, Muslim, and Sikh. This chapter argues that religious identity was not only an important axis for racialization of South Asians but it also worked to reinforce the internal boundaries within the community. Religious identity not only shaped and calibrated racial targeting but also framed the responses of South Asian groups and worked against broader panethnic solidarity in opposition to racial hostility.

In chapter 4, I analyze the dominant modes of political mobilization among South Asian Americans to interrogate the notion of political incorporation based on a unified ethnoracial identity. The political incorporation of South Asians is taking place in an institutional context that is characterized by the decline of political parties, where political parties and other institutions have made little attempt to bring contemporary nonwhite immigrants into the political process. The incorporation process is also unfolding in *the context of the demographic profile of a group defined by a lack of significant population concentration*. The lack of mobilization and inclusion of South Asians in the political process, however, simultaneously coexists with selective elite mobilization within the community that results in political incorporation being largely driven by community elites. This chapter analyzes three major modes of political engagement that rely on selective elite mobilization: (1) the trend of descriptive representation from white majority districts, (2) the prominence of campaign fund-raising as a strategy for gaining political power, and (3) the prominence of lobbying related to home country concerns. All three forms of engagement have led to the mobilization of a very narrow segment, leaving out the broader community from the political process, and in complete contrast to the kinds of ethnoracial mobilization predicted by the dominant models. Finally, the chapter contrasts the elite mobilization strategy with the newly emerging labor and low-income South Asian organizing that is producing a distinct form of mobilization.

Chapters 5 and 6 focus on the role of transnational political engagements of South Asians vis-à-vis their inclusion in U.S. politics. In chapter 5, I present evidence from quantitative and qualitative data to argue that higher levels of South Asian engagement with issues concerning home countries do not lead to depressed political participation in U.S. politics, and I demonstrate the linkages between the two spheres of political engagement. In chapter 6, I analyze distinct examples of transnational mobilizing to illustrate multiple sites of transnational political engagement, including specific forms of economic transnationalism emerging from the professional and entrepreneurial segments of the community. Analyzing the case studies of Indian American mobilizing in favor of the U.S.–India Civil Nuclear Deal in 2006 and mobilizations within the Indian American community on the issue of Hindu nationalist politics, the chapter argues that the community uses these issues not only with the intention to intervene in home country issues but also to enhance their political efficacy as a minority group in U.S. politics. The chapter argues that transnational political engagements of the community are deeply linked to the internal cleavages that challenge the idea of a unified diaspora. The analysis of political mobilizations within the Indian American community on the issue of Hindu nationalism and religious violence in India underlines the internal cleavages along the lines of religious identity that have become more pronounced with the resurgence of *Hindutva* politics in India.

In the concluding chapter, I emphasize the analytical importance of internal group distinctions for understanding the political incorporation trajectory of a minority group. I bring together the elements of a new framework of political incorporation that moves beyond the centrality of ethnoracial mobilization. The chapter puts forward a framework that analyzes the political mobilization trajectory of a group by underlining the dynamic interaction of internal distinctions such as class, religion, and nation of origin with selective and strategic uses of ethnoracial identity. Synthesizing the experiences of South Asian American political incorporation, the chapter suggests that the framework emphasizing internal distinctions is not only relevant for other Asian American groups that are similarly situated, but for African Americans, Latinos, Arab Americans, and others. Thus, I suggest ways in which the South Asian American experience might prove instructive to understanding the experiences of other groups, as well as the ways in which some aspects of their political incorporation may be considered fairly unique.

# 1

## South Asian Americans and Immigration Regimes

*Exclusion, Ghadar Rebellion, and Silicon Valley*

In this chapter, I trace the history of highly diverse South Asian American communities in the United States to underline the different phases of their formation as shaped by changes in immigration policies. I identify the specific ways in which the development of Indian, Pakistani, and Bangladeshi American communities has overlapped and diverged. The chapter engages with both the early twentieth-century and post-1965 phases of immigration to identify the creation of internally differentiated South Asian communities—the existence of which has often been ignored to foreground a sense of cohesive ethnic, or panethnic, unity. Furthermore, I situate South Asian communities in the larger context of the history of other major Asian American groups to locate shared immigration histories and settlement patterns as well as specificities of some of these communities. I show that the study of South Asian American political incorporation has important implications, not only for South Asians, but for other Asian American groups as well.

South Asian American community formation in the United States has been deeply tied to the immigration regimes that determined who was allowed to immigrate, how, and when. Asian American scholar Bill Ong Hing (1993), analyzing the relationship between Asian Americans and immigration policy regimes, argues that these communities are largely a creation of the U.S. immigration system. The social and economic lives of Asian Americans—education, profession, economic status, settlement pattern, and gender distribution—have been deeply influenced by the immigration regimes that have unfolded over the last several decades. South Asian communities, an example of this larger phenomenon, have also been produced by immigration regimes that have either enabled or disabled the influx of particular kinds of immigrants over a history spanning more than a hundred years starting at the turn of the twentieth century. The early history of South Asian immigration to the United States, similar to that of other Asian American groups, has been defined primarily by the migration of peasants and laborers who faced exclusion, racial hostility, and denial of citizenship. This history, marked by resilience on the part of South Asians in the face of all odds, produced mobilizations to contest racism in the United States and challenge colonialism in the home country. Post-1965 South Asian immigration, however, inaugurated a different phase that was initially dominated exclusively by highly educated and skilled professionals but later joined by immigrants coming from other strata of South Asian societies.

## The Tide of Turbans and Racial Exclusion

The early history of South Asians in the United States was characterized by racialized exclusion and community activism to contest racism and denial of equality, as well as the building of transnational alliances to overthrow British colonial rule in India. Historical records show that more than six thousand Indian immigrants, primarily peasants from British India's Punjab province and a small group of students, came to the western United States between 1899 and 1913 (Jensen 1988, 170–71; Takaki 1998, 294).[1] A large majority of these early migrants were Sikh peasants from the Doab region of Punjab along with Muslims and Hindus from other parts of India. A significant number of them were veterans of British colonial military forces who had traveled around the world and had no intention of going back to their small landholding economies, which were reeling under the changes introduced by British colonial policies that placed small landholders in an extremely vulnerable situation (Ramnath 2011, 17–18).

The early Punjabi migrants to the United States found work primarily in lumber mills, railroads, and construction in California and Washington state. However, their encounter with the racial structure of U.S. society was immediate and swift. Feared as cheap competitors, South Asians were driven out of employment in the railroad and lumber industries by white workers. In September 1907, for instance, the Indian community in Bellingham, Washington, was brutally attacked by white workers, and several hundred of them were forced to cross over to Canada for their protection. A similar attack on Indian workers took place two months later in Everett, Washington, where they were forcibly rounded up and expelled from the town (Takaki 1998, 297–303).[2] The Asiatic Exclusion

League took up the task of fighting the "Hindoo Menace" and asserted: "From every part of the coast, complaints are made of the undesirability of the Hindoos, their lack of cleanliness, disregard of sanitary laws, petty pilfering, especially of chickens, and insolence to women" (*The Hindoo Question in California* 1908, 8–10). Driven out of lumber mills and railroad construction by white workers, Punjabi migrants took to agricultural work that was already dominated by Asian labor from Japan and China. However, agriculture was in constant need of new labor since the Chinese Exclusion Act stopped the inflow of Chinese labor and the Gentlemen's Agreement with Japan cut the inflow of Japanese labor.[3] Despite facing persistent anti-Asian mobilization, Punjabis did find work in agriculture, and many of them even managed to buy agricultural land and become owners (Takaki 1998; Jensen 1988; Leonard 1992).

The roots of Pakistani and Bangladeshi American communities were also planted in this period. As pointed out earlier, ethnic Punjabis numerically dominated the migration from India to the United States during the British colonial period. Many ethnic Punjabis came from West Punjab, which became a part of Pakistan, created in 1947 after the end of British rule. A great majority of these Punjabis were Sikhs, but a small number of them were Muslims as well. One of the earliest Muslim communities with distinct Pakistani roots was established in Willows, in northern California. Fazal Mohamed Khan, a Punjabi immigrant who came to the United States in the 1920s and became a successful farmer and entrepreneur, helped establish a mosque in the area and was instrumental in nurturing a thriving Muslim community that later identified itself as Pakistani (Bagai 1967). However, the period from 1947 to 1965 saw only a small trickle of Pakistani immigrants since there was a numerical restriction on immigrants from most Asian and Latin American countries. According to one estimate, 1,800 Pakistanis were granted immigration status in this period. A large number of the newcomers in this period were family members and relatives of those who were already in the United States. During the 1950s and afterward, there was an increase in the number of nonimmigrant visitors from Pakistan who came as a result of deepening military and political ties between the two countries. A sizable number of these visitors, who came for education or training, went on to stay and acquire immigrant visas over time (Najam 2006, 49–50).

Bangladesh, a nation that came into existence in 1971 after a bloody separation from Pakistan, also has a long history of migration that is deeply linked to the larger history of South Asian migration to the United

States. The Muslim peddlers and seamen who came to the United States in the late nineteenth and early twentieth centuries belonged to the part of South Asia that was known as the Bengal Province in British colonial India. According to Vivek Bald (2013), one of the early streams of South Asian immigration was from the Bengal Province. These Muslim craftsmen started reaching the East Coast of the United States in the early 1900s to sell small items produced by traditional artisans and craftsmen. They brought embroidered silk—particularly the Chikan embroidery work of Bengal—and "exotic" goods, including rugs, perfumes, and a range of other items. In fact, these peddlers followed the paths and interconnections developed by the British Empire for colonial trade and administration. By the early 1900s, a small number of these peddlers were traveling extensively throughout the United States, and they routinely moved through places such as New Jersey, Atlanta, and New Orleans to cater to a pronounced appetite for anything Indian or Oriental. New Orleans's Tremé neighborhood became home to some of these Bengali Muslim peddlers who settled there and started families (Bald 2013).[4] Multiple cases were recorded of Bengali Muslim men settling down in New Orleans and marrying African American or Creole of color women in a predominantly minority neighborhood.

Another stream of migration in the early twentieth century was South Asian seamen—primarily Bengali Muslims—who jumped British ships docked at the harbors of U.S. cities. Hundreds of South Asian maritime workers, who worked in very difficult conditions on British ships, disappeared into cities such as New York and Baltimore. A loose clandestine network of South Asian workers came into existence that helped each other escape ships and find work in nearby areas. They aspired to better working conditions and wages while navigating immigration hurdles. Historical evidence suggests that this was a largely transient population that cycled through factory work and often went back to maritime work and made their way back to India. However, some decided to settle down in the United States and found spaces in working-class neighborhoods primarily inhabited by African Americans and other people of color in New York, Baltimore, and Detroit. They married African American, Puerto Rican, and West Indian women and created biracial families in neighborhoods such as Harlem in New York City. These remarkable stories about Muslim peddlers and maritime workers defy expectations and assumptions about the linear and insulated historical trajectory of South

Asian migration to the United States, as they negotiated the race and class boundaries in that period by developing strong linkages with African American and other communities of color in New York City, New Orleans, and other urban areas (Bald 2013). The early history of South Asian immigration also points to the emergence of distinct religious groups that established some of the early Gurdwaras for Sikhs, temples for Hindus, and mosques for Muslims in the United States.

Despite very restrictive social and political conditions shaped by racist social and institutional orders, a group of South Asian immigrants organized one of the most significant transnational political interventions of the early twentieth century. Different groups and ideological trends within the Indian immigrant community came together, as Maia Ramnath (2011) narrates in her book *Haj to Utopia*, to form the Pacific Coast Hindi Association (PCHA) in October–November of 1913 in the Pacific Northwest of the United States. The group was formed with the mission to advance the struggle for India's independence from British colonial occupation. Sohan Singh Bakhna, a Sikh laborer who initially worked in a timber mill, and Taraknath Nath Das, a Bengali student, intellectual, and political activist, were the founders of PCHA and coordinated the branches of the organization throughout the Sikh farming community on the West Coast. They recruited Har Dayal, by then a well-known Indian political activist who worked with the Industrial Workers of the World (IWW) in San Francisco, to edit the group's publication, called *Ghadar,* and run its headquarters, the Yugantar Ashram, in San Francisco. Within a few months of its formation, the group's membership had swelled to five thousand, with seventy-two North American branches, including those in Berkeley, Portland, Astoria, St. John, Sacramento, and Stockton. It was a unique attempt to bring Punjabi laborers and Indian student intellectuals together for a cause that was dear to both groups, and they not only reached out to South Asians across North America but also created networks among Indians serving in the British Army across the globe as well as Irish and Mexican nationalist groups (Ramnath 2011).[5]

Even as the Ghadar Party's reach expanded in the United States as well as transnationally, the legal status of Indian immigrants in the United States remained uncertain after the 1917 Asiatic Barred Zone Act that prohibited the entry of immigrants from Asia and Pacific Islands (Takaki 1998). The federal law of 1790 that had initially reserved citizenship for "free white persons" provided clear racial basis for excluding Chinese,

Japanese, and Korean immigrants.[6] However, there remained an ambiguity about immigrants from India, Syria, Turkey, and other Middle Eastern countries, as the prevailing "science of race" defined Indians and those from the Middle East as Caucasian, and the courts were open to the argument that these immigrants were eligible for citizenship on that basis (Haney-López 2006). In fact, Asian Indians and some Middle Eastern immigrants were allowed to naturalize using that argument.[7] However, the rising tide of anti-Asian and anti-immigrant sentiment in the interwar period reversed the fortunes of those Asian immigrants who claimed citizenship on the basis of Caucasian ancestry. The Supreme Court, in *U.S. v. Bhagat Singh Thind* (1923), resorted to the "commonsense," or popular, conception of whiteness to define race to rule that immigrants from India were ineligible for citizenship, since being Caucasian was not equivalent to white. The *Thind* decision not only made Asian Indians ineligible for citizenship but also led to the rescinding of U.S. citizenship of many Indian immigrants who had acquired such status.[8] Besides the dire legal consequences of this decision, making a case for naturalization rights of Indians as Caucasians ironically reflected Thind's embrace of "white superiority" and "nonwhite inferiority" reinforcing U.S. racial relations of domination and subordination (Haney-López 2006, 148–49).

The Court's decision also became the basis for the application of anti-miscegenation laws to any interracial marriages between Asian Indians and whites, and led to a denial of land ownership under the California Alien Land Law (1913). Within weeks of the *Thind* decision, California's attorney general began instituting proceedings to revoke any land purchases made by Indian immigrants. The move was devastating for the community, as a significant number of Indian immigrants lost their ownership of land and were forced to become wage laborers again. There were reports of Indian immigrants returning to India due to these changes. However, parallel stories of innovative circumventions of racial restrictions—on their rights to acquire citizenship, bring their families, and purchase property—also circulated. Negotiating the highly restrictive and racialized legal and social norms, a number of Indian agricultural landowners adopted a "front-man" strategy to purchase or lease agricultural land, working out informal agreements to have property placed under the names of white farmers, bankers, and lawyers (Takaki 1998, 307–8).

The South Asian community in this period was composed primarily of men and, as noted earlier, they were prohibited from marrying white women under the miscegenation laws in California.[9] Even if the marriage was solemnized in another state that recognized such marriages, such unions invited the wrath of the white community. Punjabi-Mexican unions, however, became fairly common, as a number of Punjabi men and Mexican women got married and started families in California.[10] Over half of the Mexican spouses were immigrants themselves, and a sizable number of them were farm laborers as well. Such interracial marriages reflected the willingness on the part of individuals of both groups to go beyond fixed ethnoracial boundaries and create new communities. These unions, however, were not easy at that time. Punjabis would generally hide such marriages from their families back in India, and there were numerous examples of hostility from local Mexican communities (Leonard 1992).[11]

Because of the combined impact of restrictions imposed on Asian migration and a significant number of South Asian immigrants returning to their home countries, a very small community of Indians existed in the United States around the Second World War. According to the 1940 Census, the Asian Indian population in the United States had dropped to 2,405, and a significant number were in the forties and fifties age group (Takaki 1998, 314). However, the community started growing very slowly once again with the passage of the Luce-Celler Act in 1946, which allowed Indian and Filipino immigrants to acquire citizenship in the United States. The act also allowed a very small number of immigrants—one hundred each year—to enter the United States from India (Leonard 1992, 163). The eligibility to acquire citizenship was a major change for Indian and Filipino communities, since they had been legally barred from naturalizing after the *Thind* judgment in 1923. In fact, Indian immigrant organizations, along with other Asian American organizations, had been lobbying the U.S. Congress for this important right. Congressional testimonies in favor of naturalization rights for East Indians given in 1945 by Mubarak Ali Khan, a rich Muslim farmer of Indian origin who had settled in Arizona, and J. J. Singh, a Sikh businessman of Indian origin based in New York City, suggest that there was a concerted mobilization by the Indian American community in support of removing this barrier (Bald 2013).

Dalip Singh Saund, a Sikh immigrant from India who came as a student and earned his PhD from the University of California, Berkeley, was an important part of the mobilization against British colonial rule and later got closely involved with the lobbying campaign to grant naturalization rights to Indian immigrants. To gain support for naturalization rights, Saund and others directed war-bond drives among Indian immigrants to gather support for U.S. participation in World War II, hoping to earn the "trust" of other Americans (Takaki 1998, 369). Saund acquired U.S. citizenship three years after the passage of the Luce-Celler Act that he had campaigned tirelessly for, and he went on to be elected to the U.S. House of Representatives in 1956 from the Imperial Valley in Southern California, serving three terms. Saund was the first Asian American to be elected to Congress, and his success in electoral politics symbolically opened doors for Asian Americans. However, despite this remarkable success, Asian Americans faced widespread discrimination and exclusion, and it was only many years after Saund's election that they would achieve significant political representation.

The early immigrants from South Asia not only showed tremendous perseverance amidst a profoundly anti-immigrant and racially restrictive environment, they also challenged the racial laws in courts and found other ways to subvert them. It is also important to note that the conditions laid down by restrictive immigration and racial laws created the groundwork for interracial alliances—often through marriages—both in cases of Bengali Muslims and Sikh pioneers. The early history of South Asian Americans demonstrates that they were simultaneously engaged in challenging racial restrictions and creating a space for themselves in the United States while building a transnational movement in support of anticolonial struggles back in India.

## Give Me Your Best and Brightest: The 1965 Immigration Act and South Asian Americans

The passage of the Immigration and Naturalization Act in 1965 opened up the possibility for large-scale immigration from Asia, even as it laid down the legal basis for future waves of immigration. The act was significant in two important ways: It abolished discrimination on the basis of race and nation of origin for the purposes of admission, and it created three major categories—family reunification, professional skills, and refugee—that remain the primary basis for immigration policy even today.[12] The 1965 immigration reform was shaped by the imperatives of the Cold War, the demands created by the growing economy, and domestic racial justice concerns. The debate leading up to the 1965 reform was framed, among many other things, as an attempt to improve the image of the United States in the international arena by abolishing immigration quotas based on racist principles (Tichenor 2002; Das Gupta 2006; Takaki 1998). The civil rights movement had created a political climate that had little tolerance for an earlier system based on explicit racial quotas that preferred certain national groups over others.

The new immigration regime was geared toward recruiting highly skilled and professional foreign labor that could help accelerate economic growth domestically and also compete with the Soviet Union's Cold War aerospace and weapons development program to give an edge to the United States in the field of science and technology (Prashad 2000). In addition, the need for more health care professionals to meet the demands created by the Medicaid and Medicare programs initiated under President Lyndon Johnson's "Great Society" plans also pushed reform in the direction of recruiting both doctors and nurses (Hing 1993, 38–39; Prashad 2000, 72–75; Das Gupta 2006, 34–35).

Because it emphasized the recruitment of skilled professionals and family members, the 1965 immigration law eventually opened doors for a highly diverse South Asian community. Different streams of immigration that followed the 1965 act included skilled professionals, those with family reunification visas, those who acquired diversity visas, agricultural workers, refugees, and undocumented individuals. The new immigration regime created a chain of migration that may have subverted the original intentions of attracting only highly educated professionals. Regardless, South Asian immigration remained broadly in consonance with the needs of the U.S. economy, which required highly skilled professionals and technology workers as well as those who could be employed in low paying jobs for other kinds of services. The community that evolved in the post-1965 period thus became increasingly diverse not only along the lines of class, nation of origin, and religion but also in terms of region, language, caste, gender, and sexual orientation, as evident in the organizational and political expressions within the community. A brief analysis of three distinct South Asian groups in the next section further demonstrates that despite a common history of immigration in the early twentieth century, these communities have also developed in distinct ways that have produced greater diversity among South Asians.

## Indian Americans

The 1965 Immigration and Naturalization Act resulted in the arrival of a new wave of skilled and highly educated professionals from India and elsewhere. A significant number of immigrants also came as higher education students in different science and technology fields who got employed after completing their training. Characterized as the "second wave" of Indian immigration, this migration produced a highly educated and economically well-off segment of Indian immigrants because of the very nature of the immigration law and its priorities. Physicians, engineers, scientists, and other highly skilled professionals filled the critical needs of the economy and were employed across different parts of the country (Prashad 2000; Das Gupta 2006; Visweswaran 1997).[13]

A temporary decline in the numbers of new professional immigrants in the 1970s occurred, partly due to a backlash fueled by fear of plum jobs going to foreigners as well as the global economic slowdown (Das Gupta 2006). However, a new phase of Indian immigration that substantially increased the number of professionals with higher qualifications and skills started in the 1990s with the computer and information technology boom that opened the door for a large number of technology workers from different Asian countries, particularly from India. The Immigration Act of 1990 created a temporary visa category—known as H-1B—for skilled workers, with an annual cap of 65,000, and allowed these workers to petition for permanent resident status during their stay in the United States. Subsequent changes—exemptions granted to universities and research laboratories to issue H-1B beyond annual limits, demand for technology workers during the Y2K crisis, and an increase in the H-1B annual cap to 195,000 from 2001 to 2003—contributed to a spike in immigration of professionals from India. Official statistics point to a dramatic increase in H-1B visas, reaching almost 200,000 annually until recently, which has made these visas a topic of heated discussion in the current immigration debate (Wong et al. 2011, 44).[14] Moreover, a sustained flow of students from India to U.S. universities for higher education, not only in science and technology but also in the humanities and social sciences, has become another important pipeline of professional immigration from India.[15]

This second wave of immigration—defined by professionals and the highly educated—has been the dominant story of immigration from India. However, the Indian community, due to inclusion (family reunification) and exclusion (undocumented immigration) provisions of the

1965 immigration act, community-specific occupational niches (motel owners), colonial histories (Indo-Caribbean), and working-class migration (agricultural and other service workers), has observed substantial diversification in terms of class and occupation. In fact, the family reunification provision of the 1965 act led to what has been termed the third wave of immigration from India that started in the 1980s (Prashad 2000; Das Gupta 2006; Leonard 1997). For those South Asians who had family members in the United States, immigration through family reunification became a viable option. The first cohort of post-1965 professional immigrants was in a position by the 1980s to sponsor their family members, who subsequently sponsored additional family members. Family visas remain the largest source of immigration for aspirants from all South Asian countries even today. For instance, in 2011, 62 percent of immigrants from the six largest Asian source countries received green cards based on family members already residing in the United States (Pew Research Center 2012a). However, the stream of immigrants who came via the family reunification provision generally had lower educational and skill levels than those who entered via the special skills provision.

Indian American-family-sponsored immigrants entered an economy in the 1980s that was in recession, and many of these immigrants settled for low-paying jobs in nonprofessional sectors. Family reunification, some argue, turned out to be a way for recruiting immigrant labor for a new economy that needed low-wage and part-time flexible labor (Das Gupta 2006, 100–101). Contextualizing the emergence of working-class, low-paid, and self-employed South Asians, Das Gupta argues: "This dynamic between immigration policies and the labor market explains the appearance of self-employed and working-class South Asians. Just as the occupational preferences of the 1965 immigration law responded to the economy's needs for professional labor, its family reunification quotas serve the interest of a service economy seeking low-wage and deskilled labor amid corporate downsizing" (101). There were other streams of immigration, such as agricultural workers, that attracted a small number of working-class Indian immigrants. In fact, the special agricultural worker clause within the Immigration Reform and Control Act (IRCA) passed in 1986 legalized a significant number of Indian workers in agriculture (Najam 2006).

The rapid increase in small-hotel and motel owners of Indian origin has received considerable media attention in recent times and points to the dynamics leading to the creation of niche businesses dominated by an ethnic community. The overwhelming majority of these Indian hotel and motel owners come from the state of Gujarat in India. In fact, a small number of early Gujarati immigrants came to the San Francisco area from India in the 1940s and 1950s and got into the local hospitality industry. They are considered to be the pioneers of the community in the motel industry (Dhingra 2012). In the post-1965 period, a number of Gujaratis migrated from Britain after the opening up of the immigration system in the United States. Many of these Gujaratis had moved there from African countries such as Kenya, Uganda, and Tanzania to which they had emigrated from India during the British colonial period as a part of the colonial trade and labor circuit.

The political turmoil in some of these African countries had forced the community to move to countries such as Britain and the United States and to negotiate the racial and economic realities of new countries, a history depicted in Mira Nair's celebrated film *Mississippi Masala* (1992). These migrants were able to bring in some of their accumulated capital, which enabled them to get a foothold in the motel business in the United States. The family reunification provisions of immigration laws further enabled the Gujarati community to expand their hold on the motel industry. According to the Asian American Hotel Owners Association (AAHOA), an established trade association primarily of Indian American hotel owners, approximately 50 percent of all hotels and motels in the United States, with a concentration in lower- and middle-budget motels, are owned by Indian Americans (Dhingra 2012; Varadarajan 1999). The dominance of Gujarati immigrants in the hotel business is evident in the fact that approximately 70 percent of Indian American hotel owners have the surname Patel, indicating their origins in a particular community from Gujarat.[16] The enviable presence of Gujarati immigrants in this industry is a testimony to the role of caste and kin networks in creating a niche business for an ethnic group.

As in the case of Gujarati motel owners, the Indian American community is composed of members who have migrated from other diasporic locations due to a complex colonial history. The Indo-Caribbean community is one such example that has a very distinct history of mobility and cultural identity that goes back to the 1830s, when African slavery was abolished and Asian Indians were brought to the European-owned sugar plantations in Caribbean islands, with the help of British colonial authorities, to work as indentured labor. The descendants of these indentured labor communities constituted a sizable part of the population of Caribbean islands, and they migrated in large numbers to the United States, United Kingdom, Netherlands, and Canada during the 1970s and 1980s driven by the economic turmoil in many of these island countries. There is a sizable Indo-Caribbean community in the United States, concentrated primarily in the New York area, which came from countries such as Guyana, Surinam, Trinidad, and Jamaica.[17] Due to their unique immigration and cultural trajectory, the Indo-Caribbean community in the United States often finds itself on the margins of the Indian American or South Asian community.

There is a sizable and fast-increasing population of undocumented immigrants in the Indian American community. A Pew Research Center report published in 2015 suggests that Indian Americans are the fourth largest group of undocumented immigrants, numbering approximately 450,000 (Pew Research Center 2015). A large number of them entered the country legally but overstayed their visa's stipulated time. Many are employed in an informal economy with low paying jobs that help them circumvent the legal documentation requirements for working in the United States.

Finally, it is important to note that the Indian diaspora across the globe has brought with it the institution and practices of caste, which consists of a rigid tradition of graded internal stratification and discrimination within the community. Caste is believed to be an important part of Indian society, and it is the single most powerful practice linked to traditional social status and notions of superiority. The Indian diasporic community carries, and indeed replicates, caste consciousness and notions of purity and pollution that are linked to discriminatory practices.[18] The presence of caste divisions among the Indian diasporic population has been highlighted in recent years by *Dalits*—people belonging to the so-called untouchable castes—who are now a significant portion of the diaspora; they have mobilized the community in the United States, Britain, and Canada against caste discrimination both in diaspora as well as in India. They have not only challenged the normalization of caste practices in diasporic locations but have used their resources and organizations to highlight the prevalence of caste oppression in India at international forums (Kumar 2003; 2004).[19]

As we have seen, the Indian American community is constituted of different streams of immigration that have brought people from diverse backgrounds, with varied resources, ethnic networks, and skills.

## Pakistani Americans

There have not been many studies of Pakistani (and Bangladeshi) immigrants in the United States, and the scholarship produced on South Asian Americans has not yet systematically focused on these communities. The history and trajectory of Pakistani American immigration can only be pieced together by drawing upon the general insights produced by the scholarship on South Asians—focused primarily on Indians—and a slowly emerging body of work specifically on the Pakistani American community.[20]

It was the 1965 Immigration and Naturalization Act that dramatically changed the scale and nature of Pakistani immigration as well.[21] Following the broad political and economic trajectory of U.S. immigration in the 1960s and 1970s, most Pakistani immigrants were highly educated and skilled professionals who filled major gaps in the U.S. technological and professional workforce. These immigrants included a very high number of physicians, engineers, scientists, and other professionals with high levels of training (Leonard 1997). Some of these professionals were directly recruited into jobs, and a still larger number came to U.S. universities to study in many of the high-demand fields and stayed on to take lucrative positions. A number of Pakistani professionals came to the United States via Britain or the Middle East, where they got their first opportunity to work abroad.

This phase of immigration helped create a stable Pakistani American community in major metropolitan centers such as New York, Chicago, Los Angeles, and San Francisco. The family reunification provision, as with immigration from India, became a major path of immigration for Pakistanis in the 1980s. Additionally, there were two other immigration laws that helped accelerate Pakistani immigration further, namely the Immigration Reform and Control Act (IRCA) of 1986 and the Diversity Visa provision introduced in 1990. The special agricultural worker clause within the IRCA in 1986 was used to legalize the status of a large number of Pakistani, Bangladeshi, and Indian agricultural workers. The 1986 act gave the workers a chance to legalize their status by demonstrating that they had worked in agricultural production for a stipulated time period. Consequently, the number of Pakistani immigrants jumped suddenly in 1991 to 20,335—an increase of almost 100 percent over the previous year—due to legalization granted by this law (Najam 2006, 52). The socioeconomic profile of these immigrants was very different from the professionals of the earlier wave, and they were more likely to take low-paying jobs in different sectors of the economy.

A new law introduced in 1990 to diversify the immigrant pool in the United States helped increase immigration from Pakistan further. The Diversity Visa, popularly known as the "Green Card lottery," is aimed at diversifying the U.S. immigrant pool and is open to countries sending relatively lower numbers of immigrants to the United States. The lottery has attracted a large number of applicants from different economic and educational backgrounds since the prerequisite is very simple: twelve years of education and recent work experience in a profession that requires a minimum of two years of training (Leonard 1997, 71). Pakistan and Bangladesh were included in the list of underrepresented countries that were eligible for Diversity Visas. Between 1995 and 2001, a significant number of Pakistani immigrants came through Diversity Visas.[22] The Diversity Visa program for Pakistan, however, was discontinued in 2002, based on the determination that it was no longer an underrepresented country in the larger immigrant pool.

The community that emerged after the boom in immigration from Pakistan in the 1990s was thus a mix of highly educated and skilled professionals alongside a large number of low-skilled workers. The flow of medical professionals, engineers, and information technology specialists, as well the trend of enrollment of Pakistani students in different fields of higher education—particularly science and technology—continued. The overwhelming majority of low-skilled immigrants who came via Diversity Visa, family reunification, and other means were mostly absorbed in the low-income U.S. labor force, finding employment in small businesses, retail stores, gas stations, taxi services, and other low-paying jobs (Najam 2006). In fact, the taxi industry in New York City, Los Angeles, and many other major cities has a sizable number of Pakistani drivers (Mathew 2005).

The post-9/11 United States has witnessed a strong backlash against Arab and South Asian Americans, with a particular focus on Muslim immigrants. The National Security Entry-Exit Registration System

(NSEERS), a special tracking and registration system focused exclusively on migrants from Muslim majority countries, impacted Pakistani and Bangladeshi communities among South Asians. They were targeted for interrogation, detention, and deportation in this period—an issue that will be discussed at greater length in chapter 3. As a result, the flow of migrants from Pakistan was negatively affected immediately after the 9/11 attacks. There was a sharp dip in the number of permanent residencies granted to Pakistanis in 2002 and 2003: nearly a 40 percent decline in two years. However, the numbers started climbing up again beginning in 2004 and reached pre-9/11 levels in 2006 (U.S. Department of Homeland Security 2007).[23] The number of Pakistani students, which underwent a similar decline after 2001, has not gone back to the previous level. The number of Pakistani students coming to the United States in 2001 to 2002 was 8,644, and has gone down to 4,935 in 2013 to 2014 (Institute of International Education 2015).

The number of religious minorities who migrated to the United States from Pakistan has been significantly higher relative to their proportion within the Pakistani population. Even though Pakistani immigrants are overwhelmingly Muslim, there are significant numbers of Pakistani Christians and Zoroastrians (Parsis) in the United States (Najam 2006, 48–52; Leonard 1997). The fast-growing Pakistani community—comprising very new immigrants and those who have been here for decades, highly skilled and those without much skills—thus constitutes a diverse group of people, and their social and political adaptation to U.S. society is highly differentiated, often shaped by socioeconomic resources at their disposal.

### Bangladeshi Americans

Between 1947 and 1965, there was very little migration of people from the area that became Bangladesh (then the eastern portion of Pakistan) to the United States.[24] However, the changes brought by the 1965 immigration reforms started a new phase, and the numbers increased after Bangladesh became a nation-state in 1971. In the initial period, a wave of immigration started that was primarily dominated by professionals and skilled immigrants with higher educational qualifications. A significant number of Bangladeshi students enrolled in U.S. universities; many of these graduates later settled in the United States with lucrative jobs. The migrants were primarily middle class and urban and were able to find relatively high-paying jobs. The number of such Bangladeshi immigrants increased consistently in the 1980s and 1990s (Kibria 2007).[25] However, many Bangladeshis with professional educations could not translate their education and skills into commensurate jobs in the United States. A number of immigrants who had managerial and professional positions in Bangladesh ended up finding work in low-paying manufacturing or service sectors (Kibria 2011, 36). Such occupational downgrading, a phenomenon common among many immigrant communities in the United States, increased the proportion of low-income individuals in the Bangladeshi community.

Similar to Pakistan, a distinct phase of immigration from Bangladesh started in the 1990s that brought immigrants of different socioeconomic backgrounds with moderate to low levels of education and skills (Stevanovic 2012). The most significant shift was produced by the Diversity Visa regime, described earlier in greater detail, that encouraged Bangladeshis to apply for U.S. Green Cards through a lottery system. It allowed people from diverse classes to apply for immigrant visas, resulting in more than a thousand Bangladeshis immigrating to the United States each year after 1990. The program transformed the nature of the Bangladeshi American community, as a significant number of people with modest means were able to migrate (Baluja 2003, 58; Kibria 2007). Similar to Pakistani immigrants, many Bangladeshis got legal status through the 1986 Immigration Control and Reform Act, which granted legal status to "aliens" who were present in the United States without legal documents. Approximately 5,000 undocumented Bangladeshis were granted legal status through this act between 1990 and 1991 (Baluja 2003, 58–59). Diversity Visas and the ICRA were thus two major paths of legal Bangladeshi immigration in the 1990s. Not unlike Indian and Pakistani immigration, family reunification visas became one of the most important ways of legal immigration for Bangladeshis as well (Stevanovic 2012, 47). The figures suggest that family reunification visas resulted in a mere 9 percent of Bangladeshi legal immigration in 1991, but this rose to approximately 30 percent in 2000 (Baluja 2003, 58).

Bangladeshis are the fastest-growing among South Asian immigrants in the United States. The newly arrived have traditionally settled in major metropolitan centers such as New York City; Washington, D.C.; and Los Angeles, but there are newer destinations, such as Detroit in Michigan, that are witnessing a sudden surge in Bangladeshi population (Kershaw 2001). Bangladeshis work both in high-skilled professional and managerial jobs as well as low-paying jobs, but a significant number of newcomers have joined blue-collar professions and low-paying service jobs. For instance, in New York City, the Bangladeshi immigrants are now a sizable segment of yellow cab drivers, a profession that was earlier dominated by Pakistanis and Indians (Stevanovic 2012, 52). They have also entered the construction industry, which now employs a significant number of workers from the Bangladeshi community. The most visible low-income Bangladeshi workers in New York City, however, are street vendors selling fruits and vegetables and those who run small kiosks across the city. The Bangladeshi American community also has one of the highest poverty rates—approximately 21 percent—among Asian American and Pacific Islander communities (National Coalition for Asian Pacific American Community Development 2013).[26]

The broader demographic trends indicate that South Asian groups are currently one of the fastest growing immigrant communities in the United States. According to the figures released by the 2010 Census, there are approximately 3.4 million people of South Asian descent in the United States, and more than 80 percent of them are of Indian origin. To contextualize the pace of South Asian American growth, the sharpest increase in their number has taken place in the last twenty years (as reported in Census figures from 1990 to 2010). The figures from 1990 and 2000 indicate that the number of Indian, Pakistani, Bangladeshi, and Sri Lankan immigrants increased by 106, 89, 249, and 84 percent, respectively (see Table 1). This trend of rapid growth continued between 2000 and 2010, with a relatively small decline in the rate of growth among Indian Americans. The data represent a baseline picture of the community. However, it is important to note that certain South Asian communities—particularly Bangladeshis, Pakistanis, and other smaller South Asian groups—are often undercounted. This could be due to a combination of factors, including the fact that non-Indian individuals need to write in an ethnicity on Census forms and neither Pakistani nor Bangladeshi is on the list of options. There is also a fear among certain immigrant populations about participating in government surveys.[27]

There are growing communities of South Asians from Nepal and Sri Lanka that have also witnessed a sharp increase in the last ten years.[28] The number of Nepalese has increased more than fivefold between the

TABLE 1

**The Numbers and Growth of South Asians in the United States**

|  | 1990 | 2000 | PERCENTAGE INCREASE (1990–2000) | 2010 | PERCENTAGE INCREASE (2000–2010) |
|---|---|---|---|---|---|
| Indian | 815,447 | 1,899,599 | 106 | 3,183,063 | 68 |
| Pakistani | 81,371 | 204,309 | 89 | 409,163 | 100 |
| Bangladeshi | 11,838 | 57,412 | 249 | 147,300 | 157 |
| Sri Lankan | 10,970 | 24,145 | 84 | 45,381 | 85 |

Source: Compiled by the author based on data from the U.S. Census in 1990, 2000, and 2010.
Note: The numbers are based on "race alone or in combination" figures from the Census data.

2000 and 2010 Census, and the number of Sri Lankans has almost doubled in the same period (SAALT 2012). South Asian American organizations are increasingly becoming aware of these communities, which have traditionally not been a major part of the larger South Asian community.

The layers created by different waves of immigration from South Asia have produced a community that is undergoing complex negotiations among different identities shaped by nation of origin, religion, class, caste, language, gender, and sexuality among others. The organizational and political developments among South Asians reflect these complex negotiations vis-à-vis internal differences within the community as well as in relation to the U.S. racial hierarchy. The organizational landscape, analyzed at length in chapter 4, suggests varied mobilizations that partly draw upon these identities. The more particularized forms of mobilizing exist alongside attempts at developing political influence by deploying broader categories such as Indian/Pakistani/Bangladeshi American as well as a panethnic identity of South Asian American.

South Asians not only belong to the same Census category as other Asian Americans, but they also have certain demographic and historical commonality with Asian American groups. Even while each group has a specific immigration and adaptation trajectory, the commonalities demand that we place South Asian experiences in the context of other Asian

American groups to underline the possible implications of a study on South Asians for the larger category of Asian Americans.

## "A Part, Yet Apart: South Asians in Asian America"

*A Part, Yet Apart: South Asians in Asian America,* the title of an edited volume published in 1999 on the relationship between South Asians and Asian Americans, aptly reflects the tensions around the placing of South Asians in the broader category of Asian Americans, especially given that the term "Asian" in the United States has been traditionally associated primarily with East Asian immigrants. In fact, the evolution of the Asian American category was initially driven by Japanese and Chinese Americans, who were later joined by Filipino, Korean, and other South East Asian communities. South Asians were the newest entrants when they officially became a part of the "Asian American and Pacific Islander" Census category in 1990. Indian Americans were placed in Census categories such as "White," "Hindu," "Other," "Non-white/Hindu," and "Asian Indian" before they became a part of this category (Koshy 1998). The quest for minority status, a common ancestry in Asia, and a shared history of exclusion and discrimination led to their inclusion in the "Asian American" category after a sustained campaign by a vocal segment of the Indian American community.[29]

However, the process of identification of South Asians with the category of "Asian American" is still evolving, and the literature on this issue is at best inconclusive. Early scholarship on identity and activism among Indian and other South Asian communities suggested that the community was distinct from Asian Americans and did not engage with or accept this identity (Shankar and Srikanth 1998; Kibria 1998; Davé et al. 2000). More recent scholarship suggests that Indian Americans are not distinct from other Asian American groups with respect to the adoption of the Asian American label. In fact, they are as likely to adopt this label as Chinese Americans, and more likely than Japanese Americans. It is important to note, however, that the percentage of Indian or Chinese American respondents who were likely to identify with the "Asian American" category was as low as 20 percent (Wong et al. 2011). It seems that there is an increasing acknowledgment of the Asian American label but only a small segment of the community is willing to adopt this identity. However, in the sphere of civic and political organizing, there is an increasing trend of inclusion of South Asians and their concerns within some of the important Asian American organizations, suggesting concerted attempts at enhancing the South Asian presence in these organizations.[30]

In the following section, I present some of the broad similarities and differences among South Asian and Asian American groups using demographic data and other patterns that emerge from their immigration trajectories in the United States. Such analyses situate South Asians in the broader category of "Asian American" and underline the extent to which the groups share a similar immigration and incorporation trajectories. To begin with the broad demographic patterns, Asian Americans have a high proportion of foreign-born members, with Indian (87 percent), Pakistani (88.5 percent), and Bangladeshi (94.5 percent) at the top, followed by Vietnamese (84 percent), Korean (78 percent), Chinese (76 percent), and Filipino (69 percent). The proportion of foreign born among Japanese Americans (32 percent) is the only exception to this trend (see Table 2). The high number of recent immigrants among most Asian American communities, with all South Asian groups having higher proportions, produces varying levels of transnational attachments among these communities, making transnational engagements an important part of Asian American political participation (as will be discussed in chapters 5 and 6). Furthermore, the relatively lower level of citizenship among Indian (56.2 percent), Pakistani (63.2 percent), and Bangladeshi (53.3 percent) immigrants in comparison to Chinese (68.7 percent), Filipino (77.4 percent), and Vietnamese (79.5 percent) Americans could be partly explained by a relatively higher proportion of foreign-born and recent immigrants among South Asians. A higher proportion of foreign-born individuals and a relatively lower level of naturalization among South Asians in comparison to other Asian American groups have important implications for their political mobilization and participation.

Overall, Asian Americans have a higher level of income and educational attainment relative to the general population, with significant variation among groups. This demographic pattern can be largely attributed to a specific pattern of post-1965 Asian immigration, discussed earlier in the context of South Asians, that brought a significant number of highly educated and professional migrants. Among the major Asian American groups, Indian ($88,000), Filipino ($75,000), Japanese ($65,390), Chinese ($65,050), and Pakistani ($60,000) Americans have relatively high annual median household incomes, whereas Vietnamese ($53,400), Korean

TABLE 2

## Demographic Comparison Among Major Asian American Groups

|  | TOTAL POPULATION | PERCENT FOREIGN BORN | PERCENT CITIZENS | MEDIAN HOUSEHOLD INCOME ($) | PERCENTAGE WITH UNDERGRADUATE EDUCATION AND ABOVE |
|---|---|---|---|---|---|
| U.S. (overall) | 317,000,000 | 15.8 | 91.4 | 49,800 | 28 |
| U.S. Asians | 17,320,856 | 74 | 69.6 | 66,000 | 49 |
| Chinese | 4,010,114 | 76 | 68.7 | 65,050 | 51.1 |
| Filipino | 3,416,840 | 69 | 77.4 | 75,000 | 47 |
| Indian | 3,183,063 | 87 | 56.2 | 88,000 | 70 |
| Vietnamese | 1,737,433 | 84 | 79.5 | 53,400 | 25.8 |
| Korean | 1,706,822 | 78 | 67.3 | 50,000 | 52.6 |
| Japanese | 1,304,286 | 32 | 78.6 | 65,390 | 46.1 |
| Pakistani | 409,163 | 88.5 | 63.2 | 60,000 | 55.7 |
| Bangladeshi | 147,300 | 94.5 | 53.3 | 45,575 | 50.9 |

Source: Author's compilation of data from a report by the Pew Research Center titled *The Rise of Asian Americans* (2012).

($50,000), and Bangladeshi ($45,575) are on the lower side of the income scale (see Table 2). Asian American communities also have a relatively higher proportion of population that has acquired undergraduate education and above. However, there is a significant variation among groups on this count too. Indian Americans (70 percent) have the highest proportion with undergraduate education and above, followed by Pakistani (55.7 percent), Korean (52.6 percent), Chinese (51.1 percent), Bangladeshi (50.9 percent), Filipino (47 percent), and Japanese (46.1 percent) Americans. Vietnamese Americans (25.8 percent) show a distinct pattern, with numbers lower than the general U.S. population (28 percent).

In terms of socioeconomic resources, considered to be crucial for political participation, the data presented above suggest that there is a fair amount of variation among Asian American groups, with South Asians having higher levels of income and educational resources. However, it is important to note that the data on political representation of South Asian

Americans, particularly in the electoral arena, suggest that this group lags behind the other Asian American groups. In 2008, eighteen Indian Americans held elected political offices at different levels, in comparison to fifty-nine Japanese Americans, fifty-five Chinese Americans, and forty-one Filipino Americans (Lai and Nakanashi 2007). The difference is significant and points to a longer history of political participation and mobilization of Japanese, Filipino, and Chinese Americans in the mainland United States and Hawaii. Possible reasons for relative lack of political representation of South Asians could include a relatively high number of new immigrants and a very high proportion of foreign-born individuals and noncitizens. Recent trends, however, indicate an increased attempt by South Asian political aspirants to succeed in the electoral arena. The election of Dr. Ami Bera to the U.S. House of Representatives from Sacramento, California, in 2012 has been an important addition to the list of South Asian elected officials. Moreover, the elections of governors Bobby Jindal of Louisiana and Nikki Haley of South Carolina have generated intense debate over the significance of conservative Republican political aspirants within South Asian and Asian American communities.

In addition to the earlier comparison of demographic patterns, a brief analysis of five major Asian American communities in the following section is helpful in creating a richer context for comparisons that situates South Asians in the larger context of Asian American immigration, settlement patterns, and political participation.

Chinese Americans, the largest Asian American group, consists of those who have been living in the United States for generations as well as newcomers who constitute more than half of the community. The group has a sizable number of professionals and entrepreneurs that came in the post-1965 period alongside those constituting the bottom rung of the labor force employed in restaurants, garment factories, and other low-wage occupations (Wong et al. 2011). Ronald Takaki, referring to the class differences, writes, "In New York City there are the 'Downtown Chinese' of waiters and seamstresses as well as the affluent and professional 'Uptown Chinese.' In Southern California, there are Chinatowns in Central Los Angeles as well as in Monterey Park" (Takaki 1998, 425). Monterey Park has been promoted as the "Chinese Beverly Hills," and many wealthy professionals and entrepreneurs of Chinese origin, who have brought a significant amount of capital with them, have settled in such areas. The other side of the expanding Chinese community is reflected in old Chinatowns where the overwhelming majority are new immigrants and the poor. The diversity within the Chinese community thus produces challenges for creating a unified politics. With increasing diversity within the community and new attempts to build political power, the politics of the Chinese American community is a complex affair that deals squarely with cleavages along the lines of class, region, homeland politics, and immigrant generation (Toyota 2010). This is an important similarity between Chinese Americans and South Asians, particularly Indian Americans. However, South Asian Americans lack the population concentration in ethnic neighborhoods, an attribute that helps build political power to some extent, and that has historically been a part of Chinese American community.

Filipino Americans, the second largest group among Asian Americans, initially migrated as agricultural laborers and constituted the largest ethnic group working on sugar plantations in Hawaii by the late 1920s (Chan 1991). The post-1965 period witnessed a new wave of Filipino migration, similar to that of South Asians, which came primarily from urban areas, with a significant number of doctors and nurses alongside school teachers (Wong et al. 2011). The family reunification and other forms of visas have, however, brought a sizable number of Filipino immigrants who found employment in low-income sectors. The community also has a large number of undocumented migrants who struggle socially and economically because of their legal status.[31] The racially stratified labor market has further accentuated the problem, pushing Filipinos into low-paying jobs (Takaki 1998). In many ways, Filipino Americans are similar to South Asian communities, with a sizable number of professional and skilled immigrants who have proficiency in the English language. The second wave of Filipino immigrants, similar to South Asians, has not been concentrated in ethnic enclaves such as old Manila Towns, and they have also not built new Filipino suburban enclaves (Takaki 1998, 432). Their settlement is thus relatively dispersed. However, a long history of Filipino Americans in Hawaii has given them a chance to gain a number of elected representatives in comparison to South Asians.

Japanese Americans have a larger proportion of native born and a relatively high proportion of U.S. citizens compared to other groups. Immigration from Japan has leveled off, and the growth in numbers is not driven by the influx of new immigrants (Wong et al. 2011). Japanese ethnic identity and political mobilization was deeply shaped by the internment of 120,000 Japanese Americans during World War II. The first generation (Issei), which worked in agricultural fields and sugar plantations and played a major role in sugar plantation strikes through vibrant ethnic associations, was very hesitant to participate in American politics after the internment was over. The second (Nisei) and third (Sansei) generations, largely middle-class professionals, became very active politically and mobilized around the issues of formal apology for internment and reparation for the surviving victims. Such mobilization deepened their sense of ethnic identity and gave them relative prominence in American politics (Chan 1991). In fact, it was because of the historical experience of internment that Japanese Americans were the first to come out in support of South Asians, Arabs, and Muslims in the wake of racial hostility and targeting that followed the September 11, 2001, terrorist attacks. However, religious diversity among South Asians and a fracture along the lines of religious identity has led to a very distinct pattern of response to racialization that has made it challenging to build ethnic or panethnic solidarity among South Asians. The trend of mobilization along religious lines among South Asians in the post-9/11 period, which will be analyzed at greater length in chapter 3, is distinctive in comparison to Japanese American mobilization experiences in response to internment.

Korean immigrants also have some similarities to South Asians in terms of a relatively differentiated community along the lines of income, education, and occupation. There was a fast growth of the community after the 1965 immigration reform, and major metropolitan centers such as Los Angeles and New York have seen the growth of neighborhoods and commercial areas with high concentrations of Korean immigrants. The post-1965 Korean immigration, like South Asian, Filipino, and Chinese, drew many middle-class and professional immigrants. A large number of Korean physicians, nurses, pharmacists, and dentists entered the United States in this period (Takaki 1998). However, many of them encountered discrimination and licensing restrictions that created insurmountable barriers to the job market—a pattern that is noted among South Asian communities also—resulting in increased self-employment through small businesses such as grocery and liquor stores (Takaki 1998, 439; Min 1995, 210). A growing segment of the working-class Korean immigrant population has become part of a highly exploitative form of ethnic entrepreneurship in which Korean employers have special access to Korean immigrants, who they exploit, since they are isolated from the general labor market by virtue of discrimination and their limited knowledge of English (Takaki 1998).

The visibility of Korean Americans, through their shops in urban areas, particularly in minority neighborhoods, has led to heightened targeting and visibility of the group in American urban and racial politics. African American communities organized several boycotts against Korean-owned stores in New York and Los Angeles in the 1980s (Kitano and Daniels 1995). The Korean American mobilization in response to consumer boycotts and general violence against the community has made the group more attentive and involved in politics. However, there are proportionally fewer Korean American elected representatives when compared to Chinese, Japanese, and Filipino communities (Wong et al. 2011). A relatively low level of naturalization, similar to South Asian communities, could be one of the factors shaping this lack of political representation.

Finally, the Vietnamese American community has had a very distinct immigration trajectory defined by an influx of refugees from Vietnam that started in large numbers following the American war in Vietnam and the fall of Saigon in 1975.[32] Due to the geopolitical context of the Vietnam War and the history of U.S. involvement, Vietnamese refugees were supported and settled generously.[33] The federal government devised a plan to settle these refugees throughout the country in order not to burden the social services of any particular city. However, the plan did not work, as Vietnamese refugees found ways to settle in places where larger Vietnamese communities were being formed. Northern Orange County, San Diego, and San Jose in California, and Houston in Texas were the most important centers. In comparison to South Asians, Vietnamese Americans (and other South East Asian communities) have far fewer economic resources, as reflected in their comparatively lower median household income and higher rate of poverty (see Table 2).

Another important characteristic of the community that distinguishes it from South Asians is a very high level of naturalization. Since most Vietnamese immigrants arrived in the United States as political refugees who did not want to return, the rate of naturalization was very high. The data show a significant difference between proportion of citizens among Vietnamese (79.5 percent) and Indian Americans (56.2 percent). Due to high levels of naturalization and population concentration in a few areas, Vietnamese Americans have gained a political foothold in Orange County, California, a hub of Vietnamese American activism with several city council members from the community alongside one member to the state assembly. A Vietnamese American, Anh "Joseph" Cao, has also been elected to the House of Representatives from a predominantly African American district in Louisiana. However, a stable base of representation for the community, scholars argue, may come from the community hubs in Orange County and San Jose in California (Wong et al. 2011).

An analysis of emerging voting patterns and party affiliations among Asian American groups reveals important political trends within these communities. In the 2008 presidential elections, Indian Americans voted overwhelmingly for the Democratic presidential candidate, Barack Obama. Data from the National Asian American Survey (NAAS) 2012 indicate that Indian Americans voted even more strongly in favor of the Democratic presidential candidate in the 2012 presidential election (Figure 1). In fact, Indian Americans were most supportive of the Democratic candidate in comparison to other Asian American groups. The survey suggested that an overwhelming percentage of voting Indian Americans (84 percent) voted for Obama, which was far higher than Japanese (70 percent), Chinese (69 percent), Korean (66 percent), Filipino (62 percent), and Vietnamese (61 percent) support for the Democratic candidate (National Asian American Survey 2012). Furthermore, a survey conducted during the 2014 midterm elections suggested that 58 percent of Indian American voters—the highest percent among Asian American groups—indicated their preference for a Democratic congressional candidate on a generic House ballot. The survey also reported that Democratic Party favorability was highest among Indian Americans (68 percent) in comparison to other Asian American groups (APIA Vote and Asian Americans Advancing Justice 2014).

Scholars of Asian American voting behavior point to a clear shift toward the Democratic Party among Asian American voters as their numbers increased sharply in the last two decades. Asian Americans, who were voting majority Republican until the 1990s, started tilting toward the Democratic Party during the Clinton presidency and are now voting consistently Democratic in high numbers (Lee 2014). Analyzing the shift in Asian American voting patterns, Karthick Ramakrishnan and Taeku Lee argue that, since 2000, the Republican Party has sharply moved to the right on issues that have been important to the community. Asian Americans differed sharply from the Republican Party on the issues of health care, immigration, and the war against Iraq. The emergence of the Tea Party, anti-immigrant rhetoric, and aggressive deployment of Christian conservative language by the Republican candidates further pushed

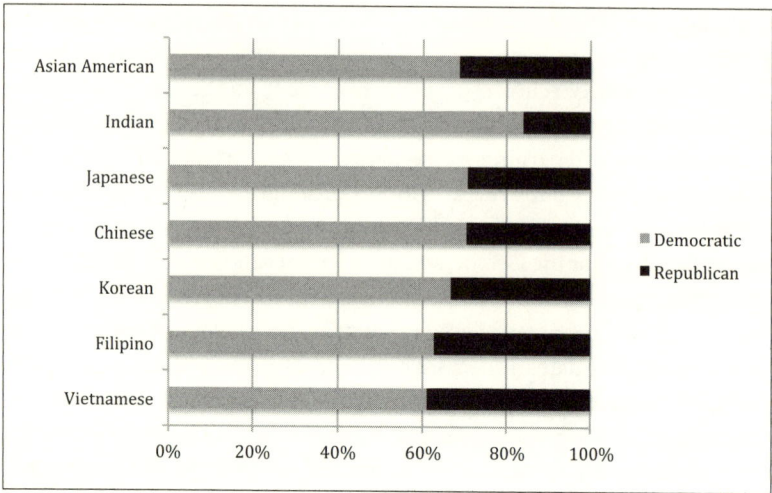

*Figure 1. Voting Patterns among Asian American Groups in the 2012 Presidential Election. Source: National Asian American Survey, 2012.*

Asian American voters away from the party (Lee and Ramakrishnan 2012). South Asians are even more sharply impacted by this trend since they are overwhelmingly non-Christian.

A Pew report on Asian American religions showed highest support for the Democratic Party among Hindu Americans as well religiously unaffiliated Asian Americans (Pew Research Center 2012b). A similar pattern was observed among Muslim Americans (Council on American-Islamic Relations 2012). The post-9/11 hostility against South Asian Americans has further accentuated support to the Democratic Party, which is considered far more open to minority communities. It is important, however, to note that approximately 55 percent of Asian Americans—and the same proportion of Indian Americans—do not identify themselves as either Democrat or Republican, indicating that this group of voters does not follow the traditional patterns of political socialization. The internal cleavages among Asian Americans along the lines of socioeconomic status, English proficiency, immigrant generation, and other demographic factors play an important role in shaping the political party identification patterns of Asian Americans (Wong et al. 2011). The underlying patterns of party identification suggest that even as they vote solidly Democratic,

South Asian Americans, alongside other Asian Americans, remain a politically volatile group in terms of party identification patterns and consequently their long-term voting loyalties.

In conclusion, South Asian communities have their own specific trajectories with distinctive features, but they share a history of social and political exclusion with other Asian American communities. Moreover, they also share with most Asian American groups a post-1965 pattern of immigration that brought a significant number of highly educated and professional immigrants, followed by waves that included those who immigrated through family reunification, as agricultural workers, and via other visas that created a low-income and working-class population within these communities. An important commonality that is highly relevant for the analysis developed in this book is the extent to which some Asian American communities are internally differentiated along the lines of occupation, income, education, generation, English proficiency, region, and so on. These distinctions have important implications for the political mobilization and incorporation of these communities. Furthermore, the settlement pattern—the existence of ethnic enclaves in some cases—of different Asian American groups is also an important factor. The preceding discussion noted how South Asians are very different from Chinese, Vietnamese, and Korean communities in this regard. Finally, the presence of a significant number of foreign-born immigrants, with varying levels of naturalization, among most Asian American groups (except Japanese) is another important commonality that significantly impacts patterns of political participation and mobilization. This feature underlines the centrality of transnational engagements for understanding political mobilization of these groups.

There is one aspect of South Asian American community that is relatively singular and requires separate treatment because of its salience. As discussed earlier, the religious diversity within the South Asian community is an important part of their community formation in the United States. The large number of Hindu immigrants from India is balanced by a significant, and equally important, Muslim population from India, Pakistan, and Bangladesh. Similarly, a long history of Sikh immigration has created a strong and vibrant Sikh American community. Christians, Parsis, Jains, and other groups also contribute to the South Asian American religious mosaic. The religious composition of Indian Americans, captured in a recent survey conducted by the Pew Research Center, indicates that Hindus (51 percent) are a majority among Indian Americans, followed by Christians (18 percent), Muslims (10 percent), Sikhs (5 percent), and others (Pew Research Center 2012b).

These different religious communities among South Asians have not only developed their own religious institutions and networks but they have also intervened in the political arena, both domestic and transnational, using their religious identities. The salience of mobilization along the lines of religious affiliations such as Hindu, Muslim, Christian, and Sikh that emerged in the context of the post-9/11 racialization of South Asians is a case in point. Religious identity is also highly important in transnational mobilizing and it assumes a fractious tone in the context of a history of religious conflicts in South Asia. The dynamics of mobilization along religious lines, accompanied by intracommunity contestations, are features that have acquired considerable importance for analyzing South Asian American political mobilizations. Since most other Asian American communities have varying levels of religious diversity, the analysis of a religious axis of political mobilization among South Asians remains important for other Asian American communities as well.

The political mobilization and inclusion of a highly diverse and differentiated South Asian American community is deeply tied to the nature of community formation shaped by U.S. immigration regimes described earlier. The focus of this study on the internal differentiations among South Asian communities, while analyzing their trajectories of political mobilization and incorporation, brings new insights to ethnic and racial politics that could have implications for similarly placed Asian American groups as well as other ethnic and racial minorities.

# 2

## Political Incorporation and New Immigrants

### Beyond Racial Solidarity

South Asian Americans have embarked on a path that has been traversed by multiple immigrant and racial minority groups with widely different outcomes. The inclusion in or exclusion from the American political process of minorities and immigrant groups has historically been a major concern for these communities and those interested in ensuring the openness of the democratic system. Questions that animate such discussions coalesce around the likelihood, pace, and trajectory of inclusion of newcomers into the democratic process: How will these groups mobilize and achieve influence in the political process? Will ethnoracial identities work as a barrier in the political inclusion of new groups, or will these identities work as a resource that can help them gain leverage in the political process? Will new immigrants adopt the path of political inclusion followed by earlier waves of immigrants, such as European ethnics during the early twentieth century, or will the U.S. racial hierarchy produce an experience closer to the African American one? To analyze some of these questions, scholars in the fields of political science and sociology have utilized the framework of political incorporation that has evolved out of a long tradition of work on newcomers as well as minorities. In this chapter I discuss the existing frameworks for analyzing minority and immigrant political inclusion and underline the need for moving beyond the dominant frameworks that have emerged from this tradition of work.

### Political Incorporation and Assimilation

The concept of *political incorporation* has emerged from broader research on minority and immigrant political participation over the last several decades. More specifically, the concept has gained currency from research in the field of urban politics that studies the political participation patterns of minority groups in major urban centers (Browning, Marshall, and Tabb 2003; 1997; Verba, Schlozman, and Brady 1995; Dahl 1961). At a very broad level, political incorporation is a study of how new social forces enter the political system, and the concept has been at the center of a longstanding investigation of ethnic succession and partisan realignment in the field of urban politics (Shefter 1986). The concept embodies the pluralist idea of inclusion that foregrounds the mechanisms and the processes through which a political system expands, balances, and accommodates new social forces.

It is relevant to note that the process of incorporation has traditionally been understood as the assimilation of new groups into the political process. However, the traditional framework of assimilation that emerged from the works of Park and Burgess (1969), Gordon (1964), and others has been either challenged (Glazer 1983) or reformulated (Alba and Nee 1997; Portes and Rumbaut 1996) to emphasize the retention of ethnic, cultural, and linguistic identities of immigrant communities and to underline the highly differentiated nature of American society in which immigrants have been expected to assimilate. Building upon a range of scholars who critiqued the assimilation approach, political incorporation literature has come to adopt a perspective that emphasizes negotiations, accommodations, and changes brought to the political process by new groups rather than a simple absorption (Minnite 2009).

Karthick Ramakrishnan, analyzing the assimilation and political incorporation literature in the fields of sociology and political science, argues that the concept of immigrant assimilation (or its more recent elaboration as "segmented assimilation") is primarily concerned with individual outcomes such as educational attainment, labor market participation, and other such attributes, and the group differences (for example, Mexican Americans vs. Chinese Americans) are identified primarily through an aggregation of individual attributes. Ramakrishnan argues that studies that primarily examine the political behavior or attitude of immigrants—party identification, naturalization, and voting behavior, among other attributes—should be classified more in the tradition of immigrant assimilation with a focus on individual political characteristics as opposed to studies that focus on institutional processes such as party organizations, bureaucracies, elected officials, legislatures, and other institutional dynamics relating to immigrant communities. The latter, he argues, belongs to the conceptual tradition of political incorporation due to its focus on political institutions, mobilization, and influence of immigrant groups (Ramakrishnan 2013). This differentiation does provide a useful analytical lens to conceptualize political incorporation in terms of distinguishing it from the framework of assimilation as well as identifying processes that constitute political incorporation. However, there is no consensus, as evident in the discussion below, about excluding individual-level processes (party identification, naturalization, etc.) from the category of political incorporation (Hochschild and Mollenkopf 2009a).

The literature on assimilation has undergone major revisions and changes, with a focus on nonwhite immigrants (Alba and Nee 1997; Portes and Zhou 1993). One of the most influential revised versions of assimilation theory is segmented assimilation. Focused primarily on individual outcomes such as educational attainment, labor market participation, and income for the second-generation immigrants, segmented assimilation theory predicts distinct integration outcomes for different nonwhite immigrant groups. The theory is particularly relevant since it came in response to an increasing realization that the contemporary process of immigrant assimilation and adaptation may be different from those experienced by earlier white European immigrants. Scholars have argued that contemporary immigrants come from a wider variety of socioeconomic backgrounds than those in previous European waves; thereby different groups will start out at different economic classes or strata of American society, and hence a single uniform trajectory of inclusion is not possible (Alba and Nee 1997; 2003; Portes and Rumbaut 1996; Suárez-Orozco and Suárez-Orozco 2001; Waldinger 2001; Zhou 1997). The theory of segmented assimilation argues that the United States is an unequal and stratified society with different "segments" to which immigrants can assimilate. It proposes three possible paths of assimilation: the first is the classical assimilation path, where immigrants acculturate and integrate into the middle class. The second is acculturation and assimilation into the urban underclass (adopting the oppositional culture of poor minority youth), leading to poverty and downward mobility. Finally, the third possible path is "selective acculturation," where a group's culture and values are preserved, accompanied by upward economic integration (Portes and Zhou 1993; Portes and Rumbaut 2001).

The broad import of segmented assimilation theory for the literature on political incorporation is that it emphasizes how different immigrant communities mobilize and enter into the political process differently, and that the existing models of political incorporation, as discussed below, point only to limited paths of incorporation that may not be applicable to all immigrant communities. However, segmented assimilation theory, with its focus on individual outcomes such as income, education, and job, does not provide any explicit framework for understanding the political participation and mobilization of immigrant groups. Following Ramakrishnan, the distinction between individual-level outcomes (income, education, and job) and group process (group mobilization, interaction with party, bureaucracy, and civic association) points to the difference between frameworks that emphasize assimilation (of individuals) as opposed to political incorporation of groups (Ramakrishnan 2013).

Segmented assimilation literature also posits inner-city neighborhoods and their underclass as a source of "oppositional youth culture" that could lead to downward assimilation of immigrant youth. This formulation has been critiqued on the grounds of minimizing the existence and impact of oppositional culture among white European immigrant youth (Perlmann and Waldinger 1997) and attributing oppositional culture only to the urban underclass instead of the immigrant working-class experiences (Alba 2005). In contrast, the political incorporation literature has foregrounded a different kind of abstraction that emerges from the urban areas where the underclass live—dominated primarily by African Americans and other minorities. This literature points to a mode of political incorporation, elaborated more expansively in the racialization model discussed below, where racial exclusion and economic and political marginalization of African Americans—the underclass conditions—has led to mobilization around their racial identity and a significant level of political success in gaining local as well as state and national representation. In fact, contemporary nonwhite immigrant communities have adopted some of the ways in which African American communities have succeeded in gaining a certain level of political leverage through such mobilizations. The segmented assimilation literature, thus, even while pointing toward significant differences among immigrant groups and their modes of assimilation, does not directly engage with questions concerning immigrant political mobilization and incorporation at the group level and completely ignores the contributions of the racial solidarity framework that emerged from the civil rights movement led by African Americans.

## Urban Politics, Political Incorporation, and New Immigrants

The recent scholarship on political incorporation has most often referred to Browning, Marshall, and Tabb's (2003) definition of the concept that emerged from the subfield of urban politics within political science.[1] These scholars consider it a multistage process that can include a range of possibilities but argue that the ultimate expression of political incorporation is the extent to which group interests are effectively represented in policy making. Elaborating further, they write:

> We measure the political incorporation of a group by the extent to which it is represented in a coalition that dominates city policy making on issues of great concern to the group. . . . Political incorporation as a measure thus refers to a range of possibilities. . . . At the lowest level, a group is not represented at all. . . . At next level there is some representation, but on a council dominated by a coalition that is resistant to minority interests. Finally—the strongest form of incorporation—a group has an equal or leading role in a dominant coalition that is strongly committed to minority interests. (Browning, Marshall, and Tabb 2003, 11)

The concept thus refers to different stages in the process including group mobilization, protest, electoral participation, representation, and policy influence. Their framework is widely used for allowing a greater operationalization of the concept thereby enabling concrete assessment through measures such as voter registration, voting, descriptive representation, and policy influence. However, this approach to studying incorporation has been critiqued for emphasizing and privileging elite representation at city councils and other policy-making levels at the cost of other processes that do not reach the level of formal representation and the policy-making process (Wong 2002).

Browning, Marshall, and Tabb studied political incorporation of minority groups—more specifically African Americans and Latinos—in the post–civil rights movement period when the focus was to go beyond protest politics, and analyze the participation of these groups in the electoral arena and their representation in decision-making bodies in major urban centers. In contrast, the recent studies on political incorporation are largely focused on new immigrant groups that are comprised of a significant number of newly naturalized citizens and noncitizens. These immigrants are beginning to participate in the political process through different ways, and some of their acts may not be captured by an exclusive focus on electoral participation and descriptive representation. Scholars studying political incorporation of these new immigrant groups—Asian Americans, Caribbeans, and Latinos—have therefore tried to broaden the concept by making it applicable to different settings and aspects of the incorporation process, particularly to immigrant groups that may not necessarily be at the stage of mobilization and group representation through the electoral process. For example, Ricardo Ramirez and Luis Fraga, broadly following the Browning, Marshall, and Tabb framework, highlight the dynamics of self-identified group formation as part of this process. They describe political incorporation as "the extent to which the self-identified group interests are articulated, represented, and met in the public policy making process" (Ramirez and Fraga 2008, 64). The formation of a group identity in the new context—the United States as opposed to the country of origin—and identifying and articulating group interests are thus also recognized as essential components of the incorporation process. Similarly, in an attempt to capture the multiple aspects of the process, Reuel Rogers defines political incorporation as the process through which new groups begin to engage with politics and eventually achieve representation and influence in government (Rogers 2006, 17). More importantly, political incorporation is seen here as a learning trajectory for new immigrant groups. Rogers writes that, "during the incorporation process, newcomers learn the rules of the game: how to identify and define themselves, how to frame their policy interests, where to draw alliances, where to position themselves within the party system, and where their ideological allegiances lie. Incorporation is, in short, a political learning process for new groups to American democracy" (2006, 18).

Michael Jones-Correa also emphasized the importance of studying incorporation through analyzing the broader dynamics that emerge when new groups start engaging with the political arena. His study of Latinos in New York City examines the hesitation among first-generation Latino immigrants to become citizens of the United States and how the resulting in-between status contributes to their marginality in the U.S. political system. The focus on such aspects of the political incorporation process is especially productive in studying new immigrant groups because it captures the specificity of their experience instead of merely focusing on the standardized measures (Jones-Correa 1998). This conception of political incorporation thus moves away from the studies that focused exclusively on outcome measures such as naturalization, rates of registration and voting, group representation, and policy benefits (Browning, Marshall, and Tabb 2003, 1997; Mollenkopf, Olson, and Ross 2001). Furthermore, recent attempts to synthesize political incorporation literature have underlined the need to conceptualize it as a wide-ranging spectrum that includes activities and outcomes of both groups and individuals. Jennifer Hochschild and John Mollenkopf, in an important volume on political incorporation that compares the United States and Europe, capture the different elements that constitute incorporation: "(1) process (2) for individuals or groups, (3) encompassing views as well as interests, (4) involving various forms of political activity, and (5) including changes caused by as well as changes to immigrants' political activity" (Hochschild and Mollenkopf 2009a, 16).

The process of political incorporation, broadly defined, can thus be analyzed by studying the numerous ways in which groups adjust to or negotiate with the norms of U.S. politics that, in turn, shape their prospects for participation and representation. I here draw upon this conceptualization of political incorporation, which relies not only on easily measured indicators such as naturalization, registration, voting, and representation but also encompasses the process of acquiring a group identity (both ethnic and panethnic) in relation to other groups, identification and articulation of group interests, axes of group mobilization, forming of organizations and alliances, adjustment to the U.S. political norms, development of ideological and policy interests, and transnational engagements. A conception of political incorporation such as the one outlined above allows for analyzing South Asians who are in the process of articulating their identity, negotiating contending ideas of common group interest or the lack of it, and mobilizing in electoral and nonelectoral arenas in both the domestic and transnational spheres.

## Models of Political Incorporation

The scholarship on minority political incorporation has a long history, beginning with a focus on the experiences of white European ethnics and Jews, which later expanded to include African Americans, Latinos, and Asian Americans (Gamm 1989; Glazer and Moynihan 1970; Handlin

1951; Pinderhughes 1987; Hero 1992; Wong 2006). Here I discuss the two dominant models that have often been used to explain minority and immigrant political incorporation: the pluralist model, termed by some as the "assimilation model," and the minority group model, also known as the "racialization approach." These two models, emerging out of different group experiences, have become the prominent approaches for analyzing political incorporation of new immigrant groups such as Latinos, Asian Americans, and Caribbean immigrants (Rogers 2006; Wong et al. 2011). Some scholars have proposed a four-fold schema of political incorporation models that further divides pluralism and racialization into subcategories (Schmidt et al. 2009).[2] However, the basic premises of the two broad models considered here remain largely the same in all other iterations.

## The Pluralist Perspective

The pluralist model of political incorporation, based on the experiences of European immigrants in the early twentieth century, holds that current nonwhite immigrants will overcome the initial prejudices and barriers to political incorporation as their European counterparts did earlier. According to this model, ethnoracial mobilization is an important part of the incorporation trajectory, and it functions as a major resource and organizing axis to enter into the political process. Contemporary nonwhite immigrants, as they gain some economic stability, will achieve full political incorporation in a gradual manner without any radical disruption to the political system. The model further suggests that ethnoracial-identity-based mobilization declines in significance with the passage of time, and there is upward mobility of the groups such that immigrants start displaying mainstream political attitudes and behavior. The political parties and other institutions, the model argues, positively facilitate this process of political incorporation (Dahl 1961; Portes and Rumbaut 1996; Alba and Nee 1997). The subsequent scholarship on European immigrant experience, however, revised this account of relatively smooth incorporation by pointing to the experiences of Italian, Irish, and other Southern and Eastern European immigrants who were racialized as undesirable and considered not fit to be a part of the broader white identity (Roediger 2005; Jacobson 1998).[3]

Precursors of the pluralist model included earlier scholarship on European immigrants that produced categories such as "assimilation" and "Americanization." The theory of assimilation was based on the notion that immigrants would gradually adapt to the social, economic, and cultural ethos of the host society and would do away with the cultural baggage transported from the country of emigration (Gordon 1964). As immigrants continued on their endeavor of acquiring formal membership in the host society, the logical culmination was single nation-state citizenship, characterized by a unitary political cultural core in the dominant position (Park and Burgess 1969).[4] The political imagery of this assimilation process was of a political boss who would receive immigrants when they first got off the ship and recruit them as a part of the city's political machine (Handlin 1951). The urban political machine was an Americanizing institution for white European immigrants, and though the entry of immigrants was made possible by immigration policy, the existing urban machine made them voting citizens (Erie 1988).

The pluralist analysis of minority political incorporation has partly drawn upon the assimilation framework that held intellectual sway in the disciplines of sociology and political science for a number of years. According to the pluralist perspective, there are multiple centers of power in society as well as politics and thus power is widely dispersed among a variety of groups and institutions. The availability of resources to a number of groups and multiple access points to the political system makes it possible for minority groups to enter the system in an incremental manner (Dahl 1982; Lindblom 1980). In his classical work *Who Governs?*, Robert Dahl deployed this framework to explain political incorporation of European immigrants and argued that the new immigrants take their first step toward political incorporation by starting to view themselves as part of a cohesive group. He argued that immigrants from the same country, often identifying with each other as outsiders when confronted with similar challenges in the new nation, come together on the basis for a common ethnic group identity. Incorporation for the European immigrants, Dahl argued, began with the emergence of ethnic politics (Italian, Irish, etc.), and the local political parties played an important and positive role in the process of incorporation. According to this framework, ethnic group politics is a transitional phase in the incorporation process, and as groups achieved upward economic mobility and political integration, their ethnic loyalties gradually melted away. However, Dahl's pluralist analysis has been criticized for its failure to explain African Americans' story of political incorporation—which he bracketed as black exceptionalism in his New Haven study—and for not giving race and skin color due importance in his model.[5]

More recent works using the pluralist framework to analyze political incorporation of Latino, Asian, and Caribbean immigrants have continued to reach similar conclusions with some modifications (Portes and Rumbaut 1996; Skerry 1993; Portes and Stepick 1993; Chavez 1991; Alba and Nee 1997). Following Dahl's depiction of different stages of political mobilization among European ethnics, Portes and Rumbaut argue that contemporary nonwhite immigrants—specifically Mexican Americans— have also followed the path of ethnic mobilization for greater political incorporation. They argue, "By mobilizing the collective vote and by electing their own to office, immigrant minorities have learned the rules of the democratic game and absorbed its value in the process" (Portes and Rumbaut 1996, 139). They thus predict complete political incorporation of Mexican Americans through a path of ethnic mobilization. Peter Skerry (1993) generalizes that formulation for other Hispanics and argues that contemporary Latino politics is no different from European ethnic mobilization earlier. Min Zhou (2004) identifies a similar pattern for Asian Americans and she argues that they, like European immigrant groups, build solidarity by living in ethnic enclaves and mobilize along ethnic lines, and this path has proven to be effective for their incorporation. For Zhou, the only difference between contemporary Asian Americans and earlier white European immigrants is that ethnic identity, mobilization, and formation of ethnic enclaves are more enduring features than they were for European immigrants.

Richard Alba and Victor Nee, while analyzing the distinctions and similarities between European immigrants and contemporary nonwhite immigrants, point out that even racialized perceptions toward the most disparaged European ethnic groups gradually disappeared once they attained some upward mobility. Irish and other groups who "initially struggled to put some racial and social distance between themselves and African Americans" were eventually able to overcome their perceived distinctiveness from other whites once they climbed the socioeconomic ladder and moved into mixed neighborhoods (Alba and Nee 1997, 845). They argue that a large section of contemporary nonwhite immigrants should be able to achieve a similar kind of assimilation and incorporation. Alba and Nee argue further that often dark skin color has been suggested as a possible barrier to social and political incorporation; however, it is not dark skin color per se but the similarity and connections to the African American group that raises the most difficult racial barriers. They refer to Asian and light-skinned Latinos in particular to make the argument that these new immigrants will broadly follow the same path of assimilation and political incorporation as European immigrants. Despite some important differences, there is a striking closeness between Dahl's analysis of white ethnic incorporation, where he bracketed African American experience as exceptional, and Alba and Nee's argument that a racial barrier to incorporation is more true for groups that appear to be connected to African Americans than for nonwhites per se. For the scholars discussed in this section, a large majority of contemporary nonwhite immigrants are destined to follow the path of political incorporation that European immigrants followed earlier and achieve complete or at least substantial incorporation.

Even as the pluralist model—both old and new variants—emphasizes the openness of the political system for newcomers and its ability to assimilate them, it also underlines the importance of ethnoracial mobilization for political inclusion. The ethnic mobilization as Irish, Italian, and Jews was an important step for gaining political voice and representation, and it was only after a sustained period of such mobilization that these groups could, to a certain extent, become a part of the mainstream white population. However, even in the case of European immigrants, ethnicity did not completely disappear, but assumed a symbolic importance (Gans 1979). In case of the newer waves of nonwhite immigrants, the ethnoracial mobilization remains even more important and almost becomes an enduring feature of how these groups mobilize. Thus, even scholars such as Browning, Marshall, and Tabb (1997), focusing on African Americans and Latinos, underlined the importance of ethnoracial mobilization. They note the fluidity and openness of the political system for achieving representation and presence in city ruling coalitions. The endurance of the ethnoracial mobilization, according to the pluralist framework, only facilitates the process but does not drastically alter the path of gradual greater incorporation for these groups. Notwithstanding some differences among pluralist scholars, this approach would predict that South Asian communities, as nonwhite immigrants, will also successfully mobilize as an ethnoracial group to achieve complete political incorporation.

## The Racialization Approach

The "minority group" or "racialization" approach takes inspiration from the experiences of the civil rights movement. It illustrates the difficulties and resistance faced by African Americans (as the paradigmatic case of a minority or immigrant group facing obstacles to political incorporation) and challenges the assumptions of the pluralist framework. The minority group model is broadly in consonance with racialization and identity-based frameworks used by scholars who consider racial and other forms of identities as important categories that determine prospects of inclusion in general (Omi and Winant 1994; Tuan 1998; Young 1990). Since the majority of contemporary newcomers to the United States are nonwhites, scholars following the racialization paradigm argue that such immigrants' paths to political incorporation will be greatly influenced by American racism. They will also follow the path adopted by African Americans in their attempt to achieve full political incorporation, a path that includes grassroots mobilization, demand for resource redistribution and political reform, incomplete and partial incorporation, and heavy reliance on group identity or linked fate (Hero 1992; Dawson 1994; Takaki 1998; Kim and Lee 2001; Tate 1994; Pinderhughes 1987).

Diane Pinderhughes (1987), using the experiences of African Americans in one of the seminal studies that illustrates minority group framework, argued that their path to political incorporation has been very different from white ethnics such as Italians and Poles. Analyzing the labor and housing markets in Chicago alongside political participation trends, she argued that blacks faced more extensive and enduring barriers in comparison to Italian and Polish ethnic immigrants, and that their political and social incorporation has not been amenable to gradual progress through incremental changes as suggested by the pluralist model. Foregrounding race as an analytical tool to understand black political incorporation, she argued: "Because race is a highly evocative American social characteristic that provokes deep political and economic divisions, it is too broad and controversial a matter to be the subject of meaningful trading, or bargaining. It does not, in short, fit a pluralist analytical framework. When political institutions handle racial issues, conventional rules go awry, individuals react irrationally" (Pinderhughes 1987, 261). The prominence of race in African American economic and social life has led to a political orientation among the black community where the primary imperative in politics is to advance the political interests of African Americans as a racial group shaped powerfully by a perception of a common group interest, or "linked fate" (Barker 1988; Pinderhughes 1987; Walters 1988; Dawson 1994).

Rodney Hero (1992), in his study of Latino political incorporation, has reinforced many of the insights from the African American experience and extended them to Latino immigrants in a compelling manner. Hero argues, critiquing classical pluralism, that minority groups are incorporating in a system that can be seen as a two-tiered form of pluralism. It allows full incorporation for whites (representing the top tier) but only marginal inclusion for Latinos, African Americans, and other minorities that face unique racial barriers and inequalities. Describing the implications of two-tiered pluralism for Latinos and other minorities, Hero argues: "Certain basic equalities and rights apply to all Americans, but because of the distinctive historical experiences and structural features of some groups, and because cultural or racial deficiencies are alleged to exist (Barrera 1979), equality is largely formal or procedural, not substantive. . . . Part of what two-tiered pluralism means is that there is a marginal inclusion of minorities in most or all facets of the political process" (Hero 1992, 190).

The effort on the part of minority groups to wield political influence, Hero argues, takes the form of a demand for redistribution requiring significant changes as opposed to incremental and regular politics. Hero distinguishes among different nonwhite groups by positing a continuum of racial disadvantage for the nonwhite groups relegated to the second tier of American pluralism. On this continuum, African Americans are on the far end, and Latinos in the middle. The two-tiered pluralism in the case of African Americans has led to the development of parallel institutions for blacks and greater residential segregation—the unintended consequence of the latter is enhanced representation in local-level politics in the post–civil rights movement period. Hero argues that Latinos have a tenuous relationship to the United States compared to African Americans due to the past history of forced occupation by the United States (for example of Mexico) and their immigrant status. Hero, however, stops short of specifying the implications of this tenuous relationship for Latino political incorporation. Hero's analysis seems to suggest that although all nonwhite groups are relegated to a second tier of political incorporation, there is a need to look at the differences in the experience of different nonwhite groups to have a better analysis of the political incorporation process of minority groups. In Hero's framework, Asian Americans are part of the second tier of pluralism that faces incomplete incorporation, but their experience would be distinct from African Americans and Latinos. This insight suggests that even while following the broad parameters of a racialization approach, one needs to develop a specific analysis for groups such as South Asians.

A number of Asian American scholars have also echoed the broader assumptions of the minority group model and underlined that Asian Americans were historically kept out of civic life through exclusion laws and denial of citizenship rights. Even though they have been valorized as a "model minority" vis-à-vis blacks in the post-1965 period, Asian Americans have continued to face civic ostracism that is rooted in the perception of "perpetual foreignness" (Kim 1999; Tuan 1998). Analyzing the contemporary barriers to Asian American civic incorporation, Claire Kim argues: "Although the bar on naturalization was lifted in 1952, white opinion makers continue to police the boundary between whites and Asian Americans by imputing permanent foreignness to the latter. They do not overtly deny civic membership to Asian Americans; yet their skepticism about the legitimacy of Asian American participation in public life and their readiness to see Asian American public figures as agents of a foreign power constrain what civic privileges Asian Americans do enjoy" (Kim 1999, 126). The long history of Asian American civic ostracism and a label of permanent foreignness are indicative of persistence of barriers to political incorporation of Asian Americans. Claire Kim's assertion is very different in comparison to the pluralist argument that sees these barriers as only transitory.

These two approaches—pluralism and racialization—in their classical forms represent two opposite ends of the spectrum as far as political incorporation of new groups into the political system is concerned. Pluralism suggests a relatively open political system that is amenable to the entry and influence of new groups and predicts a complete incorporation for them. Recent variants see some enduring ethnic features and even acknowledge the difficulties of this process but see this path as gradually succeeding for most immigrant groups. The racialization model emphasizes the enduring barriers presented by racial hierarchies and postulates an incomplete and halting incorporation for new groups and racial minorities in a manner where ethnoracial identity becomes both a resource as well an impediment to incorporation. Even though these two models are generalizations drawn from the specific experiences of European white ethnics and African Americans, they are heavily used frameworks to explain and understand the political participation and incorporation processes of recent nonwhite immigrants such as Latinos, Asian Americans, and Caribbeans. Furthermore, despite contrasting predictions about the extent and pace of inclusion of contemporary nonwhite immigrants, both models emphasize the centrality of ethnoracial mobilization for political incorporation. According to the pluralist model, this mobilization is a relatively temporary phenomenon, with some scholars cautioning that it could last longer, until the group becomes a part of the mainstream economic and political process. In case of the minority group model, ethnoracial mobilization represents an enduring feature of minority political incorporation. Thus, despite major differences about the prospects of minority incorporation, both models agree that ethnoracial mobilization is the way through which minorities and new immigrants achieve some level of political incorporation, and therefore this is the dominant framework for studying incorporation in the fields of political science, sociology, and ethnic studies.

## Political Parties, Transnationalism, and Models of Political Incorporation

The contrast between the two dominant frameworks is most visible in their assessments of a major tool of political mobilization, political parties. Drawing upon the European immigrant experience with political parties, the pluralist model paints a positive picture of political parties. The model presumes that competitive electoral politics will generally push political parties toward new immigrant groups and parties will play an important role in bringing these groups into the political process. The urban political machine and labor unions have traditionally played a major role in bringing new groups such as European ethnics into the political process. Dahl argued that party organizations and elected officials courted immigrants as ethnic constituencies and brought them into the political system. Political parties also fielded ethnic candidates for public offices to give symbolic recognition to immigrant groups and an opportunity at descriptive political representation (Dahl 1961). Political parties thus become a primary instrument through which new groups are incorporated into the political process.

In contrast, scholars who have analyzed the role of political parties and other institutions in the contemporary period have underlined the changed role of political parties vis-à-vis new immigrants. Janelle Wong argues that political parties, in contrast to their earlier role in political mobilization of European immigrants, have largely been absent from the task of mobilizing and bringing current immigrants to the political process. She attributes this lack of involvement of political parties to both structural factors, such as weak local parties, strategies of selective mobilization, and reliance on existing party coalitions, as well as prevailing assumptions of political parties about immigrants. It is the grassroots civic organizations and labor unions that are trying to fill the place of political parties in bringing new immigrants into the broader political process, she argues (Wong 2006, 199). Wong's analysis thus supports the minority group model's argument of continuing institutional barriers and points toward the existence of parallel grassroots efforts to enhance Latino and Asian American political incorporation.

The role of transnational engagements of immigrant communities in shaping their political incorporation has also not been sufficiently addressed by either of the two dominant approaches. The pluralist model, due to its moorings in classical assimilation literature, largely views transnational ties as having a negative influence on political and social incorporation of immigrants in the United States. It does not engage with the impact of transnational attachments on immigrant political incorporation beyond rejecting them as a hindrance to their political participation and incorporation. The minority group model, due to its initial focus on African American incorporation experience, has not placed much emphasis on transnationalism in theorizing political incorporation. However, recent scholarship on contemporary nonwhite immigrants that has followed the broad import of the minority group model has started questioning the conventional analysis of immigrant transnational attachments and arguing that transnational engagements of immigrant groups do not necessarily lead to a lack of civic and political participation in the United States (Jones-Correa 1998; DeSipio 2003; Guarnizo 1997; Guarnizo,

Portes, and Haller 2003; Guarnizo and Portes 1991; Lien, Conway, and Wong 2004; Ramakrishnan 2005; Wong 2006). Despite these important scholarly interventions, there is very little theorization on the ways in which transnational attachment of immigrant communities shapes their political incorporation experience in the United States.

## Beyond Ethnoracial Solidarity

As noted earlier, this book analyzes South Asian American political incorporation by situating it in the larger scholarship on immigrant and minority political incorporation and explores whether the existing frameworks that emphasize a unifying ethnoracial solidarity could be used to understand the South Asian experiences. As I show in the following chapters, an exclusive reliance on a unified ethnoracial solidarity framework, whether it is temporary, as suggested by the pluralist approach, or more enduring, as described by the racialization framework, is inadequate for analyzing the incorporation trajectory of South Asian Americans. The realities of a group that is racially nonwhite, but composed of a sizable number of highly educated and economically affluent members, and is internally differentiated in other ways, demand theoretical innovations that are absent in the dominant theories of political science, sociology, and ethnic studies.

Unsurprisingly, the dominant theories of minority and immigrant political incorporation fail to account for a diverse and relatively understudied group such as South Asians. South Asians and some Asian American groups have often been referred as "honorary whites" because of the socioeconomic profile of a sizable and visible segment of the community identified with the model minority discourse (Tuan 1998). However, the complexity of placing South Asians in the American racial order was most acutely reflected in the treatment of the group in the post-9/11 period. In fact, one of the first racial hate crime killings following the Twin Towers attack in 2001 was of Balbir Singh Sondhi, a Sikh South Asian American from Mesa, Arizona. South Asians, along with Arabs, were targeted for some of the most brutal racial attacks and killings. The events following the September 11 attacks demonstrated that the relative affluence and professional status of South Asians have not insulated them from racism. South Asians were thus seen from two different, yet related, lenses—model minority and perpetual outsider—that reflected their specific place in the U.S. racial order. The racialized discourse of model minority categorizes South Asians as "good," "hard working," and "successful" in comparison to other "problem" minorities, whereas the perpetual outsider construct, the product of a long history first emerging with Asian immigration in the late nineteenth century, has acquired a new meaning in the context of terrorism, security, and the "threat of Islam" after the 9/11 attacks.

Given the economic and educational profile of South Asians, there has been a pluralist or assimilationist expectation that they will easily become a part of the mainstream political process and that the level of South Asian American political participation and integration will be fairly high, quick, and easy. The empirical evidence, however, belies this assumption: not only is the rate of political participation among South Asians rather low but, like other nonwhite groups, they too encounter multiple obstacles on the road to becoming a part of the mainstream political process. An alternative prediction, inspired by racialization framework, postulates that South Asians, because of their nonwhite status and continued experiences with racial discrimination, will mobilize and enter into the political process based primarily on a shared ethnoracial identity—be it Indian, Pakistani, Bangladeshi American, or South Asian American. However, evidence does not support any significant increase in grassroots collective mobilizing among South Asians to challenge the growing racial hostility, even after 9/11. Instead, South Asian communities have primarily responded along the lines of religious identity.

The dominant framework of mobilization based on unified ethnoracial identity, outlined in greater detail earlier, has been widely used in the fields of political science, sociology, and ethnic studies to explain minority and immigrant political mobilization and incorporation. I here propose that internal differentiations within minority communities produce political mobilizations that challenge the framework of a unified ethnoracial mobilization. The framework presented here builds upon a relatively nascent trend of scholarship in political science and other disciplines that questions the unified group framework. I will briefly discuss two important critiques of the unified ethnoracial identity and mobilization approach before presenting my own framework.

A small group of scholars studying African Americans and Latinos have foregrounded the question of internal differentiations within these communities and the ways in which those distinctions problematize the

POLITICAL INCORPORATION AND NEW IMMIGRANTS · **67**

modes of politics based on a unified Latino or African American identity. Cristina Beltran (2010) emphasizes the fractures within the Latino community along lines of nation of origin, class, ideology, and historical trajectories of political engagement, and questions the desirability and possibility of developing political interventions that presume a unified Latino/Hispanic identity, or "Latinidad."[6] She argues that the category of "Hispanic" or "Latino" includes all individuals in the United States who trace their ancestry to the Spanish-speaking regions of Latin America and the Caribbean. Referring to the opacity of this category, she states:

> Latinos hail from Colombia, Mexico, Paraguay, Puerto Rico and beyond: more than twenty countries in all. Such inclusivity is a part of the problem: "Hispanic" and "Latino" tell us nothing about country of origin, gender, citizenship status, economic class, or length of residence in the United States. An undocumented immigrant from Guatemala is Hispanic; so is a third generation Mexican American lawyer. Moreover, both categories are racially indeterminate: Latinos can be white, black, indigenous, and every combination thereof. (Beltran 2010, 6)

The homogenizing tendencies obviously obscure the differences within the Latino community. These tendencies, argues Beltran, are not accidental, but strategic, as well as experiential and emotional. They are strategic because Latino political elites find it extremely effective to present Latinos "as a large and cohesive group capable of being mobilized around a recognizable set of issues" (Beltran 2010, 7). The homogenizing tendencies are emotive and experiential since they are partly constituted through the effects of racism. The analytical framework developed by Beltran pushes against the idea of a naturalized and descriptive unity and proposes that we see the category of Latino identity as historically and discursively created. Latinidad, Beltran suggests, is a site of permanent contestation that does not exclude certain interests, groups, and ideological trends for the sake of unity. The intervention of Beltran's important work has raised important questions about the possibility of a unified Latino politics that doesn't exclude important aspirations, categories, and ideological trends.

Cathy Cohen's work is another important intervention that raises questions about the dominant view of minority political mobilization, which accords centrality to a unified racial identity. Cohen argues that scholars have generally seen political mobilization among African Americans as representing a level of unity and consensus that is rarely seen in the political mainstream. These scholars point to trends in common political ideologies, policy preferences, and voting, and assume a stable homogeneous racial group identity and experience. As a consequence, Cohen argues, issues are defined in ways that tap into a unified racial group framework that is supposed to advance the interest of the entire community. Consequently, certain issues are termed consensus issues, and political entrepreneurs within the African American community work toward defining them so that middle-class and heterosexual men become the markers of threat or progress experienced by the entire community (Cohen 1999, 12–13).

However, there are other concerns, termed as cross-cutting political issues, that disproportionately and directly affect only a particular segment of the minority community. This argument, developed by Cohen in the context of her seminal study on AIDS in the African American community, underlines the ways in which certain segments of the community are marginalized and they never become a part of the unified group agenda. More often than not, these issues are related to a subpopulation of the larger group that is vulnerable economically, socially, and politically. Such vulnerabilities are often attached to narratives that highlight the "questionable" moral standing of these subpopulations. Drawing upon feminist theorists such as Kimberly Crenshaw and others, Cohen argues: "Issues such as AIDS and drug use in black communities, as well as the extreme, isolated poverty disproportionately experienced by black women—all issues which disproportionately and directly affect poor, less empowered, and 'morally wanting' segments of black communities—fall into this category of political issues" (Cohen 1999, 14).

Cross-cutting issues, to use Cathy Cohen's term, frontally challenge the framework of unified group politics based exclusively on ethnoracial identities. These cross-cutting issues tend to foreground identities constructed around gender, sexuality, and class that make the ownership of such concerns challenging for the mainstream organizations within minority communities. The intersectionality framework, a perspective that has emerged from the scholars who have focused on complex interactions among race, gender, and class, among others, also points to gendered and class variations in racial experiences of minority communities that requires moving beyond an exclusive racial identity framework. The intersectionality scholars emphasize the multiple identities of members in a minority community and argue that their specific oppression could only be understood through analyzing the intersection of these identities (Crenshaw 1991; Hancock 2007).

Building upon these critiques of a unified racial framework that point out the contestations and marginalizations that are produced by political strategies rooted in ethnoracial unity, I propose a new framework that gives analytical prominence to internal group distinctions such as class, religion, nation of origin, gender, and sexuality while explaining the political mobilization of South Asians. In the remainder of the book I will elaborate on how some of these distinctions produce a political consciousness and mobilization that complicates the notions of a unified South Asian American or Indian/Pakistani/Bangladeshi American mobilization. Ethnoracial identity interacts with one or more kinds of internal cleavages to shape the political mobilization trajectory of the group, which unfolds both in domestic U.S. politics as well as in the arena of transnational politics. Thus, in addition to a more comprehensive definition of political incorporation as a concept, I suggest a substantive rethinking of how internal distinctions radically mediate unified ethnoracial-solidarity-based political mobilization.

Chapter 3, on race and religion, for example, illustrates how religious identity has not only shaped the ways in which different South Asian communities have been racialized but also determined how they responded to post-9/11 racial targeting. Ethnoracial mobilization along the lines of ethnonational (Indian/Pakistani/Bangladeshi) or panethnic identity (South Asian) intersected with religious identities such as Hindu, Muslim, Sikhs, and Christians, which were evoked both in the process of racialization and in antiracist mobilizing. The political project of South Asian American mobilization in this particular instance had to thus contend with interventions and mobilizations along religious identities. The remaining chapters analyze the instances of ethnoracial mobilizations both in domestic politics and the transnational arena to illustrate the examples of mobilization that rest on a narrow segment of the community—termed "selective elite mobilization"—that generally leaves the larger community out of this process. In fact, class, occupational, and other differentiations have shaped the development of ethnic organizations within the community in a way that makes it harder to produce a politics that could possibly unify the community. However, the difficulties in producing a political mobilization that is inclusive of the broader community do not preclude mobilizations that use ethnic or panethnic tropes and resources. Different variants of South Asian or Indian/Pakistani/Bangladeshi mobilizations are being produced that speak to very specific segments of South Asian communities. The framework proposed here does not seek to replace the ethnoracial category as an important axis for mobilization, it rather seeks to underline that ethnoracial mobilization is deeply contingent on different internal distinctions, and a closer analysis reveals the specificities of such mobilizations.

# 3

## Race, Religion, and Communities

*South Asians in the Post-9/11 United States*

On March 4, 2011, two elderly Sikhs were shot multiple times by an unknown assailant driving a pickup truck in Elk Grove, California.[1] Surinder Singh, sixty-five, died on the spot, and his friend, Gurmej Atwal, seventy-eight, succumbed to his injuries six weeks later. These two Sikh men, who wore *dastars* (the traditional Sikh turban) and flowing beards, were out on their regular afternoon stroll close to a highway. There was no robbery involved, and these men did not have any known animosity. The killings evoked strong fears among South Asian Americans, particularly Sikh and Muslim communities. No one has been convicted in this case yet, and the police did not find any definitive evidence to classify these killings as a hate crime. However, there were strong speculations among South Asian communities as well as law enforcement agencies that the two Sikhs were mistaken for Muslims and that led to the hate violence against them. The incident symbolized the complex and multifaceted nature of the racialization of South Asians that will be explored in the course of this chapter.

While incidents of racial hostility against South Asians have a long history, the group has increasingly become the target of suspicion, racial discrimination, and violent hate crimes in the aftermath of the September 11, 2001, terrorist attacks. A pervasive sense of being an outsider and a target of suspicion symbolized the position of South Asians in the United States in the wake of the 9/11 attacks. South Asians straddled the attributes of model minority and perpetual outsider that defined their position in the racial order. Based on physical features and skin color, South Asians were lumped together and perceived as "strangers," "suspicious," and "terrorists." This racial positioning rendered them particularly vulnerable to hostile reactions such as the one that followed the September 11 attacks.

The racial reaction after the 9/11 attacks not only magnified the latent processes of the ongoing racialization of South Asians, but also pointed to deeper internal divisions within the community, particularly on the basis of religion. These divisions were important lenses through which South Asian communities perceived and responded to incidents of racial targeting in this period. A sixty-five-year-old New York-based community activist of Indian origin (Hindu) described the importance of these distinctions:

> There have been some incidents. . . . Because they mistake us [Indians] . . . as if we could be terrorists. I think you must have heard about Kamal Haasan; he was coming from Canada and they were not letting him enter into America.[2] That was because his name sounds like Muslim—Haasan. So he had problem, though he is an Indian Brahmin [A Hindu from "high caste"]. This happens . . . even sometime they may mistake us as Pakistanis.[3]

The multiple fissures within the South Asian community on different identity axes are clearly identified in this statement. The implicit understanding articulated above is that being a Hindu Indian should be an adequate guard from racial attacks and discrimination, and from this perspective the most worrying aspect of the post-9/11 situation is that Hindu Indians are mistaken for Muslims/Pakistanis. The quote points to the reality of the racialization of South Asians in the United States and also to the ways in which this racialization mediates the deeper identity distinctions within the group.

In this chapter I analyze the role of religious identity in the racial targeting of South Asians as well as in their countermobilization to contest such targeting in the post-9/11 period. The evidence suggests that, despite the lumping together of all South Asians on the basis of their appearance as outsiders and threatening in this period, there was also a differential racialization of Hindus, Muslims, and Sikhs. Moreover, religious identity played a significant role in shaping the reactions of different South Asian groups to the racial targeting, leading to further sharpening of the internal boundaries within the community. Religious distinctions played out in a way that constrained a unified panethnic South Asian response to the post-9/11 racial hostility. I argue that religious identity is not only an important axis of racialization of South Asians but that it also deter-mined the ways in which South Asians responded to racial hostility. I further argue that the current understanding of the development of pan-ethnic identities (Asian American/South Asian American) and mobiliza-tion does not adequately account for racialization and mobilizations along religious lines. Finally, I point to how critiques of U.S. multiculturalism provide a lens through which a greater understanding of the fragmented responses on the part of different South Asian groups can be achieved.

A significant portion of the interview questionnaire that I used for my overall project on political incorporation was devoted to racial discrimi-nation faced in general by South Asians as well as discrimination that followed in the wake of the September 11 attacks. It was instructive to note that questions about discrimination, even without any reference to the 9/11 attacks, evoked responses that invariably referred to that moment. Other interview questions that pertained to the subject of this chapter dealt with the acceptance of a panethnic South Asian identity in contrast to nation-of-origin-based identities (namely Indian, Pakistani, and Ban-gladeshi) as well as religious identities such as Hindu, Muslim, and Sikh. Finally, my analysis also drew upon the responses to questions about the reaction of South Asian communities to racial targeting in the wake of 9/11. The analysis of interviews was supplemented with reports on racial targeting published by South Asian and other civil rights groups.

## Racialization, Panethnicity, and Multiculturalism

Post-9/11 racial hostility against South Asians brought the issue of reli-gious identity to the fore, and religion formed an important element of the racialization process, alongside physical appearance, nation of ori-gin, and culture. The literature on race often traces the concept of ra-cialization to the racial formation framework that is defined "as the socio-historical process by which racial categories are created, inhabited, transformed, and destroyed" (Omi and Winant 1994, 55). This perspective emphasizes the dynamic nature of the process through which racial groups are not only formally classified—such as through census categories—but also the ways in which certain meanings and values are attributed to racial groups at the societal level. Racialization is thus the attribution of meanings and values to different groups, based on physical appearance, skin color, and other factors, both by formal institutional as well as "commonsense" social processes that does the work of defining them as racial groups. It is important to bear in mind that the racial formation framework does not refer to religion as an important element of race creation and racialization (Rana 2011). The emphasis is on the dynamic interplay among physical features, culture, national identity, and ethnicity. The curious absence of religion has important implications for analyzing groups such as South Asians because religion has historically been an important element through which the group has been racialized. For instance, the immigrants from South Asia in the early twentieth century were racialized as "Hindoos," making religion a key element in the racialization process (Takaki 1998).

An important dynamic that often accompanies racialization is the lumping together of groups into homogenous racial categories on the basis of apparent physical similarity, while internal distinctions are completely suppressed in the eyes of outsiders. Different Asian groups being seen and treated as the same is a classic illustration of this phenomenon. We find a similar homogenizing dynamic at work among other groups such as Latinos and Indigenous Americans. In fact, South Asians of different nationality, language, and religion were similarly lumped together in the post-9/11 period, as discussed through this chapter, on the basis of their physical appearance, and they all became potential targets of racial hostility.

The racialization process is directly linked to the possibilities of forming broader panethnic solidarities. The literature on panethnicity suggests that one of the important preconditions for the emergence of a broader panethnic identity is racialized lumping together of a group as homogeneous by outsiders (Espiritu 1992; Padilla 1985; Nagel 1986). Moreover, external threats lead to the intensification of group cohesion as members react in defensive solidarities and develop common interests where none may have existed before (Coser 1956; Portes 1984). The literature on the creation of panethnic identities such as Indigenous American, Latino, and Asian American identifies the situational and political dimension of the process as opposed to an exclusive primordial cultural explanation (Espiritu 1992). The history of Asian immigrants being lumped together as "Asiatic," "Oriental," and "Mongolian" at different points in history is well documented, and this process of racialization provided an important precondition for political activists to adopt the panethnic identity of Asian American as a tool to resist racialization and gain access to resources (Espiritu 1992; Lien, Conway, and Wong 2004).

Yen Le Espiritu identified protest activities, electoral politics, the creation of a census category, and formation of social service organizations as important arenas in which Asian American panethnic identity was forged. In addition, the emerging significance of a panethnic category was also a product of the political environment created by the civil rights movement and the emergence of a framework that valued mobilization of minorities on the basis of ethnoracial identity.

Expanding on the dynamics of racial lumping, one of the important arguments in the panethnicity literature is that violence and hostility on the basis of a lumped racial identity leads to increased panethnic identification and mobilization. Among Asian Americans, all group members suffer reprisals for the activities and hostility targeted against those who resemble them (Light and Bonacich 1988). Espiritu argued that violence against Asians on the basis of lumping led to intensified panethnic mobilization and contributed to enhanced panethnic organizing among Asian American communities. Analyzing the significance of the killing of Vincent Chin in 1982, Espiritu writes: "Asian Americans across the nation were drawn together by the 'mistaken identity' murder of Chinese American Vincent Chin. For some Asian Americans, the Chin case marked their first participation in a pan Asian effort. Their belief that all Asian Americans are potential victims propelled them to join together in self defense and to monitor, report, and protest anti-Asian violence" (1992, 163). Vincent Chin, a Chinese American, was "mistaken" as Japanese and killed by an unemployed white auto worker to express his anger against Japanese auto makers for causing the decline of the American auto industry. According to Espiritu, the Chin case was an important moment in the consolidation of panethnic Asian American solidarity. It showed that while political and other benefits are important factors in promoting panethnic Asian American organizations, the anti-Asian violence triggered the largest panethnic mobilization since it cut across class, cultural, and generational divisions. Espiritu predicted that if racial hostilities against Asians escalated, panethnic organizations and mobilization would also increase.

There are other studies based on quantitative data that also argue that discrimination and racial targeting lead to a higher level of panethnic consciousness and mobilizing. Analyzing the individual-level survey data on Asian Americans and Latinos, Natalie Masouka (2006) illustrated that those Asian Americans who felt that discrimination is a major problem showed a higher level of panethnic consciousness and a stronger panethnic group identity. In addition, experiencing individual discrimination also led to an increased panethnic consciousness among Asian Americans. Similarly, in a study of Asian American organizations across different metropolitan areas in the United States, Dina G. Okamoto (2006) reported that attacks against Asians in large metropolitan areas increased the likelihood of panethnic Asian American organizational activities and mobilization. It is important to note here that, as with racialization literature, panethnicity scholarship has not engaged with the issue of religion and fails to analyze how religious identity would impact panethnic consciousness and mobilization. However, the import of the panethnicity literature for South Asians in the post-9/11 period is the following: given the lumping together and racial targeting of different South Asian communities, the likelihood of a panethnic South Asian consciousness and mobilization should be strong, and yet, as this chapter illustrates, such mobilization has not occurred on a large scale. As I explain later in the chapter, there are some notable examples of mobilization on the basis of panethnic South Asian identity but they exist alongside the dominant trend of fractures along religious lines.

The final important theoretical framework for analyzing group responses to racialization can be traced to the debates on multiculturalism. The concept of multiculturalism, which signifies plural differences descriptively and the ideal of creating equal access for all groups normatively, is based on the idea of a positive acceptance of religious, cultural, and racial differences and underlines the value of recognition for minority identities (Taylor 1994; Kymlicka 1995; Kim 2004). Explaining the importance of the idea of recognition expounded by Charles Taylor, Susan Wolf writes:

> first, a failure literally to recognize that the members of one or another minority or underprivileged group *have* a cultural identity with a distinctive set of traditions and practices and a distinctive intellectual and aesthetic history, and, second, a failure to recognize that this cultural identity is of deep importance and value. The harms most obvious in this context are . . . that the members of the unrecognized cultures will feel deracinated and empty, lacking . . . a basis for self-esteem . . . obvious remedies involve publicizing, admiring, and explicitly preserving the cultural traditions and achievements of these groups. (1994, 75–76)

Borrowing from this perspective on preserving and valuing the cultures of different minority groups, multiculturalism promoted the idea of celebrating differences based on race, culture, religion, and sexuality and, thus, it emerged as a powerful critique of racism and ethnocentric domination of whites and Western/European culture.

The concept of multiculturalism, however, is critiqued on several grounds. Building on these critiques, I suggest that the multicultural framework, even while recognizing and respecting distinct cultural, religious, and racial identities, often works against broader panethnic political solidarity because of its emphasis on discrete identities. This formulation emerges from an important critique of multiculturalism, namely its tendency to essentialize a group or cultural identity in ways that do not acknowledge the fluid, situational, and contingent nature of these identities. A strong version of this critique was developed in the context of differentiating between individual autonomy vis-à-vis "scripted" group identity. In accordance with the multicultural framework that relies on the politics of recognition, demanding respect for people as blacks and gays is tied to a particular script. An individual's skin color and sexual body/orientation is not acknowledged as personal dimensions of the self but rather as qualities that make him or her a member of the group, and the individual is always expected to follow specific scripts of being black or gay (Appiah 1994).

Appiah's critique of essentializing identities and creating a particular script for an individual can be extended to group identities as well. Multiculturalism provides a framework in which groups are expected to "live" and "act" their particularized identities, and group recognition in the public realm is sought through foregrounding these essentialized identity attributes. Thus, the multicultural framework provides avenues for groups to build and promote narrow and fixed ethnic and/or religious identities in the public realm, which may not be very conducive to building a broader panethnic solidarity that recognizes the fluidity and contingency of identities.

Multicultural practices are also used to manage and control racial differences in a way that treats all differences as equal and horizontal, thereby obscuring the issue of power and dominance of whites over nonwhites (Mohanty 1993; Davis 1996; Kim 2004). Multiculturalism displaces material conflict onto cultural/literary issues: questions of power and structure are collapsed into those of cultural understanding and interpersonal civility (Carby 1992). Similarly, in the realm of religion, the pluralist framework may protect the civil rights of individuals belonging to non-Western religions, but it has not challenged the implicit hierarchical understanding that Christianity is superior to other religions in theological terms (Wuthnow 2005) or questioned hierarchies within non-Western religions. Thus, one can argue that multiculturalism's complete disregard for racial and religious hierarchies and its inability to locate the processes of continued racialization in that hierarchy sets the stage for a framework where racial, cultural, and religious differences are seen as immutable, essentialized, and benign. Consequently, groups are expected to develop their political responses through the frame of discrete religious, ethnic, and cultural differences. Analyzing the South Asian response to racial hostility, I suggest that the multicultural framework provides an alternative explanation to panethnicity theory in terms of groups foregrounding their discrete identities instead of a broader panethnic one.

With these theoretical frameworks as possible explanatory tools, the following sections analyze the racialization of South Asians alongside the patterns of community mobilization in response to racial hostility in the post-9/11 period. The analysis of South Asian panethnic mobilization or lack thereof in response to the post-9/11 racial hostility allows us to critically engage with the theories of panethnicity and multiculturalism discussed above. A brief description of the history of South Asian American panethnic identity in the United States precedes the discussion of the post-9/11 period.

## South Asian Diversity and Panethnicity

South Asians in the United States are an incredibly diverse group in terms of religion, nation of origin, class, caste, sect, region, gender, sexuality, and language. As noted earlier, religious diversity among South Asians is reflected in the presence of a wide range of religious identities such as Hindus, Muslims, Sikhs, Christians, Buddhists, Parsis, and Jains.[4] Even though a large number of South Asians in the United States are Hindus, a significant part of the community is constituted of Sikhs, Muslims, Christians, and other religious communities.[5] In fact, South Asian Muslims in the United States are the second largest group after African American Muslims (Leonard 2005b).[6] This religious plurality is accompanied by diversity on the basis of nation of origin, and there is often a slippage between the two. For instance, India is associated exclusively with Hindus, and Pakistan and Bangladesh with Muslims. However, there is a significant population of Muslims, Sikhs, and Christians in India, and the Indian immigrant community in the United States also has a sizable segment from these communities. Similarly, Pakistan and Bangladesh have Hindu, Sikh, and Christian populations.

The category of "South Asian" in the United States is a nascent one, and it is still evolving as compared to other panethnic formations such as "Asian American" and "Latino." As discussed earlier, panethnic categories are a product of several processes including cultural similarity, racial lumping, bureaucratic classification, and, most importantly, strategic adoption of broader identities by racial minorities for contesting racialization, enhancing political influence, and other such benefits (Espiritu 1992; Lien, Conway, and Wong 2004). Scholars have noted that the emergence of a South Asian identity can be traced, in part, to the student population of South Asian descent, primarily those who were either born or brought up in the United States, and their search for a collective identity on college campuses in the 1980s (Prashad 1998; Kibria 1998). Students of Indian, Pakistani, Bangladeshi, and Sri Lankan descent who were born and/or grew up in the United States found the category of South Asian a useful one since it captured their racial positioning as brown Asians with shared cultural backgrounds, who were racialized and faced discrimination but could not easily become a part of the campus Asian American organizations.

The evolution of this identity was further shaped by a number of subsequent developments. For instance, South Asian students and academics collectively questioned the marginalization of their voices in Asian American studies courses, conferences, and publications and worked toward creating a space for a South Asian identity (Davé et al. 2000). A fear of complete invisibility resulting from inclusion under the broader Asian American category also pushed the South Asian identity to the fore. In the 1980s and 1990s, a number of nonprofit service organizations, catering to different South Asian communities all across the United States, moved beyond specific nation-of-origin-based emphasis to self-consciously adopt a South Asian identification.[7] Similarly, the emergence of South Asian professional organizations such as the South Asian Journalist Association (SAJA) and South Asian Bar Association (SABA) in this period indicated the acceptance of this panethnic identity among a broader segment of the community.[8] South Asian identity is thus a combined product of a shared history and culture of the community in the South Asian region, the process of racialization in the United States, and a self-conscious adoption of this category by a significant and articulate segment of the community. Emerging through this complex process, the category acquired a certain political valence that was deployed to build solidarity among South Asians of different national origins and religious affiliations and generated critiques of identities and mobilizations around exclusive nationalist and religious identities (Prashad 1998). However, it is important to note that identities and organizations based on nation of origin (Indian, Pakistani, Bangladeshi, Nepali, etc.), religion (Hindu, Muslim, Sikh, etc.), and ethnocultural and linguistic identities (Gujarati, Punjabi, Bengali, Oriya, Tamil, etc.) remain the dominant identities within the South Asian community. The development and deployment of panethnic South Asian identity is thus in constant tension and negotiation with other particular identities. The intensive racial targeting of South Asians in the post-9/11 period brought new challenges to the South Asian panethnic category, and there was a renewed attempt by different Desi communities to renegotiate this fledgling identity.

## Post-9/11 Racialization: Racial Lumping and Religious Identity

The racial hostility toward South Asians and Arabs of all religious and national backgrounds started immediately after the 9/11 attacks, and the process of lumping of a broader segment of South Asians started with descriptors such as "Muslim," "terrorist," "Middle Easterner," "Arab," and so on. According to a study conducted by SAALT, there were 645 incidents of racial bias reported by the media in just one week after the September 11 attacks. These incidents ranged from verbal attacks to serious hate crimes involving arson, physical assault, and shootings. A wide range of ethnicities was at the receiving end of these attacks, including South Asians of different religious affiliations as well as immigrants of other nationalities (SAALT 2001). The first death resulting from the racial hate crimes following the 9/11 attacks was of Balbir Singh Sodhi, an Indian American Sikh who was shot in a parking lot in Mesa, Arizona. Human Rights Watch reported that Mr. Sodhi's killer was heard saying in a bar that he would kill the "ragheads" responsible for September 11. On the heels of Balbir Singh Sodhi's killing, on October 4, 2001, a Hindu immigrant from India, Vasudev Patel, was shot dead at his convenience store in Mesquite, Texas. His killer, Mark Stroman, also shot Rais Bhuyian, a Muslim immigrant from Bangladesh, at a gas station in Dallas, Texas. Mr. Bhuyian survived the deadly attack, but lost the vision in one of his eyes. The third victim of Stroman's revenge spree was Waqar Hassan, a Pakistani Muslim immigrant, who was shot dead in a grocery store in Dallas. Stroman later said that the anger over September 11 led him to target any storeowner who appeared to be Muslim (Singh 2002). He called himself an "Arab slayer" and believed that he should be commended for his "patriotic" work of taking revenge by killing those who looked Arab or Muslim.[9] The racial hate crimes against Muslims, Sikhs, Hindus, and others in the initial days after the 9/11 attacks are evidence of the hostility faced by all South Asians irrespective of their religion, nation of origin, class, and other distinctions. Such crimes are also evidence of a process where people of South Asian origin are racialized through lumping, and the identity of "Muslim" or "Arab" is used as a broader descriptive category for all members of the group.

The racial lumping of South Asians also points toward the fungibility of the racial construction of those "appearing to be Muslims" in the post-9/11 period. Leti Volpp argues that the category of those who appear "Middle Eastern, Arab, or Muslim" is socially constructed and heterogeneous. Persons of many different races and religions, including Hindus, Sikhs, Muslims, and Christians have been included in this category, and "Middle Eastern" or "Muslim" has become a racial signifier (Volpp 2002). Similarly, Muneer Ahmad argues that the construct of "Muslim looking" in the post-9/11 period is neither exclusively religion nor conduct based. This profile has a substantial racial content because it operates through a focus on phenotype rather than religion or action (Ahmad 2002, 2004). A significant number of hate crime attacks on South Asians and Arabs of different religious affiliations in the post-9/11 period is a testimony to this racial fungibility. Ahmad points to two assumptions underlying this fungibility: (1) all Muslims are associated with terrorism, (2) all "Muslim-looking" people are Muslims. These assumptions lead to the presumption that all "Muslim-looking" people are potentially allies of terrorism. This twin fungibility is, of course, devoid of any rationality or logic and derives primarily from a combination of fear, ignorance, and preexisting racism (Ahmad 2004, 1278–79).

The hostility experienced by South Asians in the post-9/11 period follows a long history of South Asian racial and religious discrimination in the United States.[10] In American popular culture, numerous racial slurs such as "towelhead," "raghead," "camel jockey," and "sand nigger" are used against Arab, Sikh, Muslim, and Hindu immigrants. In fact, Sikh immigrants were targets of vitriolic racial attacks when they first arrived in California and Washington in the early twentieth century. The Sikh turban even then symbolized "strangers" and "outsiders," the kind of people who could never assimilate in American society (Lal 2008). However, South Asian immigrants in the early twentieth century witnessed a process of racial lumping with a difference. All South Asians—Hindus, Muslims, and Sikhs—were termed as "Hindoos" and racialized as inferior and not fit to live and naturalize in the United States (Jensen 1988). The religious identity of "Hindoo" was thus an important part of the racialization of South Asians in that period (Takaki 1998; Haney López 2006). In contrast, the post-9/11 racialization process evoked the religious identity of Muslims to lump together all South Asians. The process of racial lumping through religious identity thus remains an important part of the treatment of South Asians, as old tropes of racialization mingle with new ones focused on terrorism, national security, and Islamic threat in the contemporary context.

The process of racial lumping in the post-9/11 period was pointed out by a significant number of Hindu South Asian interviewees. Anyone who fits a particular physical appearance—looking Muslim, Arab, or Middle Eastern—was seen with suspicion and considered a potential threat. A forty-five-year-old Hindu Indian immigrant based in Los Angeles referred to the ways in which a particular physical appearance alongside brown skin color has worked against all South Asians after 9/11: "Well, when they look at us they always think we are from somewhere else . . . because of our skin color; maybe they think that we are all terrorists or something—I don't know . . . they try to connect us to those people [terrorists] . . . there are things that scared them."[11]

All South Asians interviewed reported feeling a little vulnerable in public spaces, particularly in the days and weeks after the September 11 attacks. The possibilities of racial harassment and physical targeting seemed real. A forty-year-old Hindu New Yorker of Indian descent narrated an experience he had during his stay in Kansas City in the days following the 9/11 attacks. He said:

I remember the day 9-11 happened, at the end of the day I was going home, and my wife was to pick me up, so I was waiting in front of this bar, my very favorite bar. . . . Nearly everybody in that bar knows us, we used to go there every Thursday and Friday, my wife and I. And that day, there were two guys who probably had a little bit more to drink. So I was waiting for the car, I could hear them talking, I could hear them saying, "Is that an Arab?" and the other guy said, "I am not sure." I think there was an element of hilarity in the whole thing, but for me I was kind of feeling uneasy because I knew what had happened that day, and some of the repercussions of what could happen.[12]

It was frightening for South Asians to realize that their bodies were being construed as dangerous. Physical appearance, the dynamics of anonymity, and social distance characterizing public spaces provided an ideal setting for the construction of all South Asian bodies as suspicious.

Racialization in the post-9/11 period, however, worked in multiple ways: by lumping all South Asians into one undifferentiated category as well as by treating them differentially on the basis of religious identity. An overwhelming number of both Muslim and non-Muslim interviewees said that even though a sizable number of non-Muslim South Asians were targeted in that period, Muslims were the prime victims of racial suspicion and attacks. A fifty-two-year-old Pakistani immigrant based in New York City talked about the challenges of being a Muslim during this period. She said:

I think even people who never considered themselves to be too much of Muslim were impacted badly. Just their skin is different, their color is different. The Muslim kids, you know what they say about these kids, they look different from outside but are American from inside. Even those kids had to face things just because their name was different or they were Muslims. They had to recognize their Muslim identity. . . . It was an identity that . . . wasn't too much a part of their existence before 9-11. . . . They had to face it. A lot of people and a lot of kids have become bitter.[13]

Many of the young Muslims the interviewee referred to came from upper-middle-class families and religion was not necessarily a part of their daily existence. Yet religious identity became the dominant identifier, and Muslims of different ethnicity, class, and immigration status were targeted on that basis and, in some cases, a religious identity was imposed on them even while they themselves were not too conscious of it. A sixty-five-year-old Muslim New Yorker of Pakistani origin, talking about her son's experience, said:

> My son was at Princeton . . . my son is sort of dark skinned. He and his wife were coming out of a restaurant . . . and some white kids, who were obviously very drunk, started abusing him and saying "go back to your country," "what are you doing here"? I think what it did to my son, who came here [U.S.] when he was not even three and who has never seen himself as black. . . . But he said for the first time, I looked at myself and realized that I was not white. They were seeing me as something different.[14]

The racialization of a certain phenotype as suspicious, irrespective of class, length of stay, place of birth, and self-identification is unmistakable here. It is important to note that having a privileged background did not shield the interviewee's son from being seen as suspicious, an outsider, and threatening. The post-9/11 backlash made it clear that class privilege was not enough to insulate South Asians, Muslims in particular, from racial targeting. There is no doubt that working-class South Asians who worked at gas stations or drove taxis were much more vulnerable to violence of different kinds in public spaces, but the process of racialization through attributing certain meanings to Muslim, South Asian, and Arab identities did cut across different classes. The stark depiction of this reality in Mohsin Hamid's novel *The Reluctant Fundamentalist* (2007), also a movie with the same name directed by Mira Nair in 2013, illustrates the point poignantly. The main protagonist of the novel, Changez, a young Muslim from Pakistan and a Princeton graduate based in New York City, felt deeply the sense of being an outsider and a target of suspicion after 9/11 despite being extremely successful at his high-paying Wall Street analyst job. The suspicion and targeting of Muslims, however, acquired a completely different character when law enforcement agencies adopted a policy of systematic targeting of the group on the basis of religious identity. Such systematic targeting ended up validating the public racial reaction against Muslims and those appearing to be Muslim immediately after the 9/11 attacks.

## Muslim Racialization and Law Enforcement Agencies

After the 9/11 attacks, the U.S. government responded in two ways: (1) looking for the perpetrators of the attack outside the United States, which resulted in the invasion of Afghanistan, and (2) a domestic "war on terror," which started with the detention and interrogation of thousands of Muslims, Arabs, Middle Easterners, and South Asians. Here I briefly note some of the measures undertaken by law enforcement agencies after the 9/11 attacks that underline the systematic and pervasive nature of Muslim targeting that in turn was embodied as frighteningly transformative experiences by the interviewees.

The first round of investigations, started immediately after September 11, 2001, and termed the Pentagon Twin Tower Bombing Investigation (PENTTBOM), led to approximately 1,200 citizens and noncitizens being detained for interrogations within the first two months of the attacks and subsequently released (Akram and Karmley 2005). According to a review conducted by the Department of Justice (DOJ), it was clear from the beginning that most of these detainees had no connection to terrorism at all and their detention could only be explained by their religion, ethnicity, and nation of origin (Chishti et al. 2003). The DOJ report found that law enforcement agencies selectively followed up on dubious tips for persons of Arab or Muslim origin and accepted the arbitrary nature of arrests and designation as "special interest" by the FBI (Office of the Inspector General 2003).

A radical redefinition of immigration laws was also visible in the FBI's "hold until cleared" policy, under which the bureau required that the Immigration and Naturalization Service not release any individual until they were cleared by the FBI as not implicated in a terrorism investigation. The process of trial and "clearance" decision was secret: neither the detainee nor the public had access to the criteria by which the cases were being evaluated. According to the government's own Office of the Inspector General report, the average case took eighty days for the FBI to clear (2003). This violation of due process was justified on the basis of individuals' alien status and exceptions created under the PATRIOT Act (Akram and Karmley 2005; American Civil Liberties Union 2004a).

The "voluntary interview" program—an ironic name since the process was anything but voluntary—was also initiated right after 9/11. The first 5,000 individuals designated for interviews were claimed by the government to have "al Qaeda-related factors." The criteria used to select individuals for these interviews were: males between the ages of eighteen and thirty-three who entered the United States after January 1, 2000, on nonimmigrant visas, and who held passports from or lived in countries known to have an "al Qaeda presence." The DOJ kept the list of countries secret; however, based on the information about the people interviewed, the countries appeared to be Afghanistan, Pakistan, Yemen, Sudan, and Indonesia (Akram and Karmley 2005). Despite the DOJ's admission that the first 5,000 interviews did not produce any leads to terrorist activities, a second round of interviews was initiated in February 2002 that involved 3,000 individuals (Chishti et al. 2003).

Extending the approach of exclusively targeting people on the basis of religion, ethnicity, and nation of origin, on January 25, 2002, the DOJ announced the Absconder Apprehension Initiative to identify, interview, arrest, and deport people who had received final orders of removal in normal immigration hearings but nonetheless remained in the United States. While there was a total of 314,000 absconders present in the United States at that point, this particular initiative was focused exclusively on Muslims from Arab, South Asian, and Middle Eastern countries (Akram and Karmley 2005). By May 2003, over 1,100 of these alleged absconders had been arrested, and two-thirds of them deported destroying families in the process (American Civil Liberties Union 2004b).

The National Security Entry-Exit Registration System (NSEERS) was the most infamous of the policy initiatives that were introduced in the post-9/11 period. The program had two registration components: through port of entry and through domestic or call-in registration. Domestic or call-in registration required male nonimmigrants (people on temporary visas) over the age of sixteen from twenty-five Muslim countries to physically appear at designated INS offices with relevant documents and go through the process of verification and questioning, or risk losing their status. More than 80,000 individuals were interviewed under the program, and over 13,000 were placed under removal proceedings. The program came under intense criticism and was finally discontinued in 2005 (American-Arab ADC and Penn State University 2009). NSEERS was followed by a secret program termed Operation Front Line, coordinated by U.S. Immigration and Customs Enforcement (ICE) prior to the 2004 presidential elections, which targeted immigrants on temporary visas from Muslim-majority countries. Almost all the investigations were related to visa violations or fraudulent passports and visas, and there were no cases related to terrorism. Even though NSEERS was suspended, government agencies continued to use the data collected during the program to further target Muslims (Lichtblau 2008).

The first phase of the War on Terror, defined by policies such as voluntary interview, the Absconder Apprehension Initiative, and NSEERS discussed above, was focused on noncitizen Muslims as foreign populations, and all policy details were constructed around their links to countries of origin. However, counterterrorism policy gradually moved away from an initial focus on Muslims on temporary visas (foreigners) and toward the "radicalization" of the domestic Muslim population. This phase was defined by surveillance of the Muslim community and the extensive use of informants from the community. In August 2011, the Associated Press (AP) published a series of reports on the NYPD's surveillance program focused on Muslims in New York City and adjoining states such as New Jersey, Pennsylvania, and Connecticut. The NYPD documents leaked by the AP journalists revealed that a secret unit within NYPD's intelligence division, known as the Demographics Unit, targeted twenty-eight listed ancestries of interest (all of them from predominantly Muslim countries) and focused on gathering information about communities where terrorists might hide. Places of worship, restaurants, hookah bars, bookstores, and other places visited by Muslims were targets of surveillance. Muslim Students Associations at different New York City college campuses were also targets of the NYPD surveillance program (Goldman and Apuzo 2012; Creating Law Enforcement Accountability and Responsibility 2013). The demographic unit responsible for this surveillance program was disbanded in 2014, after these stories became public and attracted stinging criticisms by civil rights groups. However, the NYPD continues to recruit informants from the Muslim community by using its power over community members who are detained by the department for petty crimes and violations.[15] Police departments and the FBI in other major cities such as Los Angeles and San Francisco have also adopted similar practices that became controversial and faced criticism from Muslim community and civil liberty groups.[16]

A systematic targeting of Muslims by law enforcement agencies in the post-9/11 period has fueled racialization on the basis of religious identity. A forty-eight-year-old New York City–based Muslim Pakistani immigrant said: "Early on I think it was true for everyone (South Asians), but it looks like the law enforcement agencies have gone through their training and they have been told: this is a Sikh turban and this is a Muslim turban, so be aware. If you get this turban, let them go, but this turban, stop them. So they went through that change of their manual of training and it is now mostly the South Asian Muslim community."[17] Subsequently, mosques and specific Muslim neighborhoods were put under constant surveillance, causing extreme hardship and emotional distress to the community. Referring to the targeting of a predominantly Pakistani neighborhood in the Coney Island Avenue area in Brooklyn, New York, a Pakistani American activist said: "They (the FBI and NYPD) would go door to door, and they would wait in the restaurants for change of shift, and the restaurant workers working in the kitchen would come out and they would question them. There were several arrests made. Then they were people like Mr. . . . he was also arrested in a neighborhood search. It was four blocks from here. . . . There were many such arrests. People have been traumatized a lot."[18] The news of incidents such as the Coney Island Avenue police raids circulated among the Muslim communities all across the United States, and a sense of being under siege developed from hearing such stories.

The systematic targeting of Muslims by governmental agencies worked as an official validation of the racialization of Muslims as suspicious, untrustworthy, and outsiders. Many Muslims interviewed did not feel very comfortable revealing their religious identity among strangers, and they always exercised an element of caution about their surroundings. A thirty-two-year-old Muslim immigrant of Pakistani origin based in Brooklyn, New York, expressed his fears of such encounters in the following words:

> There was genuine suspicion of Muslims and defensiveness on the part of Muslims . . . just makes you walk around the streets much more carefully. I've learned to be much more defensive in public situations. Certain people get angry, not everyone. I just mean have a defensive self-protective demeanor. You just have to have an eye out on what is going on around you a little bit more. A guy with one too many beers starts asking you too many questions and you have a feeling this isn't going the right way—time to move on. I have stopped going to bars by myself, which I used to do quite often. I only go with friends. Start facing the reality.[19]

A complete racialization of Muslims as threatening, terrorist, and untrustworthy was reflected in the all-encompassing reach of the process, ranging from the actions of law enforcement and immigration agencies to innocuous encounters in workplaces, neighborhoods, and public spaces.

The construction of Muslim identity in this particular way had wider ramifications for all South Asian communities who "appeared Muslim." The approach of law enforcement and immigration agencies reflected in systematic targeting of Muslims further strengthened the public attitude of hostility and bias toward Muslims and those who appeared to be Muslim. A very high number of bias crimes against Muslims, Hindus, and Sikhs by the public in the years following the 9/11 attacks is thus inextricably linked to the approach of law enforcement and other governmental agencies that used religious and national identities to profile and target communities in the War on Terror. Legal scholars have suggested that there is a mutually constitutive relationship between systematic racial profiling by law enforcement agencies and hate violence committed by the public. Muneer Ahmad argues that the public hate violence against South Asians and Arabs is aided and strengthened by the flawed logic used in racial profiling by the law enforcement agencies. The logic that Muslims as a group are suspicious because those involved in the 9/11 attacks were Muslims leads to profiling of Muslims. Hate crimes operate on the same logic: any Muslim-looking person belongs to a larger suspicious community and is hence a possible target of racial violence on the streets (Ahmad 2002). Leti Volpp, analyzing the post-9/11 profiling and violence against South Asians and Arabs, critiques the conventional legal understanding of public versus private actions and argues that the private actions of the U.S. populace, in the form of hate violence attacks against Arab and South Asian Americans, bears a direct relationship to the explicit racial and religious profiling by the U.S. government (Volpp 2002). The hate crimes against Sikhs partly underline this insidious logic of profiling that fuels public violence against those who appear to be Muslim or Arab.

## Embodying Difference: Sikhs in the Post-9/11 United States

For Sikh Americans, the 9/11 attacks initiated a new phase that was defined by their sharply increased vulnerability to hate violence in public spaces. The increased vulnerability was apparent on September 11, 2001, itself when a Brooklyn-raised Sikh faced racial hostility on the streets of Manhattan within a few hours of attacks on the Twin Towers. Amrik Singh Chawla, who was present in close proximity to the Twin Towers at the time of attack, found himself being chased down the streets of Manhattan by a group of people yelling and calling him "terrorist." He somehow managed to safely get into a subway train and reach Brooklyn. Mr. Chawla's first act of self-protection was to take off his turban and wear his hair in ponytail for the rest of the day (Sengupta 2001). In another New York City incident on the same day, Attar Singh, a sixty-three-year-old-Sikh, was beaten up with baseball bats studded with nails in the Richmond Hill neighborhood of Queens by a group of teenagers. Mr. Singh, who had just finished his prayers in a Sikh temple (Gurdwara), was found bleeding on the street with multiple injuries. His attackers called him a "terrorist" and yelled that he should go back to his country (Vaidyanathan 2011). Such incidents of hate violence began even before the U.S. government released any information about those involved in the 9/11 attacks.

On September 12, 2001, a day after the 9/11 attacks, Mr. Sher Singh, a turbaned Sikh with flowing beard, was taken off an Amtrak train in Providence, Rhode Island, by a phalanx of police and FBI agents armed with bomb-sniffing dogs on the suspicion of possible involvement with the 9/11 attacks. Members of the crowd assembled during his arrest reportedly shouted: "Kill him," "Burn in Hell," and "You killed my brother." He was interrogated for several hours and released on the same day, but the video of his arrest was splashed on the national television as the first suspect detained and interrogated for the 9/11 attacks. The Providence Police later charged him for carrying a small ceremonial knife (*kirpan*) that is mandated by the Sikh religion (Goodstein and Niebuhr 2001). The incident was later explained as an emotional overreaction to deep anxiety created by the extraordinary attacks on the Twin Towers and Pentagon, and subsequent strain on the law enforcement agencies. However, the media splash strengthened the connection between terrorists and a turbaned male with a long flowing beard. This highly publicized incident was followed three days later by the killing of Balbir Singh Sodhi, a Sikh American, in a hate crime attack in Arizona. The killer of Mr. Sodhi, as mentioned earlier in the chapter, later confessed that he wanted to kill an Arab Muslim to retaliate against the attack on the United States (Singh 2002). In the weeks and months following the 9/11 attacks, the national and local media did not pay much attention to these incidents, and it was only through the painstaking work of Sikh and other community organizations including Arab, Muslim, and South Asian groups that these stories were pieced together and a clearer picture of public violence, particularly against Sikhs, alongside Arabs, Muslims, and South Asians, emerged.

Sikh Americans were quick to realize that they were going to be one of the prime targets of racial hostility and violence that was unleashed after the 9/11 attacks. A study conducted by the Pluralism Project at Harvard University found that the level of vulnerability and fear in the post-9/11 period was highest among Sikh Americans. The majority of Sikh respondents (64 percent) feared potential dangers of hate violence in the days and months after the 9/11 attacks. Approximately 83 percent of Sikh respondents reported that either they or someone they knew had experienced a hate crime or incident. However, a very high number of Sikh respondents (90 percent) said that neither they nor any one they knew personally had experienced deportation or detention after 9/11. A comparison with Pakistani Muslim respondents indicated that the fear of hate violence was much more pronounced among Sikhs in the post-9/11 period. A significantly lower proportion of Pakistani American Muslim respondents (48 percent) reported that either they or someone they knew experienced hate crimes or incidents in the post-9/11 period. However, approximately 33 percent of Pakistani respondents knew of someone who had been detained or deported. The study also referred to a greater concern among Muslims about their acceptance in American society and possible targeting by the government. Sikhs, however, were more concerned about hate violence, but did not express a fear of targeting by the government and indicated a higher level of acceptance in American society (Han 2006).

The difference between the experiences of Muslims and Sikhs has evolved even further in the post-9/11 period. The regime of surveillance, community mapping, and extensive use of informants defines the Muslim experience in the post-9/11 period, as discussed earlier. Law enforcement agencies continue to approach the Muslim community as a "suspect community" and are aided and abetted in this approach through an ongoing public discourse against Muslims and through the War on Terror. Sikhs, in contrast, continue to be the targets of hate violence in public places, but experience significantly less targeting by law enforcement agencies. The continuation of hate violence against Sikhs was most starkly reflected in mass killing of six Sikhs at a Gurdwara (Sikh temple) in Oak Creek, Wisconsin, by a white supremacist on August 5, 2012 (Mishra 2012). Civil rights groups and community organizations such as SAALT, the Sikh Coalition, SALDEF, and others were galvanized by this attack, and they came together to provide support to the victims and their families. They helped organize protests across the nation to amplify the voices of individuals and communities impacted by hate violence. The campaign led to a special hearing by the Senate Judiciary Committee on "Hate Crimes and Threat of Domestic Extremism." One of the important demands put forward by these groups was to improve data gathering by the FBI on hate crimes targeted at specific religious communities. The campaign gathered momentum in the wake of the Oak Creek killings, and the FBI decided to change its policy in 2013 to track hate crimes against Sikhs, Hindus, and Arabs in addition to Christians, Jews, Muslims, and atheists, who were already being tracked for hate crimes.[20]

The post-9/11 hate violence against Sikhs is often framed as something that emerged from the lack of knowledge about the group among the general population. A forty-year-old Pakistani Muslim immigrant in Los Angeles expressed this idea in the following words: "When 9-11 happened, mostly Sikh people were killed over here. Just because the Americans thought they are Muslim. It is very hard for these people [Americans] to understand about other nations . . . geographically and nation-wise, they are very naive. They don't have knowledge of other nations, religions, and cultures."[21] The incidents of attacks on Sikhs were seen as cases of mistaken identity, and many shared the interviewee's sentiment that this hostility was due to the lack of information among average Americans about different nations, religions, and cultures. Even though the Sikh beard and turban have always functioned as physical embodiments of racial and religious differences, the Twin Tower attacks changed the meaning of the Sikh turban in a fundamental way. Sikhs with turbans became easily accessible proxies for terrorism in the popular imagination. Their appearance took on a new meaning as the public perception conflated the Sikh turban with that of Osama Bin Laden's, and by implication identified the group with terrorists who were determined to harm the United States.

Sonny Singh, a musician and a community activist, wrote about his experience as a Sikh after the 9/11 attacks: "Most commonly, someone will call me a terrorist or 'Osama,' either directly to my face or to someone they are with, with the intention of me hearing it" (2011). A 2013 study conducted by the Stanford Peace Innovation Lab reported that 70 percent of Americans cannot identify a Sikh man in a picture as Sikh.

Approximately 49 percent of Americans believe Sikhism is a sect of Islam. Furthermore, respondents also tend to associate turbans with Osama bin Laden more than with Muslim and Sikh alternatives and more than with no one in particular. The study also found that 79 percent of respondents cannot identify India as the geographic origin of Sikhism. In fact, the turban itself has become an object of enmity, and it is associated with figures who have played the role of antagonist in the news and other popular narratives over the past several years.[22] The portrayal of Muslims and Arabs as well as turbaned figures in mass media and popular culture has contributed immensely to the racialization of Sikhs as figures of distrust and animosity.[23]

Despite the changed meaning of the Sikh turban in the popular imagination, the hostility against Sikhs cannot be explained away primarily as a case of "mistaken identity," since there is a long history of racialization and exclusion of the group. As discussed earlier, Sikh migration began at the turn of the twentieth century, when they first reached the West Coast of the United States and found work in agricultural fields, lumber mills, and railroads. However, they were brutally attacked as "ragheads" by white labor and became targets of race riots in Bellingham, Washington, in 1907 and Live Oak, California, in 1908.[24] Using the explanation of mistaken identity to frame the hostility against Sikhs in the United States is also belied by the experiences of institutionalized racism and discrimination encountered by the community in workplaces, the legal arena, and educational system. Major private companies have engaged in employment discrimination against Sikhs based on their appearance and use of the turban. For instance, Disney World fired a Sikh employee in 2008 because turbaned Sikhs did not conform to their conception of the "Disney look."[25]

Similarly, Sikhs have faced discrimination by different governmental agencies that object to turbans and beards on the grounds of professionalism and security. In 2001, the NYPD objected to Jagjit Singh Jassi wearing a turban to work and asked him either to resign or be fired from the job. Mr. Jassi resigned and filed a case with the New York City Human Rights Commission against the NYPD. The case eventually led to monetary compensation and reinstatement at his job. A similar case was filed in 2002 by another NYPD Sikh police officer, Amric Singh Rathour, who was removed from his job for wearing a turban, but was reinstated after the settlement of the case.[26] The U.S. military still does not allow Sikhs to serve in the military due to its strict grooming and dress regulations. Despite recent changes in grooming policies allowing for leniency, Sikhs argue that it is very difficult for them to join the military.[27] Sikhs have filed legal cases in many jurisdictions to challenge such discriminatory practices and used the right to religious freedom as one of the major arguments against discrimination. However, such legal challenges have required Sikhs to be highly vigilant and have demanded significant resources on the part of both individual plaintiffs as well as the community. Moreover, the success in challenging such discriminatory practices has been very slow.

The institutional discrimination against Sikhs has touched other facets of their lives as well. Sikh children have been barred in the past from schools for carrying *kirpan* mandated by Sikhism for observant Sikhs, and it was only after prolonged legal battles that school districts in different jurisdictions have started becoming tolerant of this religious right (Lal 1996). The Sikh community is currently engaged with another issue that impacts Sikh children disproportionately across the United States: school bullying. Surveys conducted by Sikh civil rights groups have pointed to a dire situation where a majority of Sikh students have been harassed, bullied, and physically attacked in schools because of their turbans and uncut hair. A survey of Sikh students in Queens, New York, conducted by the Sikh Coalition in 2007 reported that over 40 percent of Sikh students who wear turbans or *patkas*—a head covering often worn by many Sikh children and adults in place of a turban—have been subjected to some form of physical harassment, including hitting, punching, or disrespectful touching of the head. These students often complain to school personnel, but about one-third of their complaints go unheeded.[28]

The varied examples discussed above suggest that Sikh racialization in the United States is a continuation of an ongoing history of violence, marginalization, and institutional discrimination that has affected all facets of their lives. The multiple layers of Sikh racialization include attribution to them of exclusionary meanings such as "strangers" and "outsiders," based on their religiously mandated turban and beard, alongside racialization linked to the construction of Muslims as a "suspicious community" and "prone to terrorism." The racialization of Sikhs thus has elements that are distinctive to Sikh religious identity as well as features that are deeply connected to the racial construction of Muslims and those "appearing to be Muslims." The post-9/11 period has brought both these dynamics to the fore of Sikh experience.

## Patterns of Mobilization against Racial Targeting

Historically, those who have been racialized through a process of lumping have often demonstrated their agency by claiming certain identities and disavowing others. As discussed earlier, the panethnic category of Asian American as a racial and political organizing resource emerged in the 1960s, when groups fighting against the treatment of different Asian groups as outsiders used this for mobilization against racism and nativism (Omi and Winant 1994; Espiritu 1992; Prashad 1998). Organizations representing different Asian communities were able to turn racial lumping into a political tool that was used as a mobilizing identity to contest racism. The example of Asian Americans thus points to the agency of racialized groups in rearticulating new racial meanings and alliances. This framework is of critical importance while analyzing the responses of South Asian groups to racialization in the post-9/11 period. South Asians were not only victimized and attributed with particular racial meanings but they also contested racialization by foregrounding certain identities and avoiding others. I argue that the response on the part of different South Asian groups pointed to a racial project that was very different from the 1960s Asian American response to racialization or the consolidation of Asian American identity in the wake of the Vincent Chin killing in 1982. In particular, racial hostility and attacks against South Asians in the post-9/11 period did not elicit panethnic solidarity, as the theories of panethnicity predicted.

Interviews with community members and activists suggest that the responses of different South Asian groups to racial targeting after 9/11 broke down primarily along the lines of religious identity, with a certain amount of slippage between religious and national identity. However, there was also a trend of panethnic South Asian mobilization, which was significant though less prominent. Before presenting the analysis of interviews on this issue, it is important to add a caveat: only a few interviewees spoke openly on the question of intragroup relationships in the context of the post-9/11 racial targeting. Yet the opinions articulated by these interviewees are important because they in part explain the absence of panethnic South Asian solidarity in response to the racial hostility.

Furthermore, the analysis of the interviews presented here is substantiated by other sources as well.

Asked about the possibility of a united campaign against racial targeting after September 11, a New York–based sixty-five-year-old Hindu Indian community leader said:

> Hindus must be supporting Sikhs on that sort of campaign but
> I don't see any way that Pakistanis, Indians, and Bangladeshi can
> meet. Religion is a big divide—it really is. It is not only a feeling,
> but it is there in practical life also even in India, I think, Hindus
> don't trust Muslims, whether they (Muslims) would go for India
> or for Pakistan. This is really a problem, though it should not
> be, but it is and that can be reflected here also. Religion is a big
> factor.[29]

This statement points to the fault lines within the South Asian community and to the possible hurdles to a unified response to racial targeting. There is a clear slippage here between nation of origin and religious identity, with the underlying erroneous presumption that being Indian is equivalent to being Hindu. The statement also points to the transnational dimension of religious differences: the politics of religious conflict in India and South Asia feed into the political response of South Asian groups in the United States (as will be discussed in detail in chapter 6).[30]

A thirty-year-old activist of Hindu Indian descent working with a grassroots South Asian organization in New York City talked about the Indian Hindu community's reaction to racial targeting, arrests, and deportation in the months following the 9/11 attack. She said:

> I think they [Indian Hindus], on one hand, felt a little saved; we
> got by this time. But on the other hand, it was oh, good, it is them
> [Muslims]. And it created even sharper divisions. There is already
> all of our stuff we [Indians] bring from home about Pakistanis and
> Bangladeshis and all of that. I think it created more of that us
> and them divide. I am talking mostly about Hindu Indians here.
> Of course, there were exceptions and folks that expressed a lot
> of solidarity. Most of us who are here [in this organization] are
> Indian . . . But the Indian community, yeah, I think there was a
> real conservative response, very little visible showing of support

or solidarity with other South Asians who were being targeted. There was a desire to distance.[31]

There was a clear attempt to foreground an Indian Hindu identity and distance from identities that included others, particularly Muslims, Pakistanis, and Bangladeshis. Analyzing the responses of different South Asian groups amidst the atmosphere of fear and intimidation in the days and months following 9/11, Vijay Prashad wrote, "Rumors flew about that the Indian embassy in Washington asked its nationals to wear a *bindi*,[32] to help distinguish 'Indians' from Arabs and Afghans. . . . Talk of the *bindi* went about as a way for some to suggest it as an adequate sign of being a Hindu, or at least not a Muslim" (Prashad 2005, 585–86).[33] India's Consul General in New York, Shashi Tripathi, was reported in multiple media outlets after the 9/11 attacks, suggesting the precautions Indian Americans should be taking to avoid hate violence. He said, "We are also considering asking Indian women to wear a *bindi* as a distinguishing mark. Right now, everybody should be careful" (Nanda 2001). The reference to a distinguishing mark was in all likelihood about differentiating Hindus from Muslims and Arabs. Rajiv Malhotra, president of the Infinity Foundation and a well-known Indian American personality, was quoted by journalist Sarah Wildman on this issue: "A lot of Hindus suddenly have started realizing they better stand up and differentiate themselves from Muslims or Arabs" (Wildman quoted in Kurien 2003, 274). The relative silence of the Indian American Hindu community and most of the Indian American community organizations in the post-9/11 period, with direct and indirect attempts to foreground their Hindu identity, suggested a very particular racial project embedded in the idea of a narrow and exclusive Hindu identity. Prema Kurien (2003), in her important work on Indian Americans, also identified a Hindu-centric Indian identity as one of the major axes of response to racialization in the post-9/11 period.[34]

It is important to note that the assertion of a distinct religious identity and distancing from Muslims was happening not only among Hindu South Asians. This process could be seen as playing out, albeit a little differently, among Sikh Americans also. As noted earlier, Sikhs were faced with much more intense targeting in public spaces because of their religiously mandated turban and beard, and their responses were in relation to the exigencies of the situation. A fifty-two-year-old Indian Muslim immigrant from the New York Metropolitan Area pointed to the ways in which Sikhs reacted to the post-9/11 environment: "I have seen Sikhs with posters saying 'we are not Muslims.' It was shocking actually, but I guess I could understand, they were the ones targeted most. So that way everybody tried to distance themselves from Muslims, within the community. I had heard conversations in the Edison area[35] where they were saying they would go out of their way to show that they are different (Hindu)."[36] The Sikh organizations formed after September 11, 2001, to build an effective resistance against racial attacks were, however, careful not to follow the line of reasoning articulated in the "we are not Muslims" refrain. However, mobilization against racial targeting in the post-9/11 period among both Sikhs and Muslims developed primarily on religious lines, and there was only limited organizing across religious boundaries.[37]

The Sikh mobilization focused mostly on the attacks on Sikhs, and there was an emphasis on educating the law enforcement agencies as well as the general public about Sikh religious identity. The Muslim response was also mostly based on foregrounding their religious identity. Groups such as CAIR, the Muslim Public Affairs Council (MPAC), and the Council of Pakistani American Affairs (COPAA), which were some of the leading organizations working in that period to mobilize against racial targeting of Muslims, focused primarily on Muslim religious identity (Bakalian and Bozorgmehr 2009). In fact, the Sikh and Muslim groups mobilized their communities against racial and religious targeting successfully by deploying religious identity and used religious institutions—Gurdwaras and mosques—to increase community participation on this issue. There is no doubt that mobilization on the basis of religious identity is deeply linked to the racialization process, which deployed religion centrally alongside physical characteristics to attribute meanings such as "un-American," "untrustworthy," "terrorist," "outsider," and "stranger" to Muslims, Sikhs, and other South Asians and Arab Americans. In fact, the racializing dynamics that foregrounded religious identity also highlighted the tension between a possible South Asian panethnic identity and distinct religious identities. The earlier literature on South Asian Americans framed the tensions within panethnic identity more along the lines of nation of origin, whereas post-9/11 developments foreground the religious axis as an important factor.

Even as the South Asian category became more widely known and used in the post-9/11 period, such a category caused discomfort among some segments of the South Asian community. Some respondents noted an uncertainty about the use of panethnic South Asian coalitional identity during this period. For instance, a fifty-five-year-old leader of a South Asian organization based in the Los Angeles area pointed to the contradictory trends observed in the use of South Asian identity. He said: "I think post 9-11, there has been resistance to South Asian identity, people want to separate themselves from 'terrorists' . . . But yet at the same time, the category of South Asian is becoming more and more common too. You will see that in conversations . . . so South Asian identity is getting more attention and getting more mainstream. But a caution about South Asian identity has emerged in the post-9/11 period."[38] He conjectured that the caution against using a panethnic identity could be due to a need to distinguish oneself from a racialized Muslim identity. Overall, the intended or unintended consequences of mobilizing along religious lines further increased the challenges of building a successful coalitional panethnic South Asian identity.

While the dominant sections of the South Asian community responded in terms of exclusive religious identities in the post-9/11 period, there has also been a parallel racial project undertaken by groups emphasizing broader panethnic South Asian solidarity against racism. A number of organizations, in both the Los Angeles and New York areas, with modest influence within South Asian communities, used panethnic South Asian identity to mobilize the community against racial targeting. For instance, the South Asian Network (SAN) in the Los Angeles area worked with Muslim and Sikh organizations and played an important role in responding to the post-9/11 hate crimes and the atmosphere of fear. Similarly, South Asian organizations such as Desis Rising Up and Moving (DRUM), the Coney Island Avenue Project, New York Taxi Workers Alliance (NYTWA), Council of Peoples Organization (COPO), South Asian Youth Association (SAYA), and many small advocacy and service organizations in New York City actively mobilized against the targeting of South Asians. In particular, they rallied against special registration, detentions, and deportations and coordinated with others to develop a broader antiracial coalition against racial targeting of South Asians and Arabs. Organizations such as South Asian Americans Leading Together (SAALT) effectively worked on this issue with policy makers in Washington, D.C., and highlighted the violence against South Asians in the immediate aftermath of the 9/11 attacks. In fact, SAALT released one of the first reports detailing the widespread nature of retaliation against

South Asians and how the targets included a wide section of people of different religious affiliations (SAALT 2001).

However, the complexity of the issue of broader coalitional mobilization was recognized and reflected in conversations among activists and scholars. A special issue of the *Asian American Literary Review*, published on the occasion of the tenth anniversary of September 11, 2001, voiced this concern. Sunita Mukhi, writing in this special issue, underlined the limitations of broader panethnic mobilization by pointing to the foregrounding of Hindu, Muslim, and Sikh identities for gaining different kinds of representations (Mukhi 2011).[39] Overall, attempts at panethnic mobilizing against racial targeting and hate crimes were an important intervention within the South Asian community, but had to contend and negotiate with a parallel mode of responding to racialization on the basis of exclusive religious identities. Moreover, the mobilization by South Asian groups against hate crimes and profiling by law enforcement agencies witnessed occasional alliances of panethnic organizations (such as SAALT) with groups that were formed around religious identities (such as Sikh Coalition). More specifically, the targeted religious groups—particularly Muslim and Sikh groups—were willing to join coalitions with broader panethnic groups. However, the groups formed around Hindu religious identities largely stayed away from such coalitions.

I argue that panethnic mobilization and exclusive religious-identity-based mobilization are two distinct but related reactions to the racialization process noted above. Dominance of the lens of religious identities such as Hindu, Sikh, and Muslim in response to post-9/11 racial hostility cannot be explained solely by the very existence of different religious communities within the broader category of South Asians. Instead, South Asian religious groups also found a very specific institutional and ideological discourse in U.S. multiculturalism that enabled the consolidation of their religion-based responses. The emphasis on discrete and authentic identities, whether ethnic or religious, as opposed to politically crafted identities of solidarity, goes along with the basic orientation of multicultural institutional and discursive practices. In fact, U.S. multiculturalism defines the very trajectory for social and cultural representation of minority communities by foregrounding discrete religious and cultural identities rather than those based on coalitional solidarities. The tension between the acceptance of a solidarity-oriented panethnic category on the one hand, and a unique and authentic identity on the other, has also been noted by other scholars. Using the concept of racialized multiculturalism in the context of Asian Americans, Jerry Park (2008) notes that the process of racialization pushes Asian ethnic groups more toward the racialized category of Asian American, whereas the multicultural framework encourages the identities rooted in uniqueness and authenticity of particular groups such as Chinese, Japanese, and Korean. In the case of South Asians, however, the process of racialization (intensified after 9/11) has also contributed to responses rooted in unique and authentic religious identities.

## Multiculturalism, Authenticity, and Religious Recognition

In the final section of the chapter I briefly illustrate how religious groups deploy multiculturalism and claims to authenticity to stifle internal contestations within communities. Such claims to authenticity and exclusivity through multicultural discourses often work against constructing panethnic political solidarities discussed earlier. South Asian groups in the United States have often sought and gained recognition through foregrounding of religious identity.[40] For example, one of the most talked about instances of the recognition of Indian Americans by U.S. political institutions is the celebration of a Hindu religious festival (*Diwali*) by President Obama at the White House in 2009, a first by a sitting U.S. president. Underlining the importance of this momentous occasion, a *Washington Post* columnist wrote, "Never before had a sitting U.S. President personally celebrated the Diwali holiday, and with that one gesture, two million Hindu Americans felt a bit more like they belonged—one more reason to feel at home" (Shukla 2009).[41] Examples such as the above suggest the importance of promoting religious framing and discrete identity for the recognition of a particular community. However, recognition of a group through religious identity also poses certain challenges, which are manifested through assertions of authenticity and claims to represent the religion in ways that stifle multiplicity of voices within the community.

The controversy over the depiction of Hinduism in a California textbook is an example of assertion of the politics of authenticity deploying multicultural framework. In California, the controversy erupted in 2005 when Hindu organizations, led by the Vedic Foundation and Hindu Education Foundation, objected to the representation of India and Hinduism in a sixth-grade history book (Bose 2008). Some of the most controversial objections were over the depiction of the position of women in early Indian history and the links between the early Hindu religious texts and the caste system. The Hindu organizations protested against the stereotypical Western representation of Hinduism and even to the discussion of the unequal position of women and oppression of the "lower" castes in early India.

A prolonged period of mobilization and countermobilization was a part of this controversy, and progressive South Asian historians, along with a section of the Indian American community, pressed to stop the California textbook committee from accepting the changes suggested by the Hindu American groups. In a letter to the California Board of Education, a group of South Asian academics wrote:

> It is appropriate and legitimate for a range of voices to be heard on these issues. Yet we are troubled that a highly organized group of ideologically motivated who claim to speak for all "Hindus," seem to have dominated the curriculum committee hearing of the last week. The idea that school textbooks should assert a unified notion of Hinduism and ignore the vital and living reality of a complex and pluralistic religion; that textbook should not speak frankly about the historical relationship of Hinduism to the ongoing and debilitating inequality of the caste system, or about how the "laws of Manu" or other aspects of Hindu tradition, discriminated against women, is a disturbing distortion of history.[42]

The controversy reflected a split within the community over the understanding of Hinduism and on how to approach issues such as caste and gender inequality. The groups mobilizing on the basis of Hindu religious identity completely rejected any attempt to critically engage with these questions and positioned themselves as the sole representatives of the community. They presented themselves as a victim minority and even deployed the language of the civil rights movement, cultural rights, and multiculturalism to put forward a discourse of "respecting the culture" and an exclusive "right to represent and interpret their authentic culture" (Kurien 2007a; Bose 2008).

The episode underlined how the framing of authentic and exclusive religious identity promoted by a multicultural discourse ignores the internal contestations within the community about religion, identity, and representation. It illustrates the problems associated with using an exclusive religious framing to mobilize against racialization, as evident in many campaigns led by organizations such as American Hindus against Defamation (AHAD), Federation of Hindu Associations (FHA), and Hindu American Foundation (HAF). These groups, actively engaged with the California textbook issue, have projected Hinduism as characterized by its greatness, antiquity, tolerance, pluralism, nonviolence, and theological sophistication.[43] The groups have also worked against the negative stereotyping of Hinduism as "polytheistic," "idol-worshipping," "caste-ridden," and "misogynistic." However, they used the language and ideology of multiculturalism and recognition not only to partly challenge U.S. racism but to also impose their narrow and orthodox interpretations of Hinduism that was not open to the issues of caste oppression and gender inequality. To the extent that they challenged racism and ethnocentrism, their opposition was through a narrow prism of "authentic" religious identity that is not conducive to broader panethnic antiracial mobilizations. The example of Hindu American organizations during the California textbook controversy illustrates that religious-identity-based mobilizations always carry the possibility of adopting a frame that could preclude responding to different kinds of marginalizations within the community and building broader panethnic coalitions. Unsurprisingly, the response of Hindu groups to post-9/11 racism was thus tempered by the lens of exclusive religious identity and in the process constrained the development of a unified panethnic response.

The dominance of religious-identity-based mobilization to contest racism and violence against South Asians has thus challenged the theories of reactive panethnicity developed in the context of Asian Americans. As this chapter suggests, there is a need for recognizing the significance of religion analytically to fully understand the ethnoracial mobilization dynamics of groups defined by religious diversity. The foregrounding of religious identity to racialize South Asians in a particular manner and response from the community along religious lines underlines the centrality of this identity in the case of South Asians. However, the foregrounding of a particular religious identity, both in racialization and contestation against racialization, limits the possibility of a broader panethnic mobilization. Moreover, certain strands of religious mobilization, as illustrated through the California textbook controversy, deploy the politics of authenticity and recognition in ways that work against the possibility of addressing marginalizations and oppressions within the community.

## Conclusion

The analysis of racial targeting of South Asians in the post-9/11 period suggests that this group was racialized through lumping together on the basis of physical appearance, which existed simultaneously with differential racialization based on religious identity. The analysis further suggests that exclusive religious identities shaped the responses of South Asian communities against racialization, thereby challenging the existing understanding in ethnic studies, political science, and sociology that hostility against a racially lumped group leads to greater group cohesiveness and reactive panethnic solidarity. The centrality of religious identity in both racialization and mobilization against racial hostility is underlined in this chapter. Furthermore, the foregrounding of religious identity by different South Asian groups in response to racial hostility is in broad consonance with the multicultural institutional and ideological paradigm in the United States. Even while the multicultural framework creates institutional avenues and discursive practices to contest racism and ethnocentrism, it simultaneously provides avenues to construct, strengthen, and mobilize authentic and essentialized identities that often constrain political solidarities. South Asian political mobilization, particularly in the context of post-9/11 racialization, is thus deeply shaped by religious distinctions within the community, and the context of racialization of religious identities has further foregrounded religious identity in South Asian civic and political spheres.

# 4

# Mapping the Modes of Mobilization

South Asian Americans are highly visible in lucrative professions such as medicine, engineering, finance, business, information technology, and media, yet their political participation and representation remains very limited and sporadic. Even the examples of South Asian or Indian American electoral success—governors Bobby Jindal of Louisiana and Nikki Haley Randhawa of South Carolina, for instance—are not linked to greater mobilization and participation of South Asian Americans. Another notable trend in this regard is the appointment of a number of South Asians to positions that intersect the arenas of politics and policy. Over the years, President Obama's administration has appointed a number of South Asians in important positions, including Rajiv Shah, administrator, United States Agency for International Development; Vivek Kundra, federal chief information officer; Aneesh Chopra, federal chief technology officer; Arif Alikhan, assistant secretary for the Department of Homeland Security's Office of Policy Development; Neal Katyal, the acting solicitor general and the principal deputy solicitor general; and Kal Pen, an Indian American actor who was given a prominent liaison role at the White House.

More recently, the White House also nominated Dr. Vivek Murthy, an Indian American physician, for the position of surgeon general of the United States. The nomination hit a snag at the stage of Senate confirmation on account of opposition by the National Rifle Association (NRA) due to Dr. Murthy's pro–gun control views and he was confirmed only after a long delay. The appointment of Neera Tanden as the president of the Center for American Progress, a highly regarded liberal think tank, and the Senate confirmation of Srikanth "Sri" Srinivisan as a judge on the U.S. Court of Appeals for the District of Columbia circuit point to the increased presence of South Asians in the world of politics and policy, albeit primarily through nonelectoral means. South Asians, thus, present a puzzling picture of marginalization in terms of low levels of mass participation in the political process combined with incorporation of a selective few into high-profile political and policy positions. This chapter focuses on the contradictory trends in political participation of South Asians in order to develop a framework that adequately explains the specific trajectory of this group.

This chapter foregrounds the distinct patterns of ethnoracial mobilization shaped by internal cleavages such as occupation, class, gender, and sexuality concerns alongside nation of origin and underlines the challenges of a unified ethnic (Indian/Pakistani/Bangladeshi) or panethnic (South Asian) mobilization. In this chapter, I analyze the broad patterns of political participation and representation among South Asians through survey data and qualitative interviews. I first present an overview of voting and other forms of political participation among South Asians in comparison to other Asian American groups. The next section deals with the institutional and demographic context in which South Asians are becoming a part of the political process. In this section I analyze data from qualitative interviews on the role of political parties and the challenges of a demographic reality of a dispersed population. In the final section, I identify three dominant trends of South Asian political mobilization to note that each of them largely ignores the broader South Asian community and focuses only on a narrow socioeconomic elite. These three trends include (1) a small but growing phenomenon of South Asian candidates contesting and occasionally winning in predominantly white electoral districts, (2) campaign contributions as a significant mode of gaining political influence, and (3) primacy of lobbying among South Asians as a form of political engagement. I elaborate on these three distinct trends and point to the limited role of a unified, mass-scale ethnoracial mobilization in the political incorporation trajectory of South Asians. The chapter ends with an analysis of a distinct and parallel trend of mobilizing that is focused on low-income and working-class South Asians. For these groups, issues around socioeconomic resources come to the fore, suggesting that the dominant understanding of immigrant political mobilization, which relies on a unified ethnoracial framework, has limited value in understanding varied mobilization among South Asians. These social justice–oriented South Asian groups are increasingly moving toward multiracial mobilizing to address their important concerns.

The experience of South Asians suggests that there is limited mass-level ethnoracial mobilization, either in the context of electoral participation or other kinds of political engagement. Instead, the electoral aspirants from the community have often shown an inclination for deemphasizing their ethnoracial identity, a trend that is exemplified by South Asian electoral experiments, with some successes, from white majority districts. As I argue in this chapter, South Asian candidates in white majority districts do not rely on the votes of their co-ethnics, since these electoral districts often have negligible South Asian populations. The other mobilizing trends among South Asians primarily rely on the social and economic elite of the community and use lobbying or campaign contributions in order to gain influence in the mainstream political process. The first strategy—the trend of contesting from white majority districts—leads the group further away from ethnoracial mobilization, while the other two, centered on a narrow segment of socioeconomic elites, leaves a large segment of the community out of the process of political inclusion. Moreover, the ethnic organizing within the South Asian community has foregrounded occupational and class interests in a manner that does not easily lend itself to a broader, cross-class ethnoracial mobilization, as it is often centered on smaller niche segments of the community.

## South Asian Political Participation: The Picture from the Survey Data

The focus of this study is not exclusively on the voting behavior of South Asians, but an overview of electoral behavior, as well as other forms of participation, does provide an indication of the broad trends in mass political participation. The analysis of comparative political participation data of different ethnoracial groups suggests a participation gap on the part of minority groups such as Asian Americans and Latinos. Karthick Ramakrishnan (2005), comparing levels of political participation in California during the 2002 election cycle, analyzed indicators such as voting, signing petitions, attending local meetings, and writing to elected officials to argue that the rate of those who voted regularly was significantly lower among Latino and Asian immigrants than white immigrants. The difference persisted in three generations for which the data were reported, with the gap closing in the third generation. The gap was most glaring when it came to voting, but it narrowed on nonvoting measures of participation. Multivariate analysis suggested that differences in participation persisted even after controlling for factors such as age, education, income, gender, and home ownership. Some of these variables reduced the gap, but they did not fully account for it (Ramakrishnan 2005, 140–60). In other words, the differences in participation were not explained by these factors and clear patterns of racial differences persisted. Other studies using Census and survey data also find that voting-age Asian Americans register and vote at rates lower than their counterparts in all other major racial and ethnic groups (Uhlaner, Cain, and Kiewiet 1989; Nakanishi 1991; Lien 2001; Cho 1999; Junn 1999).

The political participation level of South Asians follows this broader trend among Asian Americans. The low level of mass political participation is clearly evident when we look at the comparative rates of voting among South Asians in relation to traditional predictors of political participation. The classical literature on political participation argues that there is a strong positive correlation between the level of political participation and socioeconomic indicators such as income and education (Verba and Nie 1972; Rosenstone and Hansen 1993; Verba, Schlozman, and Brady 1995). However, Asian Indians, with the highest average household income among all ethnoracial groups and a very high proportion of college graduates, do not show a greater level of political participation. Figure 2 demonstrates that the rate of voting among Asian Indians is not

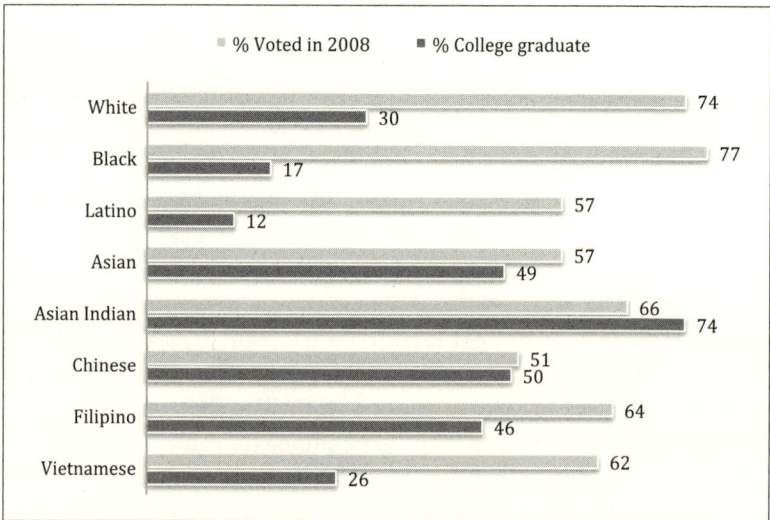

Figure 2. Voting and Educational Attainment among Adult Citizens for Select Groups. Source: 2008 Current Population Survey Voter Supplement (cited in Wong, Ramakrishnan, Lee, and Junn 2011, 6).

commensurate to the proportion of college graduates. Despite having the highest proportion of college graduates (74 percent), the rate of voting is lower (66 percent) among them in comparison to other ethnic groups who have lower levels of college graduates but higher levels of voting. Thus, the data clearly show the persistence of lower levels of political participation among Asian Indians, which goes against the common wisdom that higher levels of education lead to higher rates of participation.

The Pilot Study of the National Asian American Political Survey (PNAAPS) 2000–2001 and the National Asian American Survey (NAAS) 2008 are the two most important surveys that provide comprehensive data on voting and other forms of political participation among Asian and South Asian Americans.[1] The PNAAPS data on voter registration and voting among adults suggest that South Asians have lower levels of registration and voting compared to other Asian groups (see Table 3). Thirty-nine percent of South Asians registered to vote in comparison to 75, 62, and 49 percent of Japanese, Filipino, and Chinese, respectively. The rate of voting is also lower among South Asians (36) compared to Japanese (63), Filipinos (47), and Chinese (41). However, if participation beyond

TABLE 3

**Percentage Distribution of Political Participation by Ethnic Groups**

| | TOTAL REGISTERED | TOTAL VOTED IN 2000 | TOTAL PARTICIPATION BEYOND VOTING |
|---|---|---|---|
| Chinese | 49 | 41 | 35 |
| Japanese | 75 | 63 | 55 |
| Korean | 48 | 34 | 39 |
| Vietnamese | 43 | 39 | 33 |
| Filipino | 62 | 47 | 50 |
| South Asian | 39 | 36 | 57 |

Source: Pilot National Asian American Political Survey, 2000–2001 (Lien, Conway, and Wong 2004, 161).

Note: Distribution does not take into account eligibility requirements for registration or voting.

TABLE 4

**Percentage Distribution of Political Participation by Ethnic Groups among Those Eligible for Registration and Voting**

| | REGISTERED TO VOTE (AMONG CITIZENS) | VOTED IN 2000 (AMONG REGISTERED) | PARTICIPATION IN ACTIVITY BEYOND VOTING |
|---|---|---|---|
| Chinese | 78 | 84 | 35 |
| Japanese | 88 | 83 | 55 |
| Korean | 87 | 71 | 39 |
| Filipino | 79 | 76 | 50 |
| Vietnamese | 65 | 92 | 33 |
| South Asian | 78 | 93 | 57 |

Source: Pilot National Asian American Political Survey, 2000–2001 (Lien, Conway, and Wong 2004, 163).
Note: Analysis is confined to citizens only. All figures are in percentages.

voting—which included signing a petition, calling a public official, and participating in local meetings—is taken into account, South Asians (57) have a higher level of participation as compared to Japanese (55), Filipinos (50), and Koreans (39). When eligibility for registration and voting is taken into account (the analysis is confined to citizens only), South Asians are closer to other Asian American groups in terms of registering. Once registered, South Asians turn out to vote at a higher rate than other Asian American groups (93) (see Table 4). Similarly, in this category, South Asians are higher than other Asian American groups in participation beyond voting (57).

The NAAS data report low naturalization rates among South Asians, a trend underlined by PNAAPS data as well. According to NAAS, Asian Indians lag behind other Asian American groups in terms of citizenship acquisition (see Table 5). Only 49 percent of adult Asian Indians are citizens, in comparison to significantly higher percentages of Vietnamese (76), Filipinos (72), Japanese (70), Chinese (67), and Koreans (61). The rate of voting in the 2004 elections for Asian Indians (among all adults) was significantly lower (33) than the average rate of voting for all Asian

TABLE 5

**Citizenship and Voting Rates by National Origin**

|  | CITIZEN | VOTED IN NOV. 2004* | VOTED IN NOV. 2004** | VOTED IN THE 2008 PRIMARIES* | VOTED IN THE 2008 PRIMARIES** |
|---|---|---|---|---|---|
| Asian Indian | 49 | 65 | 33 | 42 | 18 |
| Chinese | 67 | 57 | 39 | 45 | 23 |
| Filipino | 72 | 65 | 48 | 53 | 32 |
| Japanese | 70 | 79 | 55 | 54 | 34 |
| Korean | 61 | 60 | 37 | 35 | 17 |
| Vietnamese | 76 | 68 | 51 | 39 | 23 |
| TOTAL | 64 | 65 | 45 | 46 | 24 |

Source: National Asian American Survey, 2008 (Wong et al. 2011, 55).
Note: *adult citizens **all adults. All figures are in percentages.

Americans (45). However, the rate of voting among Asian Indians with citizenship was 65 percent, which is still lower than Japanese (79) and Vietnamese (68), but at par with the average Asian American voting rate (65). Overall, the data provide a mixed picture of South Asian political participation. The level of participation is equal to other Asian American groups—these groups already have relatively lower participation in comparison to other ethnoracial groups—if the analysis is confined to citizens only, and South Asians have a higher level of participation on measures beyond voting. However, the level of political participation, particularly voting, goes down drastically among South Asians due to the lower rates of naturalization. This trend of low naturalization among South Asians is broadly in line with Latino and Caribbean immigrants, who generally postpone their decision to naturalize in anticipation of returning back to their home countries (Jones-Correa 1998; Rogers 2006). To further understand the relatively lower level of mass political participation among South Asians, it is also important to analyze the institutional context in which the group is engaging with the political process.[2]

## Participation, Political Parties, and Demographic Realities

There are two important aspects of the current institutional context and demographic reality that have significant implications for South Asian political participation: (1) the historical evolution and changing role of political parties and candidates in mobilizing ethnic and minority communities, and (2) the emerging demographic pattern of South Asians, characterized by a population with low residential density.

It is also important to note that South Asian political engagement in the United States occurs in a larger context that generates political apathy and low participation and does not encourage new groups to participate in the political process. Referring to this political environment, a New York–based South Asian community leader said:

> I would argue that the U.S. presents for anybody, including the white Americans, one of the most restrictive political spaces for engagement. Just look at what is happening across the U.S. In what ways are Americans actually involved with politics? Leave alone immigrants, but in what ways are fully nationalized fifth or eighth or tenth generation Americans involved with politics. . . . It is a fairly depoliticized community as a whole. As a nation and a community, this is a community that is tremendously depoliticized. So, with that as a context now let's ask the question what chances does an immigrant stand in terms of really getting engaged in American politics. It is a very difficult task—in this kind of context one really needs to ask is the immigrants' distance from political involvement here really surprising?[3]

The quote refers to the larger context in which immigrant political incorporation is taking place today. The broad trend of secular decline in voting—with a few recent exceptions—and other forms of political participation alongside the reduced role of political parties in mobilizing citizens do not create an environment conducive for engagement of new immigrants. The South Asian experience suggests a trend where political parties are reluctant to mobilize new immigrants even though they are expected to approach all segments of the citizenry irrespective of race, class, gender, sexuality, and immigration history. A number of South Asian community leaders pointed out that while political parties—both

Democratic and Republican—do not reach out to new immigrants, they remain open to people from the community who approach them. Explaining the outlook of political parties to South Asian immigrants, a community activist of Indian descent based in New York City said:

I don't think they [political parties] are going around and asking for us to participate, because the system is well established and they don't see any reason to bring anybody new into the fold. If you are involved in politics in our country [India], you know we go around and try to get everybody. . . . Here they do not have to do that because there are only two parties. Secondly, in any election not even 35 percent of the people participate [*sic*]. The rest of the people either do not care or they do not have the time to care. So political participation itself is relatively low and that is why parties are not that much active . . . they are not actively pushing people to join them. There is no push. I have never seen that push to make members, no. That is why they are not coming to look for Indians or Pakistanis. They are not looking because they have a system in place.[4]

When asked about South Asians who approach political parties to get involved, he said:

I don't think it is a bad experience . . . I live in a place called Westchester County; it is not a city, it's a suburb. There are not that many minorities there. Because I have political ambitions or whatever you call it, and I was in a political party before [in India], so I wanted to join a party here. So I talked with the Democrats and they were happy to take me into their party and they started inviting me. I think if you go there and say that I wanted to get involved, they would be very happy to take you in.[5]

The experience of South Asians suggests that the onus is on the group and individuals within the community to initiate the process and approach political parties for any kind of recognition and representation. Political parties, however, are reluctant to mobilize and bring new groups into the political process. In fact, parties do not see the need for involving new groups as long as their voting blocks and coalitions are intact.[6]

Some of the interviewees also point to the apprehension on the part of political parties and candidates in including new voters. A South Asian community leader of Bangladeshi descent, who unsuccessfully contested a state assembly seat in Queens, New York, stated:

> Political parties are afraid; they don't want to see people (new immigrants) registered. I am a commissioner, one of the commissioners in New York City for the voter assistance commission. Even in the budget, we don't get enough money from the system . . . the people in the system don't want to see more people getting registered, because then somebody new will come and beat them. And again, I can talk about New York City, because the majority of people in the neighborhood now are colored people, immigrants. If they will become registered, the power equation will be changed, so they don't want it. They say yes, we have to do this, but when practicality comes, they don't give any money, they are not encouraging you.[7]

The concerns articulated by South Asians find resonance among other minority groups as well. Current scholarship on new immigrant groups unequivocally suggests that there is a persistent gap in the mobilization of racial minorities by established political parties (Jones-Correa 1998; Ramakrishnan 2005; Wong 2006). This phenomenon is in contrast with past waves of immigrants—the Europeans in the early twentieth century—who were incorporated largely due to the mobilization efforts of political parties and candidates, especially the urban political machines (Cornwell 1960; Dahl 1961). The contemporary Latino and Asian immigrant groups, however, have seen community organizations of different kinds—social service, labor, ethnic and religious—playing a far more important role than political parties in bringing them into the political process. These organizations work toward a broader political involvement of immigrant groups rather than focusing exclusively on registration and voting (Wong 2006). Nonetheless, the activities and mobilizations of these community organizations have a limited reach, and they are mostly focused on the low socioeconomic strata of these communities. They cannot match the scope and resources of the political parties in mobilizing and bringing new groups to the political process. Thus, one of the most important implications of the declining role of political parties has been the relative absence of an important instrument that facilitated eth-noracial mobilization in the past. Even when political parties and candidates are forced to go to new groups due to the competitive dynamics of the electoral process, they are very selective in mobilizing only certain segments of the immigrant pop-ulation. The extent of mobilization is limited to registered voters and, in the case of presidential elections, to those located in battleground states (Wong 2006). For instance, there have been serious attempts to mobilize Latino voters only in selected battleground states in the recent presiden-tial elections. Groups such as South Asians, which are numerically not large and not densely concentrated in any one area, have almost negligi-ble influence on electoral outcomes and, as a result, they are even more overlooked and marginalized by political parties and candidates.

A dispersed residential settlement of South Asians further com-pounds their marginalization in the political process. The demographic pattern of the group has historically been different in comparison to most other immigrant communities. South Asians settled in different parts of the United States in the post-1965 period due to the waves of immigration driven by professions such as medicine, engineering, and other allied fields. Unlike most other ethnic groups, South Asians have historically not created ethnic neighborhoods because of these specific patterns of immigration and accompanying socioeconomic diversity (Shukla 2003). The community is settled in urban as well as suburban areas that make the traditional mode of ethnic political mobilization through neighbor-hoods difficult. Many of the interviewees spoke about the double mar-ginalization of the group stemming from their racial minority status as well as the lack of numbers in particular areas required to affect the elec-toral process. A South Asian community leader of Indian descent from New York City, talking about the community's involvement in local pol-itics, said: "Getting involved in local school district politics and city council politics, I think, is a matter of building concentration and den-sity. This politics works only if you build density . . . the South Asian community is dispersed, unlike Mexican immigrants—or the Chinese community, which is significantly concentrated in certain locations . . . those densities are not available to South Asian immigrants, therefore, the process is much slower."[8] The lack of density creates both internal constraints in terms of developing a critical mass to intervene effectively in the political process as well as external constraints in terms of the ability to attract political parties and candidates to engage with the group at a sustained level. A South Asian community leader, explaining the reluctance of political parties to engage with the community, said: "I don't think political parties are making enough attempts to bring the community into the political process—absolutely not. Maybe because they don't feel we have numbers—like Hispanics or African Americans. Yes, if any of us has a real ambition then, yes, they will probably say, alright, let's involve him. But on their own, I don't see anybody approach our people to join politics."[9]

An increasing concentration of South Asians in some parts of the Borough of Queens in New York City, however, is fast producing a demand for redistricting to facilitate South Asian electoral representation. A group of South Asian activists have formed an organization called Taking Our Seat to demand redistricting of the existing city council districts that would keep areas with a South Asian concentration in one district. They have focused on two neighborhood clusters for this purpose: Richmond Hill and South Ozone Park, and Briarwood and Jamaica Hills. South Asian activists argue that the western boundary of District 28 has been drawn in a way that leaves out a section of South Asians and their important institutions in the Richmond Hill and South Ozone cluster of neighborhoods out of that district. They demand that the western boundary be moved to accommodate more South Asians. Similarly, South Asians in the Briarwood and Jamaica Hills area are divided between districts 24 and 29 in a way that reduces their concentration and political efficacy. The group has thus made representations to keep South Asian political interests in mind while redrawing these districts.[10] However, such trends are still fledgling, and they have not yet found their full expression.[11] The possible political space for ethnoracial mobilization has slowly emerged in some other parts of New York City due to the increased community concentration. Clusters of Bangladeshis in Parkchester, the Bronx, and Pakistanis on Coney Island Avenue, Brooklyn, have created communities of South Asians that are aspiring for political recognition through community mobilizations. Similar patterns can be seen in the suburban town of Edison, New Jersey, where the Indian immigrant community has seen a moderate concentration (Berger 2008; Palash Ghosh 2013; Tung 2011). Similar patterns are emerging in the Bay Area in northern California. Notwithstanding these emerging small pockets of concentration, the dispersed population remains the dominant pattern of settlement among South Asian immigrants.

While traditional modes of mobilization building upon population concentration have largely eluded South Asians, their dispersal in different parts of the United States has opened up possibilities for new experiments in political representation. This chapter elaborates on some of the new ways in which South Asian Americans have tried to gain representation and political influence. These methods indicate a move away from the traditional modes of representation that relied heavily on unified ethnic mobilizations. The trends of electoral representation from heavily white areas, gaining political influence through campaign contributions, and other forms of selective mobilization on transnational issues are some of the important examples discussed below. In effect, mass ethnoracial mobilization of the traditional kind has become much less important in charting out a path for political participation and representation of the community.

## Political Incorporation and Selective Elite Ethnoracial Mobilization

The dominant models of political incorporation, as noted in chapter 2, predict that the path to minority political participation and eventual incorporation depends on ethnoracial mobilization. The mobilization could be for a limited period until the group becomes a part of the mainstream political process or it could continue for a longer period in face of persistent barriers. Evidence from interviews and analysis of other data, however, suggests that there is limited mass-level ethnoracial mobilization among South Asians. The political incorporation trajectory of the group is rather characterized by attempts at representation and political influence through selective mobilization aimed at a narrow segment of the community. The following three dominant modes of political participation among South Asians describe how the politics of selective elite mobilization, in contrast to a broader ethnoracial one, is shaping their political incorporation trajectory.

### South Asian American Representation and White Majority Electoral Areas

The analysis of available data on South Asian political representation suggests a unique trend: growing cases of South Asians contesting and succeeding from areas and electoral districts that are primarily white majority with a relatively smaller minority presence. These contests generally do not involve mobilizing South Asians in any significant manner. A number of interviewees, speaking about South Asian Americans contesting for political offices across the U.S., cited Bobby Jindal, the current governor of Louisiana who was first elected in 2007, as an example of the success of South Asians in the political arena. South Carolina governor Nikki Haley followed Jindal's example in 2010. Both these Republican governors are of Indian American origin, and they built a political strategy that primarily appealed to white voters. Furthermore, both these candidates converted to Christianity at different points in their lives, and they deployed their religious identity to overcome the ethnoracial difference that they represented. They appealed to their conservative white Christian electorate by using their Christian faith. They do not consider themselves as representing South Asians or Indian Americans in any manner and did very little in terms of mobilizing Indian Americans.

Besides these two very high-profile examples, an analysis of Indian American candidates who ran for local, state, and federal offices in recent years suggests that the majority of Indian American candidates contested and even succeeded in areas that did not have a significant South Asian or Asian American population. Table 6 provides the racial composition of the electoral districts where Indian American candidates ran for and/or won state or federal offices. A large number of these electoral districts are overwhelmingly white, and Asian Americans are only a very small part of the population. The places where these candidates contested from, and in some cases also succeeded, included Georgia, Ohio, Iowa, Louisiana, and Kansas—states with miniscule South Asian populations. A significant number of successful South Asian contestants were from overwhelmingly white majority districts. The analysis of electoral district patterns suggests that the white population was more than 60 percent in an overwhelming number of electoral districts—approximately 72 percent—where South Asian candidates ran. However, we also see a few examples from Chicago, Maryland, Washington, California, and New Jersey where electoral districts are racially mixed (Table 6). They do point toward a possibly different electoral strategy relying much more on cross-over appeal to different racial communities. Notwithstanding these examples, there remains a fairly strong trend of South Asian candidates contesting from primarily white majority areas with little or no reliance on co-ethnics.

TABLE 6

**Indian Americans Who Ran for State- and Federal-Level Offices and Racial Composition of Their Districts (2001–2014)**

| NAME | ELECTORAL DISTRICT | RACIAL DEMOGRAPHIC (PERCENTAGES) |
|------|-------------------|----------------------------------|
| Tony Patel (D) (State House of Rep.) | 47th District, Georgia | 74 (W), 11 (B), 11 (AS) |
| Harmeet K. Dhillan (R) (State Assembly) | 13th District, California | 56 (W), 10 (B), 21 (AS) |
| Ashwan Madia (D) (U.S. Congress) | 3rd District, Minnesota | 89 (W), 4 (B), 4 (AS) |
| Raj Goyale* (D) (State House of Rep.) | 87th District, Kansas | 75 (W), 11 (B), 7 (AS) |
| Paul Chadha (D) (State Assembly) | 26th District, Illinois | 6 (W), 67 (B), 4 (AS) |
| Jonathan Bedi (D) (State Senate) | 5th District, Illinois | 24 (W), 65 (B), 3 (AS) |
| Subodh Chandra (D) (State Attorney) | Ohio | 85 (W), 12 (B), 1 (AS) |
| Raj Peter Bhakta (R) (U.S. Congress) | 13th District, Pennsylvania | 87 (W), 6 (B), 4 (AS) |
| Shyam Reddy (D) (Secretary of State) | Georgia | 65 (W), 29 (B), 2 (AS) |
| Jay Goyal* (D) (State House of Rep.) | 73rd District, Ohio | 87 (W), 10 (B), 4 (AS) |
| Jay Rao (R) (Secretary of State) | North Carolina | 72 (W), 22 (B), 1.4 (AS) |
| Supriya Christopher (D) (State House of Delegates) | 84th District, Virginia | 68 (W), 20 (B), 7 (AS) |
| Swati Dandekar* (D) (State House of Rep.) | 36th District, Iowa | 97 (W), 0.5 (B), 0.5 (AS) |
| Bobby Jindal* (R) (Governor) | Louisiana | 64 (W), 33 (B), 1 (AS) |
| Upendra Chivukala* (D) (State Assembly) | 17th District, New Jersey | 56 (W), 20 (B), 14 (AS) |

TABLE 6 (*continued*)

| NAME | ELECTORAL DISTRICT | RACIAL DEMOGRAPHIC (PERCENTAGES) |
|---|---|---|
| Kumar Barve* (D) (House of Delegates) | 17th District, Maryland | 62 (W), 12 (B), 14 (AS) |
| Nikki Haley* (R) (Governor) | South Carolina | 78 (W), 13 (B), 5 (AS) |
| Ami Bery* (D) (U.S. Congress) | 3rd District, California | 66 (W), 8 (B), 12 (AS) |
| Manan Trivedi (D) (U.S. Congress) | 6th District, Pennsylvania | 88 (W), 4 (B), 4 (AS) |
| Jack Uppal (D) (U.S. Congress) | 4th District, California | 85 (W), 1 (B), 5 (AS) |
| Syed Taj (D) (U.S. Congress) | 11th District, Michigan | 83 (W), 5 (B), 8 (AS) |
| Upendra Chivukula (D) (U.S. Congress) | 7th District, New Jersey | 81 (W), 4 (B), 9 (AS) |
| Ricky Gill (R) (U.S. Congress) | 9th District, California | 56 (W), 8 (B), 14 (AS) |
| Pramila Jaypal* (State Senate) | 37th District, Washington | 41 (W), 23 (B), 25 (AS) |
| Ro Khanna (U.S. Congress) | 17th District, California | 33(W), 3 (B), 52 (AS) |

Sources: Compiled by author based on USINPAC data, media sources, and the 2000 and 2010 U.S. Census data.

Note: W = White; B = Black; AS = Asian; *Successful contestants.

Commenting on the trend of representation from white majority districts, a South Asian community leader of Indian descent from New York said:

Now we have a young man from Louisiana (Bobby Jindal) and we have four or five assemblymen from different states—New Jersey, Maryland, Minnesota, Wisconsin, etc. . . . we have won elections from areas where there are very few Indians. They (South Asians/Indian Americans) could do it because they are educated people. Take an example of Louisiana—there are not too many Indians there, there is no support for Indians there. Similarly, the assemblyman from New Jersey is not from a constituency with a high number of Indians. If he can win from a non-Indian community to state assembly, the people who really work hard and have the same goal to get what they want, I think they can get it.[12]

The implicit belief reflected in this statement is that talented South Asians have a chance equal to others of winning from primarily white districts. The model minority construct further bolsters the view that South Asians can succeed in these electoral arenas due to their education, talent, wealth, and hard work. A Pakistani American mayor of a primarily white New Jersey town argued along similar lines. He attributed his victory to the role he played in solving the problems of local schools. That was an important consideration for people who voted for him, he asserted. He further said:

I felt somehow that people resonated with my ideas and they were more interested in that. They were seeing that I was interested in the best quality education, that my own educational background with a Ph.D. degree was a plus for them. That they heard from someone who was an educator, because I was also teaching. I would teach economics and other courses at Rutgers or other universities. And now I've been teaching for seven years at the University of Phoenix online. So recognizing my professional background, I believe, was more important for people.[13]

The trend of electoral success from white majority areas is also reflected in the 2007 election of Harvinder Singh as the mayor of Long Island Village, a prosperous New York town with a 95 percent white population. A reporter for the *New York Times,* analyzing this election, wrote, "He is a part of what political analysts see as a new pattern: while minority candidates are usually propelled into office from densely populated enclaves of their own ethnic groups, a small but recently growing number of Indian American officeholders has been getting elected in communities across the nation where they are the tiniest of minorities" (Vitello 2007). According to the *New York Times,* a high level of education, ability to speak English, and crossover appeal are some of the characteristics of this group, which allow them to succeed in the electoral arena. Another example of such a candidacy is that of Reshma Sujani, who contested and lost the Democratic primary in 2010 against incumbent Congresswoman Carolyn B. Maloney from the 14th Congressional District in New York City. The 14th Congressional District represents the wealthy Upper East Side, along with some modest areas in Queens and the Bronx. Prominent Wall Street figures and affluent segments of the Upper East Side supported Reshma Sujani's candidacy. Even though she lost the primary, what is significant is that she ran mainly on her accomplishments on Wall Street, while ethnic identity and mobilization were extremely marginal to her candidacy.[14]

The view that South Asians can succeed in politics because of their education, economic status, professional experience, and problem-solving abilities comes with the belief that race and color are no longer barriers for political representation of minority groups. A significant number of South Asian candidates across the nation have adopted an explicitly deracialized strategy of political representation, in which their racial and cultural differences are deployed to strengthen the pluralist discourse of the openness of the political system for newcomers. They represent the American dream: anyone who wants to succeed can ultimately make it. The South Asian candidates typically refer to their immigrant life stories as examples of the perseverance of their families against all odds in a new country. Furthermore, they deploy the trope of the American dream to mark their achievements and underline the inclusiveness of the U.S. sociopolitical structure.

Such candidacies produce a different model of minority politics that does not challenge racial hierarchy and may not lead to greater inclusion of new groups in the political process. The example of the two Indian American Republican governors—Nikki Haley and Bobby Jindal—is highly pertinent in this regard. Their political and electoral strategies demonstrate clearly that their ascension to power was achieved only through affirming a political framework that is hostile toward minorities and immigrants, and they have not worked toward creating a racially inclusive politics in the states where they were elected. All South Asian candidates running in heavily white majority districts have not necessarily adopted similar political ideologies, but it is important to recognize that deracialized campaigns and the deployment of the model minority discourse produce a distinct politics that is not conducive to making space for minority communities in the political process. This is in contrast to a significant number of minority candidates who, even as they try to build cross-racial appeal, deploy the civil rights movement's discourse of greater racial equality and representation for minority groups.

The 2012 congressional election cycle witnessed a total of six Indian American candidates—the highest number in a single election cycle—who vied for seats in Congress. They ran in California, Pennsylvania, Illinois, New Jersey, and Michigan, five of them as Democratic Party candidates, and one as a Republican. The only success came for Ami Bera, an Indian American physician, who defeated the incumbent Republican member of the House of Representatives from the 3rd Congressional District in California and became the third South Asian American member of Congress (Dalip Singh Saund and Bobby Jindal were the other two). The *New York Times,* analyzing the performance of Indian American candidates in 2012, referred to the professional and economic success of Indian Americans in the United States and pointed out that five out of the six candidates were either engineers or doctors. The analysis cautioned that perhaps the professional success of members of the community cannot be easily translated into political success.[15]

The trend of Indian American candidates entering different levels of electoral politics continues. The victory of Neel Kashkari, an Indian American investment banker who served as an assistant secretary of the Treasury under President George W. Bush, in the California Republican primary for governor in 2014 is another high-profile example of increased interest of Indian Americans in the electoral arena. Most of these Indian American candidates, as argued earlier, do not rely on South Asian votes and support, and they deploy a mode of political mobilization that is largely devoid of co-ethnic mobilization (except for the trend of appealing to co-ethnics for campaign contributions that I will discuss later). The only notable exception to this trend was the candidacy of Ro Khanna, a Democratic Party aspirant from the 17th Congressional District in California, who challenged the incumbent Democratic congressman, Mike Honda, a veteran Asian American congressman, in both the primary and general elections for the seat. The 17th Congressional District, home to the widely known technology hub Silicon Valley, is the only Asian majority district in the mainland United States, and it has a significant number of Indian Americans. The mobilization of Indian Americans was a major part of Khanna's candidacy, alongside courting the technology sector based in the area.

Asian American groups also tend to share the experiences of South Asians that have emerged in the electoral arena. Scholars point out that most Asian American candidates outside the state of Hawaii follow a strategy of mainstream or crossover appeal that is in complete contrast to other minority groups such as African Americans or Latinos. Elected representatives from Asian American communities in the mainland United States have emerged from districts where Asian Americans constitute substantially less than 50 percent of the population. In fact, of the fifty mainland congressional districts with the largest Asian American populations, Asian Pacific Americans represented only two in the 105th Congress. A majority of state- and federal-level Asian Pacific American elected officials (on the U.S. mainland) represented non-Asian districts (Lai et al. 2001). This trend is in complete contrast to African American and Latino elected officials, for whom representatives from both these groups are elected from districts with a substantial number of co-ethnics in the electorate.[16] Among African American federally elected representatives in 1982, fourteen out of seventeen representatives came from districts where African Americans made up 40 percent or more of the population. Among Latino elected officials in 1982, seven of ten Latino congressional representatives were elected from districts where Latinos made up 50 percent or more of the population (Espiritu 1992; Moore and Pachon 1985).

Latino politics scholar Matt Baretto (2010) has emphasized the increased importance of Latino candidates for co-ethnic mobilization. He argues that the particular electoral context surrounding the campaign of a Latino candidate—endorsement by prominent Latino leaders, coverage by Latino media, registration drives by Latino organizations, and involvement of Latino churches—creates a mobilization leading to higher rates of Latino voting and a strong level of support for co-ethnics. With a sharp increase in Latino population and a higher level of population density in selected areas, the role of Latino voters in the electoral success of Latino candidates has become increasingly important. The current trajectory of most Asian American representation, however, relies heavily on mainstream or crossover appeal, where the ability of these candidates to appeal to different racial groups is highlighted (Rodriguez 1998). Asian American scholars have correctly identified this trend of political representation, but they have stopped short of spelling out its implications for the political incorporation trajectory of the group.

A closer look at the electoral strategy of many Indian American candidates suggests that these campaigns drew heavily upon the rhetoric of postracial politics, which actually deemphasizes race and color.[17] The campaigns of both Bobby Jindal of Louisiana and Nikki Haley of South Carolina are testaments to this trend. Both these candidates did occasionally evoke their ethnic heritage, but those references were not central to their electoral strategy. In the case of the two governors, as mentioned earlier, their Christian religious faith was deployed heavily to compensate for their ethnoracial difference. Indeed, one of the important prerequisites for succeeding in white majority electoral districts is to run a deracialized campaign that treats the ethnic and racial identity of the candidate as peripheral to the electoral strategy. This approach to electoral politics among minority candidates is in complete contrast to the classical models of political incorporation that considered ethnoracial mobilization as critical to the representation of minority groups both in electoral as well as nonelectoral arenas.

The trend of political representation among South Asians, thus, frontally challenges the centrality of ethnoracial mobilization in the political representation of minority groups. It challenges the conventional understanding that greater representation is a product of increased ethnoracial participation and mobilization of a minority group. Given the new trend of electoral success, there might be a greater representation of South Asians without any significant mobilization and increase in political participation of the group as a whole. Hence, the incorporation of the group may be highly incomplete and selective, with a few elected representatives at different levels. Consequently, there could be much less inclusion of the larger community as a whole and fewer actual policy initiatives in favor of the group.

## Political Power through Economic Strength

The lack of mass mobilization by political parties and candidates among South Asians simultaneously coexists with a selective targeting of a small section of the community for campaign contributions. Journalistic reports in ethnic as well as mainstream media have often noted that there has been a significant trend of organizing political fund-raising events within the South Asian community. The stereotypical stories of influential and wealthy first-generation South Asian immigrants getting photographed with political leaders and candidates because they made hefty political contributions abound within the community. The extent of involvement of Indian Americans in political fund-raising was reflected in a spat between senators Hillary Clinton and Barack Obama during the 2008 presidential primaries. The controversy was over a fund-raiser organized by Indian Americans for Hillary Clinton, where she jokingly made a remark alluding to her closeness to the community: "I can certainly run for the Senate seat in Punjab (India) and win easily."[18] The Obama campaign, in a memo titled "Hillary Clinton (D-Punjab)'s Personal Financial and Political Ties to India," criticized Clinton for fundraising from the community on the grounds that she cochairs the Senate's India Caucus and has favored outsourcing of jobs to India in return for large-scale campaign contributions by Indian Americans.[19] The Obama campaign had to ultimately withdraw the memo because it ended up collapsing the distinction between Indian Americans and India as a nation by suggesting that Clinton was bound to represent the interest of India, since she was taking contributions from Indian Americans.[20]

A significant number of community members as well as leaders interviewed for this study also referred to how financially successful South Asians were courted for political contributions. In turn, the South Asian community, particularly Indian Americans, has come to think of campaign contribution as an important means of developing political influence. A number of interviewees pointed to this emerging trend and argued that it could be a possible way to counter the lack of political influence resulting from a relatively small number of South Asians, combined with a low-density residential pattern. There is a widely shared view among South Asians that the way to political empowerment lies in exploiting their financial leverage and that the group should move quickly from asserting their cultural and religious identity to developing political clout. According to this view, the political parties and candidates may not care for the community's votes, but they will certainly care about its ability to contribute. An Indian American leader from the Los Angeles area puts the relationship between political incorporation and fundraising in the following words:

> Our strength is the finances, the funds we can raise for them, more so than the votes that we can deliver them. . . . I would say so far, our majority strength lies in our ability to raise funds for

them. The Indians are professionally, business wise, everywhere; but in the political process, we are not so much. . . . Most of our strength comes from raising funds for the political people . . . we are not there at the stage where we can demand power from our voting rights, our voting power. Even though we try to throw in a number there; that number is still very small for a political person to depend mainly on us. We are too spread apart, so at the local level we cannot play any role at all in terms of votes. . . . Money wise, yes, we do, because for whatever reason, Indians do donate for political parties. And with that strength, you can sit with them and talk to them . . . is that the way to go? No, I don't think that should be the only way to go, but it always helps.[21]

A similar trend can be seen in the Pakistani American community as well. Both Los Angeles and New York area Pakistani American leaders report that their votes are not as much a target of mobilization as their money is. A Pakistani American activist from Los Angeles, speaking of the trend of fund-raising, said: "Money is more important and that is what they [political parties and candidates] are targeting—they are not going out for the vote. I have not seen anyone going out to try to get more votes from our community. Again, Pakistanis are dispersed. You are not going to see them in one area. South Asians maybe more so, but again, politically when they [political candidates] come in, I see more emphasis on fundraising."[22] This emphasis on fund-raising as a means to political power is in sharp contrast to other minority groups such as African Americans and Latinos. It also differs from the historical experience of European ethnics.

Wendy K. Tam Cho and Suneet Lad (2004), in their analysis of political behavior of Asian Indians, argue that there has been a steep increase in the volume of contributions to federal campaigns, political action committees, and party organizations. Analyzing the political contribution figures from 1980 to 2000, they show that contributions by Asian Indians have burgeoned from almost negligible to approximately $8 million in a single election cycle. The number of contributors also rose from a few hundred to approximately 8,000 separate contributions. A rising trend of campaign contributions suggests that South Asians give importance to this form of political engagement and considers it a way to gain political leverage. However, the Cho and Lad study did not point to the increasing importance of South Asians as organizers of fund-raising events for major campaigns during which significant amounts of contributions were bundled together.

Analysis of campaign contribution trends in the 2008 presidential primary elections gives further insight into the level of involvement of South Asians in the fund-raising efforts for both Democratic and Republican presidential candidates. An article in the monthly *Little India* focused upon what is known in political fund-raising parlance as "bundlers" (Mehra 2008). As federal law caps individual election contributions to a candidate in an election cycle to $2,700, bundlers have become critical to candidates for raising bigger amounts. These bundlers typically package and bundle donations from friends, family, business, and professional associates by organizing private and public fund-raising events. These kinds of contributions constitute a significant part of the funds raised by candidates in any election. In the last fifteen years, bundlers have become extremely important for fund-raising in presidential elections. The analysis by *Little India* of 2,493 bundlers reported by Public Citizen—a public interest watchdog group—during the presidential primaries of 2008 revealed that there were twenty-one Indian Americans on that list, along with a few Pakistani American bundlers (Mehra 2008). Almost half of these Indian American bundlers raised money for Senator Hillary Clinton, the rest of them were divided between senators Obama, Edwards, and McCain, and Governor Romney.

In the 2012 presidential elections, the role of South Asian bundlers was even more pronounced. An analysis of the list of bundlers released by the Obama campaign underlined the increasing importance of South Asians in the arena of campaign contribution. The information released by the Obama campaign and published by the Center for Responsive Politics identified the names of bundlers and the range of amounts (exact amounts were not provided) that they collected on behalf of the campaign.[23] The data presented in Table 7 were compiled by the author on the basis of South Asian name recognition and confirmed through information available about them in the public domain. Research indicates that there were at least twenty-four South Asian bundlers—an overwhelming majority of them Indian Americans, alongside a few Pakistanis—out of a total of 769 bundlers reported by the campaign. These individuals collected amounts ranging from $50,000 to $500,000 or more, and they played a major role in creating the financial war chest of the Obama reelection campaign. The list suggests a very significant presence of South

Asians among those who organized major fund-raising events for Obama's reelection campaign. A number of these South Asian bundlers were later nominated by the Obama administration for important and prestigious positions, as listed in Table 7. Similar patterns of fund-raising for state- and congressional-level elections have been reported by ethnic news- papers. Apart from prominent businesspeople and professionals from the South Asian community who organize fund-raisers on a regular basis, organizations such as U.S.–India Political Action Committee (USINPAC) and Pakistani American Public Affairs Committee (PAKPAC) also play an important role as far as political fund-raising is concerned. USINPAC and PAKPAC have both contributed significant amounts to congressio- nal candidates on a bipartisan basis.

Given the overall number of South Asian Americans in the United States and their levels of political participation and representation, their share in fund-raising activities seems to be fairly high. Most of the fund- raisers organized by South Asian individuals rely upon the wealthy sec- tions of the community as well as others who they work or socialize with. The prevalence of this form of political engagement suggests that there is a wide gap between the community's contribution to fund-raising and their involvement in other forms of political participation. Further- more, through the process of fund-raising, a very small segment of the community manages to garner political influence with important politi- cal institutions. The important role of wealthy South Asians as major campaign contribution bundlers has led to their political appointments in different capacities and charted a different path of representation and political clout. However, this clout is achieved through the mobilization of a very narrow and elite segment of the community that is not connected to wider political mobilization and empowerment.

It is important to note that the strategy of gaining political influence through economic clout is linked to a discourse among South Asians that describes the American Jewish community as a model for achieving political empowerment. A Los Angeles–based community leader of Indian descent exhorted the community to follow the Jewish model and move from making contributions for building temples to developing political influence. He said:

> The Indian community was not used to giving political contribu-
> tions in India. Only some very high-level people gave any political
> contributions in India. They [Indian Americans] still think that

TABLE 7

**South Asian American Bundlers Who Organized Fund-Raising for President Obama during His Reelection Campaign in 2012**

| NUMBER | NAME | ETHNICITY | AMOUNT ($ RANGE) | APPOINTMENT |
|---|---|---|---|---|
| 1 | Rajiv Fernando | Indian American | 500,000 or more | International Security Advisory Board, State Dept. |
| 2 | Deven Parekh | Indian American | 500,000 or more | Board, Overseas Private Investment Corporation |
| 3 | Shefali Razdan Duggal | Indian American | 500,000 or more | Member, United States Holocaust Memorial Council |
| 4 | Reshma Saujani | Indian American | 500,000 or more | |
| 5 | Amy K. Singh | Indian American | 500,000 or more | U.S. President's Advisory Committee on the Arts, John F. Kennedy Center for the Performing Arts |
| 6 | Raj Goyle | Indian American | 500,000 or more | |
| 7 | Imaad Zuberi | Pakistani American | 500,000 or more | |
| 8 | Kamil Hasan | Indian American | 200,000 to 500,000 | |
| 9 | Sunil and Gabrielle Sabharwal | Indian-Hungarian American | 200,000 to 500,000 | U.S. alternate executive director, International Monetary Fund (Sunil) |
| 10 | Sanjay Mody | Indian American | 200,000 to 500,000 | |
| 11 | Shelly Kapoor Collins | Indian American | 200,000 to 500,000 | |

TABLE 7 (*continued*)

| NUMBER | NAME | ETHNICITY | AMOUNT ($ RANGE) | APPOINTMENT |
|---|---|---|---|---|
| 12 | Frank F. Islam | Indian American | 100,000 to 200,000 | General Trustee, Board of Trustees of the John F. Kennedy Center for the Performing Arts |
| 13 | Deepak Chopra | Indian American | 100,000 to 200,000 | |
| 14 | Shoukat Hussain Ali | Pakistani American | 100,000 to 200,000 | |
| 15 | Khalid Hasan* | | 100,000 to 200,000 | |
| 16 | Kavita Tankha | Indian American | 100,000 to 200,000 | |
| 17 | Girish Reddy | Indian American | 100,000 to 200,000 | |
| 18 | Didi Saluja | Indian American | 100,000 to 200,000 | |
| 19 | Nomi Husain | Pakistani American | 100,000 to 200,000 | |
| 20 | Nirmal Mulye | Indian American | 50,000 to 100,000 | |
| 21 | Maneesh Goyal | Indian American | 50,000 to 100,000 | J. William Fulbright Foreign Scholarship Board |
| 22 | Imad Husain | Pakistani American | 50,000 to 100,000 | |
| 23 | Anu Duggal | Indian American | 50,000 to 100,000 | |
| 24 | Chandoo Hasan | Pakistani American | 50,000 to 100,000 | |

Source: The Center for Responsive Politics (see https://www.opensecrets.org/pres12/bundlers.php); the information about political appointments was obtained via open media sources by the author.
Note: *Khalid Hasan was listed as South Asian American in different media sources, and specific country of origin could not be obtained.

giving to political parties or candidates is useless or that contributing to temple is better. If the Indian community has a fundraising event for a congressman, we have to pull them to come and attend the function. Look at the people who have mastered the art of political involvement, the Jewish community. And look at their control. The Indian community with their financial strength could do better. However, there is a difference. Whereas the Jewish community has already built their temple, the Indian community is contributing heavily to build their temples. The next generation or third generation when the temples are built, maybe the importance will be the political contribution to control their agenda.[24]

The mainstream media has also noted the Indian American groups' fascination with the Jewish lobby. Following the publication of a highly controversial book on the Israeli lobby, Mira Kamdar, in an op-ed in the *Washington Post,* noted both the undue influence of the lobby in U.S. politics as well as the admiration it evoked among a large section of Indian Americans.[25] Kamdar wrote: "With growing numbers, clout and self-confidence, the Indian American community is turning its admiration for the Israel lobby and its respect for high-achieving Jewish Americans into a powerful new force of its own. Following consciously in AIPAC's (American Israel Public Affairs Committee) footsteps, the India lobby is getting results in Washington—and having a profound impact on U.S. policy" (2007). The success of the Jewish community in developing a strong voice on American foreign policy vis-à-vis Israel struck a chord with some of the Indian American organizations. Commenting on the perceived similarity between the two groups, a report in the *New York Times* noted, "Indians often say they see a version of themselves and what they hope to be the experience of Jews in American politics: a small minority that has succeeded in combating prejudice and building political clout" (Banerjee 2007). This reference was more common among Indian American interviewees than Pakistani and Bangladeshi Americans. The discourse of a Hindu/India and Jewish/Israel alliance against the threats of Islamic terrorism has also strengthened admiration for the Jewish lobby (Prashad 2005; Kurien 2007b).

It is important to note here that the invocation of the Jewish American experience of political incorporation is done in a very selective manner by some of the Indian community organizations in their quest for political influence. This invocation completely ignores the early history of grassroots mobilizing and multiracial alliances built by Jewish American groups against racial and religious discrimination, and the role played by the community in building up progressive alliances and movements in different American cities (Sonenshein 1993; Glazer and Moynihan 1970). What gets highlighted in the current discourse is the centrality of Israel in contemporary Jewish mobilization and how the community's political clout rests upon their economic strength.

The importance of campaign contributions in gaining political influence has significant implications for the trajectory of South Asian political incorporation. Similar to the trend of representation from white majority districts, this mode of political engagement suggests a path that relies primarily on the affluent and elite members of the group, thereby precluding any attempts at mobilizing the broader community.

The fund-raising prowess of the Indian American community has also led to a distinct trend among South Asian electoral candidates reaching out to their co-ethnics across the country for campaign money. As noted earlier, most of the South Asian candidates do not need to reach out to their co-ethnics for votes because of the demographic reality of their districts—a very small south Asian population in most cases. However, selective outreach for campaign money is becoming a big part of the strategy that South Asian candidates definitely implement. Nikki Haley, while running for governor of South Carolina, went on fund-raising tours across the United States that took her to all the major cities with a sizable Indian American population. According to one estimate, she attended at least half a dozen major fund-raising galas organized by Indian Americans and raised nearly a quarter of a million dollars at these fund-raisers.[26] Similarly, other South Asian candidates for congressional or state-level contests have relied on the affluent donors within the community (Railey 2015). It is evident that the increase in the number of South Asian candidates is leading to a particular kind of mobilization of co-ethnics focused on political fund-raising. However, it is the affluent and elite segments of the community that are being mobilized as a part of the increased electoral candidacy of South Asian candidates and not the broader community at the grassroots level.

## Ethnic Organizations, Lobbying, and Selective Mobilization

South Asians have primarily turned to ethnic organizations for civic and political engagements (in the absence of parties courting them), and one of the most important forms of political engagement is lobbying around issues concerning home countries (which will be discussed in further detail in chapter 6). The dominance of lobbying has important implications for political mobilization of the community in terms of who gets mobilized. I argue that lobbying as a form of political activity only brings a very narrow segment of the community into the political process. In addition, these efforts are exclusively organized along the lines of countries of origin, leading to tensions among the different organizations representing Indians, Pakistanis, and Bangladeshis. Moreover, the divergence stemming from campaigns around national identities point toward the problems in developing a political mobilization strategy based on a broader South Asian identity.

Before looking at the trends in lobbying in greater detail, it is important to map the existing ethnic organizations among South Asians. There are a significant number of organizations active in both the broader Los Angeles and New York metropolitan areas that cater to specific ethnic identities among South Asians. These ethno-cultural organizations range from those based on ethnic and linguistic identities such as Tamil, Telugu, Gujarati, Punjabi, and Sindhi to groups rooted in national identities such as Indian, Pakistani, and Bangladeshi. The primary purpose of these organizations has been to create a space for people from similar backgrounds to share, celebrate, and maintain their cultural identities in the United States. In addition, these networks serve important functions, ranging from the development of professional and business connections to the creation of social spaces for arranging marriages.[27] Even though these organizations do not explicitly pursue the goal of advancing the political participation of the community, it is common for them to invite political leaders, both from the United States as well as the country of origin, to their programs.[28] These organizations also become a part of lobbying campaigns around issues of home country. Another set of ethnic organizations that have traditionally been a major part of South Asian community organizing is professional ethnic associations. These organizations have played a major role in mobilizing South Asians pursuing certain occupations—generally a narrow segment of the community—for their professional advancement, and they have often pitched in to support lobbying campaigns.

## Occupational Ethnic Organizations and Selective Mobilizing

An important feature of South Asian ethnic organizations in the United States is the way in which different waves of incoming professionals have shaped the nature of organization building in the community. In fact, occupational and class interests have often dominated the organizational landscape within the community. As noted earlier, a significant part of the early post-1965 Indian, Pakistani, and Bangladeshi immigration was skilled professionals who immigrated in response to the changing requirements of the U.S. economy. In fact, the process of community building has been deeply reflective of the occupation-based immigration trajectory of South Asians, and some of the most stable and powerful ethnic organizations were formed along the lines of professional identities. The American Association of Physicians of Indian Origin (AAPI) was founded in 1984 in the midst of challenges that physicians of Indian origin encountered due to cultural barriers and bias against international medical professionals. Recent scholarship on Indian American physicians has pointed to the privilege enjoyed by these professionals due to their occupational status but also underlines how they have to constantly negotiate the racialized and gendered social order where occupational status becomes an important tool to counter marginalization (Murti 2012). AAPI was one of the earliest and one of the most well-known ethnic organizations among Indian immigrants. The organization, currently representing 41,235 physicians and 12,000 medical students, residents, and fellows of Indian origin, has been focused on enabling the professional success of its constituents and has used legislative and other forms of lobbying to raise demands specific to the group. AAPI's annual conventions are major events that have sizable attendance, and they enable participants to network and benefit from the organization's membership base.[29]

Similarly, the Association of Physicians of Pakistani Descent of North America (APPNA), founded in 1977 and one of the earliest Pakistani community organizations, represents the interests of Pakistani-origin physicians in the United States and Canada.[30] Responding to the post-9/11 targeting of Pakistanis in the United States, APPNA has started taking up the issue of profiling of Muslim doctors and the hurdles faced by them in getting work visas and green cards. The American Association of Bangladeshi Engineers and Architects (AABEA), founded in 1984 to support engineers, architects, and information technology professionals within the Bangladeshi community, has been a pioneering professional organization. The Association of Pakistani Professionals (AOPP) and Association of Pakistani Scientists and Engineers of North America (APSE-NA) have similarly worked with professionals of different fields within the Pakistani American community. The continuing relevance of these organizations is reflected in the fact that they are the most enduring associational formations within the South Asian community. Their work has primarily been focused on professional advancement of a smaller segment of the community, even as they put some resources into charity work in their respective countries of origin and occasionally support lobbying campaigns to aide their home countries' interests.

The importance of occupation-based professional South Asian organizations has continued, as the community witnessed the formation and growth of newer professional organizations in the 1980s and 1990s, indicating professional diversification within the community. One of the most important examples is the Asian American Hotel Owners Association (AAHOA), an organization of hotel and motel owners of Indian descent that is dominated by Gujarati immigrants from India. AAHOA was founded in 1989 at a gathering of Indian hotel and motel owners in Atlanta, and it evolved into a very powerful organization spread across different states.[31] It represents 11,000 members owning more than 20,000 hotels and motels that are worth 128 billion dollars in property value.[32] The group has not only become a critical support system for hotel and motel owners of Indian descent but has also acquired an important place in the larger Indian American community because of its organizational, financial, and lobbying prowess.[33] The group plays an important role in supporting its members by introducing a professional model of corporate management, working with franchises for fair treatment of owners, and lobbying with governmental agencies to better serve the needs of owners. AAHOA has consistently utilized the model minority construct, showcasing the success of the Indian American community in medicine, technology, education, and business, as leverage with American institutions and businesses (Dhingra 2012, 152–58).

The information technology boom in the 1990s led to the creation of organizations such as the Indus Entrepreneurs (TIE). It is a group primarily of Indian American entrepreneurs who started new information technology businesses in the Silicon Valley and elsewhere and wanted to create an organization to network with their co-ethnics in the field. The group has become a global network of South Asian entrepreneurs—it is formally open to South Asians other than Indians—with approximately 11,000 members and sixty chapters. According to one estimate, it is one of the largest diasporic ethnic entrepreneur associations across the globe that has seen sustained membership growth. The group has successfully implemented the model of using established entrepreneurs to mentor at least five aspiring members in their field (Newland and Tanaka 2010).

Some ethnic professional organizations have very intentionally adopted a broader South Asian identity. The South Asian Bar Association (SABA) and South Asian Journalists Association (SAJA) are prime examples of such initiatives. One of the important distinctions between these South Asian formations and country-of-origin-based organizations is that the former generally stay away from country-specific lobbying activities. This is the case because many issues tend to emphasize the interests of only one particular country, making them potentially divisive for South Asian organizations. For instance, the lobbying campaign in support of the U.S.–India Nuclear Deal was led by Indian American organizations and generally avoided by South Asian groups. Since the deal was not seen favorably by the Pakistani and Bangladeshi American communities, the South Asian groups presumably wanted to avoid alienating their constituents belonging to different national origins (Mishra 2009).

It is evident that there is a rich tradition of ethnic organizations within the South Asian community, and occupation-based professional ethnic groups have been a huge part of the associational life in the community. These professional groups were the earliest associations and, besides their specific work for their membership base, they still remain highly relevant within the community, both in terms of effectiveness in intervening in domestic U.S. politics as well as transnational issues. The most important implication of these professional ethnic organizations for our purposes is that they are largely organized along the lines of class and occupational interests represented by different professional groups. Even though national identities such as Indian or Pakistani American have been traditionally deployed for creating associations and mobilizing co-ethnics, they are deeply embedded in occupational and class interests tied to particular professions and aimed only at a smaller segment of the group. Thus the specific nature of occupation-based ethnic organizing has a limited role in broader ethnic mobilization of South Asian communities.

### Nation-of-Origin-Based Associations and Lobbying

There are some important South Asian groups that are organized exclusively on the lines of national identity. Some of these organizations have more regional U.S. presence, whereas others have a national impact. An important feature of these groups is that they are constantly in flux, and, depending on their leadership and other local factors, they can range from being influential to completely marginal. Organizations such as the National Federation of Indian Americans (NFIA), Indian American Forum for Political Education (IAFPE), Associations of Indians in America (AIA), National Council of Pakistani Americans (NCPA), USINPAC, PAKPAC, and Federation of Bangladeshi Associations in North America (FOBANA) are important examples. Most of these organizations engage in transnational politics by maintaining a strong and continual contact with political parties, leaders, and government officials in their respective countries of origin. They often reflect nationalistic ideologies emanating from the country of origin, and they also lobby with the U.S. Congress and policy-making bodies on issues relating to their home countries.

The Indian American community has been so heavily involved in lobbying activities that they have been able to create one of the largest ethnic caucuses on the Hill. The influence of this lobby can be gauged from the fact that the House Congressional Caucus on India and Indian Americans has 176 members, and the Senate India Caucus has 37 members (Kurien 2007b). This strength was reflected in the passage of the U.S.–India Civil Nuclear Deal in the Congress in 2007, a deal that was very important for the government of India in order to gain the status of a legitimate nuclear state. The lobbying by the Indian American community in favor of this deal and its significance for transnational politics is analyzed in greater detail in chapter 6.

USINPAC, founded in 2002, is one of the most important groups representing the Indian American community in Washington, D.C. It routinely organizes fund-raisers on a bipartisan basis for candidates contesting for congressional and other offices. The group has emerged in recent times as a significant player on the Hill and showed its influence during the nuclear deal campaign. John Newhouse, in an important piece in *Foreign Affairs*, underlined the emergence of the Indian American lobby and argued that India's U.S.-based lobby is the only one that can get close to the influence of the powerful Israel lobby. He located the strength of the India lobby in the prosperous Indian American community that owns a significant number of companies in Silicon Valley and other places (Newhouse 2009). There is, thus, a clear recognition that Indian Americans have been able to influence members of Congress primarily because of the community's financial strength.

The Pakistani American community has also been putting considerable resources into lobbying activities in Washington, D.C., on issues relating to Pakistan. PAKPAC, organized on similar lines to USINPAC, defines itself as: "a nationwide, membership based, non-profit lobbying organization . . . PAKPAC's mission includes advancement and strengthening of U.S.–Pakistan relations. It is organized to be a unified voice on issues and concerns common to the Pakistani American community. PAKPAC's focus includes an active environment to foster greater political and civic engagement amongst the Pakistani Americans."[34] PAKPAC has helped create the Congressional Pakistan Caucus that works on Pakistan and Pakistani American issues.[35] One of the important aspects of lobbying by these South Asian groups is that Indian and Pakistani counterparts are often in conflict with each other as far as representing the interest of their home country is concerned. The ongoing tensions between India and Pakistan often spill into the political mobilizing done by these two groups in the United States.

The dominance of lobbying activities among different South Asian groups has been a longstanding feature of their political engagement in the United States, and it has influenced their mode of political mobilization. Since the lobbying campaigns are by nature not oriented toward mass participation, they end up primarily as activities involving the selective elites of the community. The experience of the Indian American community during the nuclear deal campaign showed that this mode of political engagement only activated the wealthy, educated, and well-connected members (Mishra 2009). In fact, the elite mobilization by lobbying campaigns does not trigger processes that lead to participation of the wider sections of the community. In addition, the mode of lobbying also brings the nationalistic orientations of the groups into play, which often works against the creation of a broader panethnic South Asian identity.

## Toward a Politics of Social Justice

Parallel to the dominant trend of selective elite mobilization, there is a growing form of organizing among South Asian Americans that can be termed a politics of social justice and transformation and which is moving fast toward multiracial mobilizing. Even while focused on South Asians, these organizations have increasingly acknowledged the importance and necessity of multiracial mobilization. As discussed earlier, there is a sizable segment of working-class and low-income South Asian Americans, and their number has grown rapidly in recent years. They are employed as taxi drivers, gas station attendants, construction workers, domestic workers, and in other low-paying service jobs. The process of reaching out to this segment started primarily through service-oriented nonprofit groups that have specialized in working among Asian American and South Asian low-income populations. Both Los Angeles and New York have a number of such service, advocacy, and social movement–oriented organizations—mostly nonprofit—that focus on the working-class, underprivileged, and undocumented sections as well as gender and sexuality rights. The South Asian Network (SAN), South Asian Public Health Association (SAPHA), Satrang, Los Angeles Taxi Workers Association (LATWA), and South Asian American Voting Youth (SAAVY), all based in the Los Angeles area, are some examples of organizations dedicated to service and advocacy. The number of such organizations in the New York Metropolitan Area is greater than in Los Angeles. Some of the important organizations in this category are the New York Taxi Workers Alliance (NYTWA), Workers' Awaaz, Andolan, Desis Rising Up and Moving (DRUM), South Asian Lesbian and Gay Association (SALGA), Sakhi, Manavi, Chhaya CDC, and Adhikar.

Because organizations of South Asian Americans have traditionally been dominated by associations of affluent professionals and entrepreneurs, the history of South Asian American labor and low-income organizing is quite recent. Recent scholarship on working-class South Asian organizing points to the late blooming of labor organizing—primarily in the 1990s—as the number of South Asians in low-income jobs increased at that time, especially in sectors traditionally ignored by the established labor organizations (Mathew 2005; Das Gupta 2006; Varghese 2006). According to a recent survey, the South Asian low-income population in New York City is primarily employed in the following five occupations: taxi driving, domestic work, retail, construction, and restaurant labor.[36] In fact, most of the labor in these five sectors is immigrant labor—both documented and undocumented—and that of people of color. South Asians are more likely to join these occupations because of the low barriers for entry and the existing ethnic networks. It is important to note that South Asian low-income and labor organizations have responded to the challenges faced by labor organizing in informal sectors where labor laws and other regulations have been largely absent.

One of the important initiatives in labor organizing started when activists working with the Coalition Against Anti-Asian Violence (CAAV) in New York City started organizing yellow-cab drivers against the violence they faced. This work, within the broad framework of CAAV to counter violence against Asians, started in 1992 as a workers' project called Lease Drivers Coalition (LDC). The organizing among South Asian taxi drivers began initially as a response to the vulnerability of these drivers to police and passenger violence and responded to the vulnerable status of these taxi drivers as newcomers. In 1992, approximately 40 percent of taxi drivers were South Asians, and a large number of them faced violence and some were even killed on the job (Das Gupta 2006, 228). The project against violence soon turned into labor union work that started raising the issues of living and working conditions faced by taxi drivers. Bhairavi Deasi, one of the project coordinators of antiviolence work in CAAV, led the effort to form a new labor union among taxi drivers. A small group broke away from the parent organization—CAAV—to form the New York Taxi Workers Alliance (NYTWA) in 1998 that decided to focus on working conditions, wages, and exploitation of taxi drivers by the Taxi and Limousine Commission that oversees this complex industry.

NYTWA currently has a membership of 17,000 that includes South Asian, African, Caribbean, Latino, East Asian, European, and African American drivers, among others. The alliance has been able to secure many gains for taxi drivers since its inception and has succeeded in building a strong organization led mostly by the drivers themselves. One of the major political actions undertaken by NYTWA was the taxi drivers' strike in May of 1998 against the new rules imposed at that time that increased the burden of penalty on drivers. This strike brought NYTWA into the limelight and demonstrated the power of this traditionally non-unionized workforce. The strike, on May 13, 1998, with a participation rate of 98 percent, was considered to be one of the most successful in the city's recent history (Mathews 2005; Das Gupta 2006). The outcome was a partial reversal of some of the penalties that were started under the new rules. The success of the strike also demonstrated the emergence of a union that could effectively represent migrant workers who were considered to be marginal to traditional labor politics.

Since its founding, NYTWA has also been instrumental in getting taxi drivers' wages increased by 35 to 45 percent. It fought to implement the first ever Living Wage Standard for U.S. taxi drivers, which was achieved in 2004. Other important achievements of NYTWA include negotiating the inclusion of taxi drivers in 9/11 federal disaster assistance; recovering lost income due to unlawful license suspensions; changing numerous antiworker policies and regulations governing the taxi industry; and providing discounted or pro bono legal, financial management, and health services.[37] In 2011, NYTWA took a major step toward becoming a national union and was chartered to build the National Taxi Workers Alliance, the 57th union of the AFL-CIO. In fact, NYTWA is the first charter for nontraditional workers since farm workers in the 1960s, and the first one ever of independent contractors. South Asians remain a huge part of the taxi drivers' population in New York City, with increasing number of Bangladeshis joining the industry, and NYTWA's multiracial leadership continues to reflect the strong presence of South Asians.

The Los Angeles area also witnessed the emergence of a taxi workers' union in recent years with the involvement of South Asian taxi drivers and progressive ethnic organizations active among South Asians in the area. The South Asian Network (SAN) in Los Angeles played an important role in rebuilding a taxi workers' organization when South Asian taxi drivers reached out to the organization. The Los Angeles Taxi Workers Alliance (LATWA) was formed in 2005 after an incident of harassment of a South Asian taxi driver at Los Angeles International Airport (LAX) by the airport transportation authorities. The taxi drivers went on a brief strike to protest against the harassment, and the incident proved to be a major catalyst for the formation of a new taxi workers' organization. Since the driver at the center of the LAX incident was a South Asian, a sizable network of South Asian drivers got involved with the mobilization. They reached out to SAN and its executive director at that time, Hamid Khan, for legal and organizational support. SAN became an important part of the organizing effort and the process of creating a new labor organization. LATWA was soon representing taxi drivers of different ethnicities, including Latinos, Egyptians, and Africans, in addition to South Asians. The union raised the issues of scrapping mandatory uniform requirement for drivers, fare increases, and a flat rate for short-distance rides from LAX. The organization worked with the Los Angeles City Council on many of these issues and succeeded in having some of these demands met. Being a multiracial organization, LATWA has also dealt with the problems encountered in organizing taxi drivers due to the ethnic divisions among them, which garage owners have often tried to exploit. The organization has been able to move forward despite all odds. Many of the leaders of LATWA had been involved with social movements in their home countries, particularly Pakistan and Egypt, and their experiences in organizing have helped the group negotiate many of the challenges of movement building. The organization has a membership base of over 1,300, and it has succeeded in developing alliances with other labor and ethnic organizations (Leavitt and Blasi 2009).

The 1980s and 1990s also witnessed the creation of women's organizations that focused on the issues faced by South Asian American women, particularly domestic violence. The model minority characterization of South Asians—Indian Americans in particular—has always been based on the presumption that these minority groups have approximated the ideals set by mainstream Anglo-Americans by upholding two traditionally cherished American values: (1) family unity and (2) individual economic success through hard work (Abraham 2000). The importance of "traditional family values" in Asian cultures fits this discourse perfectly. However, the formation of South Asian women's organizations in the United States was an acknowledgment that the space of family was not sacrosanct, and issues such as domestic violence needed to be addressed publicly. The South Asian women's organizations questioned the moral solidarity within the community that did not want to recognize domestic violence and patriarchal practices.

Maanavi and Sakhi were two South Asian women's organizations that came into existence in the late 1980s in the New Jersey/New York area initially to conceptually challenge patriarchal practices and the notion that immigrant women are the bearers of culture of the community. However, soon they were asked to intervene in individual cases of domestic violence within the community. Founded in 1985 in suburban New Jersey, Maanavi, a registered nonprofit organization that is managed by a small staff and a team of volunteers, has been focused on violence against South Asian Women. However, they defined violence in the broadest possible way that included all social conditions or individual actions that kept women subjugated (Das Gupta 2006; Abraham 2000). Maanavi's work focused on survivors of domestic violence from the community and developed resources and skills to provide them shelter, give them legal support to deal with violence, as well as address the immigration issues they faced. Sakhi, founded in New York City in 1989, also focused on domestic violence, adopted the path of publicly raising this question within the South Asian community. It developed tactics that publicly held the perpetrators of violence accountable by highlighting the incidents in the communities where they lived (Das Gupta 2006; Abraham 2000). While their services were available for all South Asian women, Sakhi expanded its services to include domestic violence faced by working-class South Asian women who were employed in the middle-class household as domestic workers. Both these organizations have struggled to strike a balance between their role as service providers and work toward transformative politics that could challenge the patriarchal structures in the larger community.

Sakhi's work with domestic workers was short lived, but it initiated important developments as far as organizing South Asian domestic workers was concerned. A steady population of South Asians, primarily women, started joining domestic work in the 1980s, both in South Asian households as well as others. These women workers were primarily newcomers from South Asian countries, but there were some who had lived in the United States for a while and undergone downward class mobility. South Asian employers prefer women from their homelands due to a range of cultural and structural reasons, especially because they can exercise greater control over them and pay less. South Asian domestic workers in turn seek South Asian employers because of a perception that they are less particular about legal documentation. Language and dietary considerations also play a role in choosing a South Asian household over others (Das Gupta 2006, 215). However, South Asian domestic workers are often forced to work in abusive conditions, with demands of uninterrupted service, and they are paid well below the prevailing industry wages.

Because Sakhi was one of the few organizations focused on gender oppression of South Asian women in the area, when the organization was approached in the 1990s by many South Asian domestic workers, it did not have the resources and a program focus to deal with domestic workers' issues. But many of these workers were able to avail themselves of services such as legal referrals, English as a Second Language (ESL) classes, and skills training that were put in place for South Asian women of all classes affected by domestic violence. However, the constant need to deal specifically with the cases of domestic workers led in 1994 to the creation of the Domestic Workers' Committee (DWC) inside Sakhi that slowly started dealing with issues of unpaid wages and abusive and exploitative working conditions. Linta Varghese, analyzing the emerging tension inside Sakhi between service-oriented work to help the survivors of domestic violence and a worker-oriented organizing approach, writes: "The tension between activism and service provision, worker and survivor, exploded around an articulation of class and the ways that class positioning dictated the work of the organization, and in 1997 a majority of the Sakhi board decided to dissolve the DWC, effectively ending its work on domestic workers' exploitation" (Varghese 2006, 193).[38] The debate around this issue became very intense and engulfed the entire organization. In fact, it was indicative of a larger move that some South Asian organizers were making in the direction of a working-class organizing model. The emergence of NYTWA as a labor organization that broke away from CAAV—an organization focused on violence against Asians—was another important example of this shift.

Two important organizations—Workers' Awaaz (founded 1996) and Andolan (founded 1998)—continued the work that Sakhi started with domestic workers (Abraham 2000; Bhattacharjee 1992; 1997; Varghese 2006). They organized South Asian domestic and other low-wage workers and developed as membership-based organizations that believe in the idea of workers' leadership. Adopting a model of organizing that emphasized community-based mobilization, the Workers' Awaaz joined forces with the National Employment Labor Project (NELP), the Asian American Legal Defense and Educational Fund (AALDEF), and the New York University Immigrant Law Clinic to pursue unpaid wage cases, offer ESL classes to bring in new members, and provide information on workers' rights. They held periodic know-your-rights workshops and published a know-your-rights handbook for domestic workers (Varghese 2006). The organization also fought many legal cases to recover back wages for domestic workers.

One of the high-profile cases fought by Workers' Awaaz was against a South Asian doctor couple—Manjit and J. B. Chadha—who forced a live-in South Asian domestic worker to work sixteen hours a day without any break and with no overtime payment. They fired her once she protested against her working conditions. The prolonged legal and political fight in 2000 led to an out-of-court settlement of 50,000 dollars of unpaid wages and other compensation.[39] This high-profile case highlighted the exploitation and abuse of South Asian domestic workers within the community and led to a series of mobilizing steps that brought many more cases to the organization (Varghese 2006). Due to varied organizational challenges faced by a worker-led group, Awaaz's work slowed down considerably in recent years. However, the organization played a major role in highlighting South Asian domestic workers' plight and experimenting with innovative ways of organizing.

Andolan is another important organization focused on South Asian domestic workers to emerge out of Sakhi's DWC. Initially, the people who founded Andolan worked briefly with Awaaz. Andolan is also a worker-led association, and one of the important activists of Andolan, Nahar Alam, was a Bangladeshi woman who had been employed as a domestic worker in the past (Das Gupta 2006). Rights education and advocacy have often been combined with collective action, such as protesting in front of the households that were implicated in exploiting and abusing domestic workers. The group has devised innovative ways to reach out to domestic workers, who are generally secluded in the households of their employers, through advertising in ethnic newspapers and distributing pamphlets in places such as Jackson Heights—the South Asian ethnic commercial hub in Queens—where many of these domestic workers often came with their employers. Andolan fought multiple legal cases on behalf of individual domestic workers and succeeded in reaching settlements.

Andolan has also been doing extensive work as a part of multiracial and multiethnic coalition (especially with Filipina, Thai, African, and Caribbean domestic workers) through Domestic Workers United (DWU) to establish industrywide labor standards. Due to their efforts, the New York City Council passed a bill in 2003 that established minimum standards for the industry and provided legal avenues to enforce these standards. Andolan, alongside other domestic workers' organizations, campaigned successfully to get the Domestic Workers Bill of Rights passed in 2010 in the state of New York. This landmark legislation for the first time recognized the rights of domestic workers to be protected by all the major labor laws pertaining to other workers. Another important campaign that Andolan has undertaken is to stop diplomatic immunity of UN employees in order to ensure that such immunity is not used to shield abusive employers from accountability for their treatment of domestic workers.[40]

Organizations of the South Asian labor force are expanding further to those South Asians employed in retail and restaurant work. South Asian businesses in ethnic commercial hubs such as Jackson Heights in Queens, New York, and Pioneer Boulevard in Artesia, Los Angeles, employ a sizable number of South Asian workers. The civil rights unit of SAN in Los Angeles has been reaching out to these workers in ethnic businesses in the Pioneer Boulevard area, and they have taken up cases of salon, retail, and restaurant workers.[41] The awareness and mobilization of South Asian workers was reflected in a major legal victory, when employees of two Indian restaurants on Pioneer Boulevard—Jay Bharat Foods Inc., doing business as Jay Bharat; and Standard Foods LLC, doing business as Standard Sweets—recovered nearly $95,000 in back wages following an investigation by U.S. labor regulators that determined that workers were not being paid the minimum wage.[42]

In New York City, DRUM, working primarily among Bangladeshi and Pakistani communities in Queens, and Adhikar, active among Nepali immigrants, have reached out to low-income South Asian workers in different sectors to educate them on their labor and civil rights. A report titled "Workers' Rights are Human Rights: South Asian Immigrant Workers in New York City," released by DRUM and the Urban Justice Center in July 2012, identified low-income occupations such as construction, retail, domestic work, restaurant, and taxi driver that have seen increasing numbers of South Asian workers. The report identified the fact that South Asian workers are consistently underpaid—receiving less than the industry wages—and work in hazardous conditions while facing harassment by employers and law enforcement. Moreover, most South Asian workers in these sectors have little to no benefits.[43]

The recent organizing effort among construction workers is another important example of the expansion of labor organizing among South Asians in New York City. The growing presence of construction workers from the South Asian community was reflected in the formation of New York Construction Workers United (NYCWU). In 2007, NYCWU, along with AALDEF, filed four lawsuits involving six South Asian construction workers and five contractors to recover unpaid wages. The legal action signified the growing number of South Asian construction workers in the city and attempts to organize them for better wages and working conditions. According to NYCWU, many of these workers put up with abusive conditions and low wages because they are undocumented and afraid of being reported.[44]

The South Asian American community has also witnessed the emergence of organizations and social spaces that have provided visibility to the issues of sexual orientation and sexuality within the community. The concerns of LGBTQ South Asian Americans have gained visibility within and outside the community through these organizations. The South Asian Lesbian Gay Association (SALGA) in the New York area, which was initially named the South Asian Gay Association in 1991, has provided a safe space for the Desi queer community and has enabled them to negotiate their visibility within the South Asian community as well as larger LGBT community spaces that have not been very open to Desi queers. Similar efforts were made in other cities in the 1980s and 1990s that led to Desi LGBTQ groups such as Trikone (San Francisco), MASALA (Boston), KhushDC (Washington, D.C.), and Satrang (Los Angeles). These groups have worked toward countering the dominant ways of thinking within South Asian communities that make LGBTQ issues invisible by excluding them from larger conversations that do the work of defining who South Asian/Indian/Pakistani/Bangladeshi Americans are. These organizations also emerged out of the frustrations of Desi LGBTQ individuals with the mainstream gay and lesbian organizations that made South Asians feel marginal and did not address the specificity of negotiating sexual identity in the cultural context of South Asian communities (Das Gupta 2006).

The most well-known example of the struggle for Desi queer visibility within the larger South Asian community spaces is the history of mobilization by SALGA along with other progressive allies against the ban on gays and lesbians from marching in the annual India Day Parade in

Manhattan. The India Day Parade in Manhattan is traditionally held to mark the day India achieved independence from British colonial rule, and it has become an occasion to celebrate the Indian American community, following a long tradition of parades in the United States to assert ethnic pride of immigrant communities. Mainstream Indian American organizations were opposed to providing a space for LGBTQ Indians, claiming that they were not a part of Indian culture. SALGA, along with other organizations, protested every year outside the parade, questioning the conservative and heteronormative outlook of parade organizers. SALGA was finally allowed to march in 2010, after many years of protest and negotiation with the parade organizers who had not let the group march with the parade after 2000 (Venugopal 2010). The controversy became a way to highlight LGBTQ issues in the broader South Asian community. However, participation in the parade itself as an end goal was an issue of debate within SALGA, and there was some discomfort within the organization about the nature of the parade, particularly the kind of nationalism it espoused (Gopinath 2005).

South Asian American LGBTQ groups have also developed significant transnational engagements with LGBTQ issues in South Asia. They have been playing an important role in building linkages with LGBTQ groups in South Asian countries and have worked toward highlighting the social and legal restrictions on the sexual lives of LGBTQ individuals. The 2013 Supreme Court judgment in India, upholding the legality of Article 377 of the Indian Penal Code, which criminalizes homosexuality, led to mobilization by a number of South Asian American LGBTQ organizations, who asked the government of India to stop criminalizing the sexual choices of individuals (Lakshman 2013). The organizing work around the issue of sexuality and sexual orientation among South Asian Americans has acquired strong visibility within the community in recent years and remains in constant contestation and negotiation with the larger community.

National-level advocacy organizations of South Asians focused on social justice mobilization have also come of age in the last ten to fifteen years. South Asian Americans Leading Together (SAALT), founded in 2000 in the New York area and moved to Washington, D.C., in 2005, is one of the most important organizations of this kind. Besides doing community work in New York, New Jersey, and the Philadelphia area, the organization started working toward building its capacity as an advocacy group that could represent the growing South Asian American population—particularly low-income and working-class segments and those impacted by racial and religious profiling—to policy makers and others. Before SAALT registered its presence in policy-making circles, South Asian American concerns were mostly channeled through the existing progressive Asian American organizations. However, South Asian issues have been traditionally marginal to the dominant Asian American organizations. South Asian American organizations working in different parts of the United States found a strong ally in SAALT that could amplify their voices. On the initiative of SAALT, thirty-two South Asian organizations from twelve regions of the United States came together in New York City in June 2008 to announce the formation of the National Coalition of South Asian Organizations (NCSAO). The coalition was a result of attempts by many of these organizations over the last several years to develop a comprehensive coordination among South Asian organizations working in different regions of the United States (SAALT 2015).

The important issues identified by the coalition included equal and full participation in the civic and political process for all, enforcement of civil rights and civil liberties for all, gender equality within the South Asian community, immigrant rights and reform, rights for gays and lesbians, and empowerment of South Asian youth.[45] SAALT has also built alliances with groups such as the Detention Watch Network, National Network of Immigrant and Refugee Rights, and National Council of Asian Pacific Americans to build a broader movement on issues such as deportation, detention, immigration policy, and issues pertinent to larger Asian American communities. SAALT has been extremely effective in highlighting the ongoing profiling of South Asians and Muslims in the post-9/11 period and helped educate other Asian American organizations about the critical importance of this issue for the larger South Asian and Asian American communities. It has also been effective in amplifying the voices of low-income and working-class South Asians and has worked toward producing a counternarrative to the model minority discourse about the community.

It is important to note that most South Asian organizations active among low-income and working-class populations are constantly struggling with issues of financial viability. Most of these organizations are nonprofit associations that are dependent on funding from different government agencies as well as private foundations. Even though the South

Asian community has seen the emergence of different kinds of progressive and social justice–oriented organizations working among low-income segments in the last two decades, there is a clear recognition of the challenges that these organizations encounter. Many of these organizations are not able to survive due to financial constraints and the challenges of working among marginalized segments of the community.

Notwithstanding all the challenges, the South Asian community is witnessing a robust growth of organizations and campaigns that are focused on working-class and low-income segments of the community. Some of these groups practice a service-oriented model that creates specific services such as ESL classes, skill development, and legal services for their membership. However, others emphasize organizing that focuses on movement building, creating leadership from the rank and file, and building organizations that could be self-sustaining. A significant number of South Asian organizations practice a combination of the two approaches. With an increasing number of South Asian immigrants joining the ranks of working-class occupations, the growth of working-class and low-income-oriented organizations has been responding to needs that have not been met by the traditional community organizations or affluent professional associations discussed earlier. A different kind of mobilization strategy is deployed by these organizations, which evokes their marginalization and oppression, and most of them do not use the discourse of the model minority that is fairly common among professional and middle-class South Asian organizations. Moreover, most of the working-class-oriented organizations have also moved in the direction of multiracial organizing, which creates organizations that are open to other ethnoracial groups in similar conditions. The organizing that has emerged through these organizations is very distinct from the elite mobilization strategies that were analyzed earlier, though they still remain largely within their particular sectors while working toward the larger goal of social justice involving the community and society as a whole.

## Conclusion

The political incorporation of South Asians is taking place in an institutional context that is characterized by the declining role of political parties in mobilizing new immigrants and the unique demographic profile of the group. Political parties and other institutions have made little attempt to bring contemporary nonwhite immigrants into the political process. South Asians as a group are, thus, marginalized in the political arena both as a result of this institutional lacuna and because of a lack of a significant population concentration that could provide them political efficacy as a voting group. However, this lack of mobilization and inclusion of the broader South Asian community simultaneously coexists with selective targeting of narrow segments that results in elite mobilization.

The analysis of interviews and other data suggests that the three major trends of political engagement among South Asian immigrants—representation from white majority districts, prominence of campaign fund-raising as a strategy for gaining political power, and the focus on lobbying—end up reinforcing selective elite mobilization, which precludes large segments from getting drawn into the political processes. The elite mobilization is particularly striking, given the presence of diverse interests in the community. The trend of elite mobilization speaks to the internal differentiation within the community and the process through which a particular segment of the community starts representing the community in the larger political process. The economic and professional elite may wish to represent the entire South Asian community, but they are not inclined to bring a cross section of interests within the community together. The broader trend within the South Asian community, as evident from the diverse nature of community groups, is the presence of differentiated interests that seek distinct articulation. The larger ethnoracial mobilization of the community has to contend with these differentiated articulations.

The emerging parallel trend of mobilization within the South Asian community, focused on the working-class segments of the community that have been joining occupations that are low paying, with minimum protections and benefits, further complicates the task of a unified ethnoracial political mobilization. This trend of political mobilization is different in terms of its constituency and reach, and it is bringing new voices into community spaces as well as the larger political process. The issues, targets, and strategies of mobilizing are very different in the case of low-income and working-class organizations in comparison to the professional associations of South Asians and they are also more inclined to adopt the path of multiracial organizing. The internal distinctions along the lines of nation of origin, class, profession, education, and sexuality and gender concerns limit the possibilities of a unified ethnoracial political mobilization that cuts across these differences. In conclusion, the dominant frameworks emphasizing exclusive ethnoracial mobilizations fail to account for the internal dynamics within the community outlined above.

# 5

# Transnationalism and Political Participation

*The Challenges of "In-Between" Americans*

In this chapter I focus on transnational engagements of South Asian Americans and analyze the ways in which such engagements impact the political participation of the group in the United States. Using both survey data and interviews to analyze the relationship between transnational engagements of South Asian immigrants and their participation in U.S. politics, I challenge the received wisdom that ongoing involvement with the home country is detrimental to immigrant political socialization and participation in the host country. I analyze the transnational behavior of South Asians in relation to other Asian American groups and point to some of the similarities and differences. Finally, I argue that involvement with transnational issues often becomes a conduit to engage with political institutions in the United States.

Many social scientists have asserted that one of the major impediments to immigrant political socialization in their adopted country is their continued attachment to the home country. In other words, strong attachment and involvement with political issues of the home country leads to lack of participation in the host country (Huntington 2004; Schlesinger 1992; Glazer 1983). Benedict Anderson termed diasporic nationalism "long-distance nationalism" and argued that the diaspora's engagement with the country of origin is not anchored in their location in the nation and, hence, it is a "responsibility-less" engagement. He further argued that this long-distance engagement is accompanied by non-engagement with the polity and society of places where these immigrants are actually situated (Anderson 1992). Moving beyond this limited debate on whether continuing attachment to the home country hampers immigrant political participation in the United States, recent scholarship has pointed to the ways in which transnational attachments shape groups' political engagement in the United States. For instance, the immigrant status of being "in-between" two countries as well as "home country cues"—a term used by Ruel Rogers to underline the importance of home country political socialization—have impacted immigrants' decisions on when and whether to naturalize and their development of strategies to deal with race politics and racial discrimination in the United States (Jones-Correa 1998; Rogers 2006). I develop this line of analysis further in this chapter and the next one to argue that transnational engagements become a necessary part of the political incorporation trajectory of immigrant groups and that internal cleavages such as class, religion, language, gender, caste, and sexuality often shape their transnational mobilizations as well.

### Does Engagement with Home Country Mean Less Participation in U.S. Politics?

I analyze here survey data pertaining to the impact of transnational attachments on the political participation of South Asian Americans in the United States. The analysis is based on data from the 2000–2001 Pilot Study of the National Asian American Political Survey (PNAAPS) and the 2008 National Asian American Survey (NAAS).[1] It is important to note that PNAAPS included a relatively small number of South Asians (141), hence the generalizability of the results is limited, given the small subsample. However, since there has been very little systematic study of South Asian immigrants, and this was the first survey of Asian American political attitudes and behavior to include this group, it does provide a baseline and preliminary understanding of South Asian immigrants' political participation in the United States in relation to their transnational attachments. It also provides a comparison point for surveys on South Asians that were conducted after 2001. The NAAS dataset included both a larger Asian American (5,159) sample and South Asian (1,150) subsample (Wong et al. 2011; Ramakrishnan et al. 2012). Thus, both these analyses together do provide a basis for drawing conclusions about the transnational political behavior of the group in relation to political participation in the United States. Moreover, the quantitative analysis is complemented by qualitative data collected through in-depth interviews with South Asian community members and activists.[2]

To analyze the broad patterns of transnational attachments and political participation of South Asians in the United States, bivariate analyses of PNAAPS data were completed.[3] The results reveal the patterns of

TABLE 8

**Asian Americans' Attachment to Country of Origin**

|  | CONTACT WITH COUNTRY OF ORIGIN | FOLLOWING NEWS IN COUNTRY OF ORIGIN | PARTICIPATION IN POLITICAL ACTIVITY OF COUNTRY OF ORIGIN |
|---|---|---|---|
| South Asian | 76* | 57 | 6 |
| Non South Asian | 59 | 63 | 6 |

Source: Author's compilation and analysis of data from Pilot National Asian American Political Survey, 2000–2001.

Note: *p ≤ .01. All figures are in percentages.

transnational attachments and political participation in the United States among South Asians in comparison to other Asian Americans (Non South Asians) in the aggregate. Measured in terms of the frequency of contact to the country of origin, South Asians demonstrate a remarkably high level of transnational attachment in comparison to other Asian groups (see Table 8).[4] The data suggest that South Asians (76 percent) are significantly more likely to maintain close contacts with their country of origin than are other Asian Americans (59 percent).[5] The data from NAAS (Table 9) suggest a similar pattern. The percentage of Asian Indians (87 percent) who communicated with family and friends is higher than Chinese (74 percent), Filipinos (67 percent), Japanese (59 percent), Korean (82 percent), and Vietnamese (74 percent).[6]

The second measure of transnational attachment utilized by PNAAPS was attention to news stories from the country of origin. Fifty-seven percent of the South Asian respondents paid very close attention to news in the country of origin, in comparison to 63 percent of other Asian respondents. However, the difference is not statistically significant—in fact, South Asians are almost equally attentive to the news in their country of origin as compared to the rest of Asian Americans. The overall number suggests that the proportion of South Asian respondents paying close attention to news in the country of origin is high (Table 8). The qualitative data based on interviews also suggest a high level of attention to news related to the home country, with widespread use of the Internet, phone,

TABLE 9

**Transnational Participation of Asian Americans**

| | ASIAN INDIAN | CHINESE | FILIPINO | JAPANESE | KOREAN | VIETNAMESE | TOTAL |
|---|---|---|---|---|---|---|---|
| Communicated with Family or Friends | 87 | 74 | 67 | 59 | 82 | 74 | 75 |
| Sent Money | 38 | 27 | 57 | 12 | 17 | 58 | 36 |
| Involved in Politics | 5 | 5 | 4 | 1 | 1 | 2 | 4 |

Source: National Asian American Survey, 2008 (Wong et al. 2011, 78).
Note: All figures are in percentages.

social media such as Twitter and Facebook, and ethnic TV channels focused on coverage of South Asian countries.

Turning to another indicator of transnational attachment, the NAAS data suggest that a sizable percentage of Asian Indians (38 percent) send money to their country of origin. Two Asian groups—Filipino (57 percent) and Vietnamese (58 percent)—indicated a higher percentage of participation in this measure than Asian Indian immigrants (Table 9). However, the numbers suggest that a sizable segment of Asian Indian immigrants maintain regular transnational attachments by sending remittances.

The data on a fourth measure of transnational attachment, participation in activities concerning the politics of the country of origin, indicate that there is a very low level of participation in such activities among Asian Americans. In fact, PNAAPS data reported that only 6 percent of both other Asian American and South Asian respondents participated in any political activity regarding the country of origin (Table 8). The NAAS data also report that only 5 percent of Indian Americans participated in such activities (Table 9). The evidence from scholarship on other immigrant groups also suggests that direct participation in political activities related to the country of origin is rather low among immigrants (DeSipio, 2003; Guarnizo, Portes and Haller, 2003). However, qualitative analysis and participant observations suggest that South Asians participate in a range of activities related to the home country that pertain to social, developmental, and religious issues. These activities are not political in the formal sense, but they are part of a broader social engagement with the country of origin. The qualitative data also suggest the existence of a rich array of organizations involved with different issues relating to the home countries. However, both the qualitative and the quantitative data do suggest that there is a gap between transnational political participation and other forms of transnational attachments such as maintaining regular contact, paying attention to the news from the home country, and sending remittances. Direct involvement with the politics of the country of origin is thus limited to a relatively small group, but intensity and impact of such engagements are quite visible in South Asian communities. A detailed analysis of some of these groups among Indian Americans is undertaken in chapter 6.

The bivariate analysis of the NAAS data additionally provides important insights into the relationship between transnational attachments and the political participation of South Asian immigrants in the United States. It shows that there is no significant association between sending money home and involvement in U.S. politics. In other words, those who send money back home on a regular basis are not any less likely to get involved in U.S. politics. In fact, there is a weak positive relationship between remittance activity and U.S.-based political participation. Home country political activism exhibits a weak negative association with voting, but with regard to other types of political participation in the United States, the relationship is positive. For instance, political contributions in the United States tend to be more frequent among those South Asians who take part in homeland politics (23 percent) than among those who do not participate in country of origin politics (12 percent). In a similar vein, contacting a government official is more likely among those who take part in homeland politics (33 percent) than among those who do not (8 percent). In addition, those who take part in homeland politics are more than twice as likely to protest and more than three times as likely to work with others to solve a community problem in the United States (Wong et al. 2011, 78–79).

Recall that South Asians tend to maintain more transnational attachments than other Asian Americans. Yet the PNAAPS data on political participation of South Asian immigrants in the United States indicate that they are high to moderate on different indices of political participation. On measures that indicate participation beyond voting (signing a petition, calling a public official, participating in a protest, etc.), there is a distinct difference between the participation rates of South Asians and the rest of Asian Americans. Fifty-five percent of South Asians engage in one form or another of nonvoting participation, in comparison to 38 percent of the rest of the Asian population. The difference between the two groups is statistically significant at a .01 level, and, in terms of absolute numbers, it is also relatively high (see Table 10). Similarly, a higher number of South Asian respondents (72 percent) take an interest in politics, as compared to the rest of the Asian sample (61 percent), and the difference between the two groups is statistically significant. A remarkably high percentage of South Asians (92 percent) show high familiarity with the electoral process for presidential elections, in comparison to the rest of the Asian sample (73 percent), and the difference is statistically significant. South Asians (25 percent) are also more likely to become members of ethnic organizations, in comparison to the rest of the Asian groups (11 percent). Almost 90 percent of registered South Asian voters cast their ballot, in comparison to 82 percent of the rest of the Asian American registered voters in the sample. However, this difference is statistically not significant. It is important to note that these analyses do not control for resources such as education or income, so one must be cautious about assuming a direct relationship between transnational attachments and political participation. In other words, some of these differences might be driven by differences in education and income.

Another set of important indicators of political participation used for this analysis is related to citizenship. There are two measures that relate to citizenship: (1) the expectation to become a citizen in the near future and (2) the rate of naturalization. The results suggest that there is no difference between the South Asian subsample (74 percent) and rest of the Asian sample (72 percent) as to the expectation to become a citizen in the near future (Table 10). However, the two groups differ on the rate of naturalization (Citizen). The analysis shows that a lower proportion of South Asians (44 percent) are citizens in comparison to the rest of the Asian American groups (62 percent). The difference is statistically significant at a .01 level of significance. The bivariate analysis thus suggests that South Asian immigrants display both strong transnational attachments as well as a relatively high level of political participation in the United States, with the sole exception of naturalization.

The results from the cross-tabulations presented above do highlight important trends and relationships, but they do not control for the

TABLE 10

**Political Participation of Asian Americans in the United States**

| | VOTING (AMONG REGISTERED) | PARTICIPATION (NONVOTING) | INTEREST IN POLITICS | FAMILIARITY WITH PRESIDENTIAL ELECTIONS | BELONGING TO ETHNIC ORGANIZATIONS | CITIZEN | EXPECT TO BECOME CITIZEN (AMONG NONCITIZENS) |
|---|---|---|---|---|---|---|---|
| South Asian | 90 | 55* | 72* | 92* | 25* | 44 | 74 |
| Non South Asian | 82 | 38 | 61 | 73 | 11 | 62* | 72 |

Source: Author's compilation and analysis of data from Pilot National Asian American Political Survey, 2000–2001.

Note: *p ≤ .01. All figures are in percentages.

influence of factors such as education, income, length of stay, and other variables. Two separate multivariate regression analyses were conducted using the PNAAPS data to analyze the relationship between transnational attachments and political participation in the United States after controlling for potential intervening variables. The first examined political participation beyond voting among South Asian immigrants, and the second analyzed naturalization among South Asian immigrants. The naturalization analysis was limited to those who had lived in the United States as permanent residents for five years or more.[7] The independent variables of interest are South Asian, transnational attachments, and discrimination; other variables, including age, income, education, length of stay in the United States, and citizenship (in the analysis of participation beyond voting), served as controls.

South Asians are more likely to participate in political activities other than voting compared to other Asians in the sample, even after controlling for standard demographic variables such as income and education (Table 11).[8] Given the higher median income and higher level of education among South Asian immigrants, an argument can be made that their higher rate of political participation is primarily due to their higher income and education. But, the multivariate analysis indicates that South Asians participate at higher rates than other Asians even while controlling for education and income.

The analysis indicates that Asian Americans who maintain high levels of transnational attachment to their countries of origin, including frequency of contact and attention to the news, are also likely to exhibit high political participation beyond voting in the United States. The associations are statistically significant and clearly confound the common understanding that continuing attachment to the country of origin is detrimental to political participation in the United States. In the case of South Asians only, the relationship between political participation in the United States and transnational attachment is positive (.242) but not statistically significant (Model II, Table 11). A close look at these relationships suggests that engaging in transnational activities does not limit South Asian political participation in the United States. However, the interaction effect between South Asians and transnational attachment is negatively related (–1.074) to acquisition of citizenship, and the relationship is statistically significant. South Asians who are more transnational are less likely to naturalize than those who are less transnational (see Table 12).

TABLE 11

## Multivariate Analysis of Association between Transnationalism and Political Participation

|  | MODEL I. BETA COEFFICIENT (STANDARD ERROR) | MODEL II. BETA COEFFICIENT (STANDARD ERROR) |
|---|---|---|
| South Asian | .819* | .496 |
|  | (.241) | (.524) |
| Age | .004 | .004 |
|  | (.006) | (.006) |
| Family Income | .147* | .145* |
|  | (.052) | (.052) |
| Educational Attainment** | .097 | .097 |
|  | (.061) | (.061) |
| Citizenship | .455* | .463 |
|  | (.187) | (.187) |
| Political Interest | .402* | .402* |
|  | (.088) | (.088) |
| Years in the United States | .017 | .017 |
|  | (.011) | (.011) |
| Participation in Transnational | .334* | .306* |
|   Activities | (.117) | (.123) |
| Interaction Effect between South Asian |  | .242 |
|   and Transnational Participation |  | (.350) |
| N | 768 | 768 |
| Percentage Predicted Correctly | 67.6 | 67.4 |

Source: Author's compilation and analysis of data from Pilot National Asian American Political Survey, 2000–2001.

Note: *p ≤ .10. Dependent variable is participation in U.S. political activities other than voting.
** Missing values for this variable were replaced by mean educational attainment.

Scholars working on Latino and Caribbean immigrants have also analyzed the lag in naturalization among immigrant groups. Michael Jones-Correa (1998), in his work on New York City Latino immigrants, argued that Latinos generally postponed their decision to naturalize because, in their minds, naturalization in the United States was a major

TABLE 12

**Multivariate Analysis of Association between Transnationalism and Naturalization**

| INDEPENDENT VARIABLE | BETA COEFFICIENT (STANDARD ERROR) |
| --- | --- |
| South Asian | 1.20 |
| | (.782) |
| Age | .009 |
| | (.007) |
| Family Income | .024 |
| | (.068) |
| Educational Attainment | .035 |
| | (.079) |
| Political Interest | −.091 |
| | (.109) |
| Years in the United States | .127* |
| | (.018) |
| Transnational Attachment | −.146 |
| | (.151) |
| Interaction of South Asian and Transnational Attachment | −1.074* |
| | (.510) |
| N | 577 |
| Percentage Predicted Correctly | 76.3 |

Source: Author's compilation and analysis of data from Pilot National Asian American Political Survey, 2000–2001.

Note: *$p \leq .10$. Dependent variable is citizenship (analysis includes immigrants only).

step toward severing their ties and ending the possibilities of going back to their home countries. He termed this mind-set a politics of "in-between," where immigrants do not want to commit to one place at the expense of the other. Reuel Rogers (2006), in his work on Caribbean immigrants in New York City, similarly argues that a number of these immigrants took longer to naturalize because of their persistent belief that they might decide to return to their home country. However, both authors also argue that postponement of naturalization does not necessarily mean complete nonengagement with civic and political processes in the United States. Even though noncitizen immigrants are not fully a part of the formal political process in terms of having voting rights, they do get engaged through various civic and political associations. South Asian immigrants show a higher level of civic and political engagement than other Asian Americans who naturalize sooner than South Asians. The overall analysis suggests that their high level of transnational attachment does not lead to lesser political participation in the United States. The lag in naturalization, hence, should not be seen as a complete lack of civic and political engagement. Rather, it suggests attachment to both the countries, and in some senses resistance to perceived breaking off from the country of origin.

## To Belong "Here" and "There"

Interviews with community members and activists also provide evidence that questions the framework emphasizing a zero-sum relationship between political participation in the United States and various forms of attachments and engagements with the country of origin. The interviewees provide a nuanced picture that reflects the simultaneous existence of multiple engagements tied to a complex ethnic identity. The interviews also reflect the impact of recent ideological and institutional shifts that are more tolerant of hyphenated identities and multiple attachments compared to an earlier period in American history. In the early twentieth century, the Americanization campaign aimed at European immigrants, with assimilation being the reigning credo, was much less tolerant of ethnic and linguistic identities and transnational attachments (Handlin 1951). However, with the gains of the civil rights movement and multiculturalism becoming a part of the larger social and political discourse, different ethnic identities, cultural practices, and the transnational attachments of immigrant communities are relatively more acceptable than in earlier eras of immigration. The majority of South Asian community members and leaders interviewed for this project asserted that it was legitimate and desirable to engage with the country of origin and that they felt comfortable with their dual identities and engagements. This general view about acceptability of transnational engagement, however, was calibrated by the post-9/11 environment that put the needle of suspicion on South Asian and Arab immigrants, particularly Muslims, leading to increased scrutiny of their transnational connections and ethnic and cultural practices.

A majority of the interviewees spoke about the need to be involved with both the country of origin and the United States and how both these involvements come naturally to South Asian immigrants. Talking about political participation in the United States and connection to the country of origin, a Bangladeshi community activist based in Los Angeles said:

> In my opinion Bangladeshi immigrants should not sever connection from their country of origin. The reason being that keeping in touch with the country of origin doesn't stop any one from getting involved in this society—both in politics and everything else. . . . Most of the countries in the third world have a very huge percentage of their revenue coming in from their expatriate workers and many of them have their family back home and they send money back home and Bangladesh is no different. . . . Immigrants from countries such as Israel are very, very active in the politics of Israel. They vote in Israeli elections. People from our part of the world at least do not vote, they may take an interest in the politics of the home country. I think people who connect most actively with the country of origin are people from Israel. They vote, lobby, fight for it, and I have not heard any body criticizing that.[9]

This statement draws upon the history of different immigrant groups, specifically Israeli immigrants and the relationship between Israel and the United States that eases transnational engagements, to make the argument that there is nothing wrong with keeping strong links with Bangladesh and that does not necessarily affect their political engagement in the United States. When asked whether Bangladeshi immigrants participate adequately in the political process here, he responded that there is not much participation because Bangladeshis are the most recent immigrants and a majority of them are still in the process of settling down. The reason for a lower level of participation, he argued, cannot be attributed to a strong attachment to the home country, but it is due to a host of reasons, including the lack of efforts by political parties and other institutions.

A thirty-five-year-old second-generation community leader of Indian descent in Los Angeles, commenting on political participation in the United States and attachments to home country, said:

> I do agree that when you make a new country your home, you should play an active role in the political process here. . . . But that does not mean that you check out your identity, your background, your heritage. I believe you can do both, and there is no conflict between the two whatsoever. You can play an active role in your adopted country as well as play a role in your country of origin. . . . Just because we come from a certain country that does not mean we should deny our heritage and wherever we came from. . . . There are people of diverse backgrounds in this country, and they celebrate their cultural heritage. . . . The American tradition is that no one has to forego one's identity.[10]

Clearly, there is a connection being made here between engagements with home country and an individual's ethnic identity. Attachment to home country is seen as an affirmation of an ethnic identity, and it is important for South Asians to have this relationship, particularly when they are seen in this country as "different." The statement also underscores multiple reasons that drive immigrant communities to have involvements with their country of origin.

As discussed earlier, both the qualitative and quantitative data confirm that active engagement with the politics of the home country is confined only to a small group. Interviews also support the general consensus that there is no large-scale mass political engagement with countries of origin. However, it is important to note that the active involvement of a small section of the community with homeland politics is accompanied by the keen interest of a larger segment of the community. A Pakistani community leader from Los Angeles pointed out:

> A very small number of people here [in the Los Angeles area] get involved in the politics of Pakistan. . . . But community in general is at the top of what's going on in Pakistan. . . . There is not a lot of participation, but the interest is there to have a healthy political cycle in Pakistan. . . . It is my advice to all the people coming from

our part of the world that they must be aware of and be a part of the political process here. . . . But it is also an unwritten responsibility for all immigrants to do something for their country of birth. . . . It is a part of human responsibility. . . . Whatever you achieved in this country because of your abilities, a small part of that success belongs to your country of origin, birth.[11]

The distinction between active engagement with home country politics as opposed to having an interest and following news is an important one. However, the continuing interest of a large segment in terms of following news and keeping track of political developments suggests that a wider segment of the community is engaged in some form with social and political developments in the home country. Technology and social media have made it even easier to keep connected with real-time political developments in home countries. An immigrant from India who has lived in the United States for the last thirty years also echoed sentiments about keeping informed about the home country even while participating in the host country. She argued:

I would say that when you come to this country and become a citizen of this country, you have to belong to this country and participate in the political process. . . . But at the same time it does not mean that you can forget from where you came, because everything is global. . . . There is no question of my country is this and the other is that. . . . It is a question of accepting the fact that you belong to both the countries and you have responsibility to both countries.[12]

Despite the lack of a mass level of participation in political issues relating to countries of origin, there is strong support for dual involvement. A Pakistani community member said:

If someone tells me to remove the Pakistan part from yourself, I can't do that. But if someone says get involved here [in the United States] then I would agree with that person. I totally disagree with people who consider this country as a money milking machine and do not get involved in anything locally. . . . To me a politically aware person should be involved on both sides. . . . I vote here, pay attention to politics, and decide issues based on current events. This does not stop me from getting involved or paying attention to the politics in Pakistan.[13]

There seems to be a widespread consensus among interviewees that it should be natural for South Asians to be involved with both the home and the host country. However, the need for a greater engagement in local politics was constantly reiterated by community members.

Many community members and activists did express concerns about the lack of participation by South Asians in U.S. politics. Many of the interviewees felt that the community is more oriented toward homeland politics than local or national U.S. politics. Here they seemed to share the view of scholars who argued that transnational engagements negatively affect participation in the United States. However, as noted earlier, it would be simplistic to argue that interest and orientation toward homeland issues and politics is the reason why South Asian immigrants participate at a lower level in U.S. politics. As argued in previous chapters, there are multiple reasons for lack of participation by the South Asian community in U.S. politics, including an overall institutional and political context of general low political participation, racial barriers, lack of mobilization of South Asian Americans by the political parties, outsider status, and the preoccupation of the group with the need for economic stability, especially as first-generation immigrants. A Bangladeshi immigrant in New York City, talking about participation in U.S. politics, said, "[There is less participation] here because maybe they don't know English or they can't follow the political process of this country, perhaps, they don't understand it. . . . I see too much Bangladeshi politics here and very little of American politics."[14] The majority of immigrants are apathetic to the political process, but those who get engaged have to deal with institutions and organizations central to the U.S. political process, and they do not find it welcoming and inviting. Another Bangladeshi immigrant in New York City, talking about the inclination of the community to get engaged with organizations oriented toward the home country, said:

> They are not confident. They do not feel comfortable associating themselves with mainstream America. I think it is because of their personal upbringing . . . they may think that it may not be easy for them to find a comfortable position or place in

mainstream American politics. . . . It is much easier for them to take an interest in *Desi* (South Asian) politics. Because for them, the mainstream American politics is a completely new arena. And they are afraid they may not be recognized or, I mean, they may not be able to make any impression. It is very hard for them. Whereas in *Desi* (South Asian) politics, many of them were already involved in politics before coming to the U.S. . . . So, when they come here, it is easier for them to carry on with their political mission with Bangladeshi politics rather than taking interest or joining mainstream American politics.[15]

Even though this statement was made in reference to the Bangladeshi community, similar opinions were expressed about Indian and Pakistani immigrant communities as far as engagement with mainstream U.S. politics was concerned.

The reiteration of the need to get more involved in U.S. politics thus comes with the recognition that there are barriers to overcome. In fact, the interviewees themselves suggest that South Asian American immigrants who are oriented toward political and civic engagement find it easier to get involved with South Asian ethnic organizations. These ethnic organizations, in most cases, have strong engagement with issues relating to the country of origin (in some cases with domestic U.S. politics as well), making it easier and more natural for South Asian immigrants to engage with them as compared to mainstream American political institutions. The presence of a large number of ethnic and occupational organizations, discussed in chapter 4, among South Asians is a testament to the growing importance of this trend.

Here, a comparison with early twentieth-century European immigration and its analysis by the pluralist model is quite instructive. The pluralist model, as discussed in chapter 2, argued that European immigrants were first mobilized on ethnic lines and then political parties and other institutions courted these ethnic organizations, which played an important role in the political incorporation of Europeans (Dahl 1961). The experience of South Asian immigrants, however, suggests that ethnic organizations are not being approached by contemporary political parties, and they are more isolated from the mainstream U.S. political process than the ethnic organizations of earlier European immigrants. The pluralist model would have us believe that ethnic organizations are the vehicle through which new immigrants gain entry into the U.S. political process, but the experience of South Asian immigrants and their ethnic organizations suggest that they face relative isolation from mainstream political groups and institutions. The other side of this relative isolation and nonengagement is South Asians' ability and ease in connecting and engaging with home country political groups and institutions. The connections of South Asian immigrants to groups and institutions of home countries have intensified in recent years with changes in the approach of home countries as well as the United States in creating dual political and legal attachments, which will be discussed in greater detail in chapter 6.

## Conclusion

The evidence from quantitative and qualitative data suggests that transnational engagements of different kinds remain a significant part of the South Asian American community. Both bivariate and multivariate analyses of PNAAPS and NAAS data indicate that transnational engagement—among South Asians as well as the other Asian Americans—of different kinds do not have a negative impact on political participation of the groups in the United States. The only exception in the case of South Asians was the rate of naturalization: South Asians with higher levels of transnational attachments showed a tendency to naturalize at a lower rate. Even though only a small segment of the immigrant community is directly involved with political activities focused on home country issues, the interest in home country politics remains very high, and there are multiple organizations within the community that are deeply involved with transnational politics. Community members continuously express desires to find ways to keep connected with the social and political developments in their home countries. The South Asian experience suggests that immigrant political incorporation cannot be neatly divided into involvement with host country and home country issues, and many instances of pure home country political concerns have pushed the group into greater engagement with political institutions and power centers in the United States. The next chapter further elaborates on the trajectories that have emerged as South Asian communities have tried to develop political and organizational frameworks that speak to dual attachments.

# 6

# Diasporic Nationalism and Fragments Within

Multiple sites of engagement inform the social and political lives of South Asian immigrants, as discussed in chapter 5, and political involvement in both the home and host countries is intertwined. In this chapter I analyze concrete examples of current transnational involvements of the Indian American community in order to illustrate the multiple impulses behind such engagements and how they relate to internal cleavages within the community. Diasporic mobilizations often use the discourse of a unified community by deploying a diasporic nationalist framework—projecting a unified community along the lines of a "nation outside the nation"—to produce a politics that maintains the seeming coherence and unity. However, transnational engagements also produce political contestations within diasporic communities over the meanings and directions of the "nation" (home country) and how particular groups are placed therein. In this chapter, I discuss three contemporary examples of transnational involvement that are emblematic of the contours of Indian American transnational political engagements. First, I describe cross-border engagements by Indian American entrepreneurs and professionals from the information technology sectors as an example of new forms of transnationalism that illustrate how particular constellations of class, technology, and emerging global business practices shape transnational practices of Indian American economic elites. Second, I discuss a major moment of transnational political mobilization represented by the U.S.–India Civil Nuclear Deal in 2006, which was enabled by professional ethnic associations and the Indian American elite, who presented it as a moment that unified the community. Third, I discuss pro- and anti-Hindu nationalist mobilizations and how changing political situation in the homeland created conditions for mobilization in the United States, in the process highlighting the fissures within the Indian American community. The analysis presented in this chapter provides new ways of thinking about the transnational lives of immigrant communities by foregrounding the attempts at unifying mobilizations as well as differentiations and contestations within the group. All three examples also demonstrate the ways in which dual interests—both home and host country—continue to shape the lives of immigrant communities.

## Diaspora Theory: Contestations on Identity, Belonging, and Nationhood

One of the dominant frameworks for understanding immigrant transnational lives has come from theories of diaspora. The concept of diaspora expresses broadly the experiences of travel, loss, longing, and long-distance involvement in a manner that transcends nation-state identification and highlights the enduring conceptual importance of both home and host countries in immigrant lives. The concept has become instrumental in interrogating and critiquing notions of identity and belonging rooted in territoriality, purity, and authenticity. Furthermore, the framework of diaspora also questions the idea of a pluralist nationalism that does recognize ethnic/immigrant differences inside the nation-state but ignores the transnational lives of these communities. The diasporic theorists, acknowledging the importance of home country attachments, assert that the sense of immigrant identity is not separatist and isolationist but rather partly grounded outside the time/space of nation-state. Diasporic discourses thus underline the immigrant sense of being part of a continuous transnational network where homeland figures as a prominent (though not an exclusive) place of attachment (Braziel and Mannur 2003).

The idea of diaspora is often deployed as a critique of the nation-state because of diaspora's extraterritorial location and attachments. Diaspora theories that emerged, initially through the works of Stuart Hall and Paul Gilroy in the 1980s and 1990s, moved the concept away from its classical orientation toward homeland, return, and exile. They used it to underline an identity that negotiates differences and hybridity and to formulate a politics that is inclusive of multiple identities, attachments, and concerns (Hall 1990; Gilroy 1993). However, the nonessentialist notion of identity that constitutes the core of this tradition of theorization of diaspora exists alongside a conception of diaspora that follows the myths of origin and purity that form the bedrock of the nation-state project

(Gopinath 2005, 7). As I illustrate in this chapter, the vocal support from the Indian diaspora for Hindu nationalist politics is a prime example of the originalist and purist orientation within the diaspora that has serious implications for Indian American political involvement in both home and host countries. I also illustrate that this orientation to diaspora encounters multiple fissures within the community that challenge the tropes of nationalism and unified community.

The groups marginalized in this purist and essentialist diasporic discourse draw upon the subversive potential of the concept of diaspora to articulate their experiences and challenge the nationalistic project. Gayatri Gopinath, in her important work on queer diasporas, argues that bringing queer experiences into diasporic discourses captures desires, practices, and subjectivities that are generally considered outside the conventional diasporic and nationalist imaginaries. Gopinath argues, "A consideration of queerness . . . becomes a way to challenge nationalist ideologies by restoring the impure, inauthentic, nonreproductive potential of the notion of diaspora" (2005, 11). Bringing the queer into diaspora not only challenges a particular construction of the nation but also asks for reimagining diaspora differently. Others have pointed to the issue of caste privilege and how people from Dalit, or oppressed, castes struggle to find a space within the upper-caste-dominated Indian American diasporic community. Thenmozhi Soundarrajan, talking about her experience growing up in the United States as a member of a formerly untouchable caste, says, "Many Americans and Indians can't imagine what it looks like to pass. For my family it was finding ever clever ways to sidestep the 'jati' [caste] question, attending temple functions and never speaking about 'our community' in public functions ever" (Soundarrajan 2012). The recent attempts by Dalit, or oppressed, caste Indian American groups in the United States to highlight the prevalence of caste-based discrimination in India as well among Indian Americans in the United States challenge a particular conception of diaspora that normalizes the predominantly upper-caste composition of the community.

Similarly, Indian American minority religious communities, such as Muslim, Christian, and Sikh, bring up the distinctive concerns of these groups both in the United States and India and challenge a majoritarian (Hindu) conception of diaspora. The transnational political engagements of these groups emphasize the heterogeneity of the Indian American diasporic community and the distinctiveness of their political and social concerns. Thus, attempts to create a seamless homogenous construction of diaspora run into contrary subjectivities and social cleavages that require us to think about diasporic communities and transnational engagements in a more complex manner. My analysis of the transnational political engagements of South Asians in the United States is informed by perspectives brought by diaspora and transnational scholars who have challenged the dominance of nationalist and assimilation frameworks and proposed an interrogation of the contestations and fissures within diasporic communities. Vijay Prashad (2000) and Kamala Visweswaran (1997), for instance, point out that the professional- and managerial-class composition of the post-1965 Indian diasporic population in the United States, engendered by globalization and transnational capitalism, produces specific forms of transnationalism embedded in their class position. The class composition and immigration trajectory thus become critical in analyzing the transnational engagements of diasporic communities. In this context, one of the most important and distinctive forms of transnational engagement among Indian Americans has emerged from the professional and entrepreneurial segments of the community dominated by the IT, health, and biotech industries.

## Information Technology Investment, Entrepreneurship, and Cross-Border Engagements

Given the socioeconomic and occupational profile of the Indian American community, a very important part of transnational engagement pertains to the professional and entrepreneurial aspects of their lives. This section focuses on information technology entrepreneurs and professionals illustrating the specificity of transnational engagements based on occupational and class resources that produce particular kinds of transnational networks with business, social, and political elites. A new phase of globalization has created the conditions that have introduced new dimensions to economic transnationalism including call centers; outsourcing of different kinds of work; and cross-national business firms that rely on movement of data, people, jobs, and ideas across continents. Thomas Friedman termed this increased level of flow "the flattening of the world" in his book *The World Is Flat: A Brief History of the Twenty-First Century.* He used multiple examples from India—Bangalore in particular—to explain new forms of interconnections in the global economy that have created jobs, businesses, and services thriving on the hypermobility of data and the ease of communication. Friedman refers to different kinds of outsourcing, such as services provided through call centers, accounting work (he wondered if his tax returns were being filed by someone in Bangalore), medical services such as reading CT scans and MRIs, and the software and back office needs of all kinds of companies in the United States and Europe, through Business Processing Outsourcing (BPO). He terms this phase Globalization 3.0, which he characterizes as enabling individuals from different parts of the world, as opposed to nation-states, to be empowered and to benefit from the process (Friedman 2007). Friedman's analysis has been sharply critiqued for presenting a view of globalization—termed as neoliberal—that completely disregards the historic inequality among nations as well as inequalities within countries such as India and China. While Friedman describes these countries as beneficiaries of globalization, he ignores the fact that some sections of society benefit, but others get further impoverished and marginalized in the process (Smith 2005). Notwithstanding this important critique, Friedman does point to the intensification of globalization that centrally concerns India and the United States, particularly a segment of Indian American professionals and entrepreneurs who are deeply engaged in such processes through their work, investment, and business choices.

Scholars have argued that human-capital-rich immigrant communities can be an international business asset, and a combination of preference, knowledge, and ability to pay make the members of diaspora willing customers and investors. Their knowledge of the needs and capabilities of both host and home countries in specific areas of business make them useful intermediaries (Kapur 2010). A segment of the Indian American community has indeed come to acquire the resources, network, and inclination to occupy this position through their transnational activities. To fully understand the present phase of transnational engagement among Indian diasporic business, financial, and professional elites, it is important to contextualize some of the important shifts in diasporic engagements with India. Even though there is a fairly long history of the Indian diaspora's engagement in trade, business, and finance in different parts of the world, diasporic business involvement with India had very little economic impact until the late 1980s. Scholars attributed the nonengagement of the Indian business diaspora with the home country to the fact that Indian diaspora was based in many of the newly independent countries (Africa and Caribbeans) that imposed severe restrictions on trade and other economic activities with other countries. More importantly, India also espoused a framework of economic nationalism that led to a relatively closed economy with major restrictions on trade and investment (Kapur 2010; Bose 2008).

A significant change in approach toward diaspora came about in the 1990s, with the liberalization of the Indian economy, which was a highly contentious policy initiative that led to major changes allowing for greater foreign investment and trade alongside other policy initiatives. The move led to the privatization of public-sector companies and reforms that curtailed labor rights and weakened labor unions.[1] The changes also coincided with the emergence of relatively affluent Indian immigrant communities in North America and Britain. However, the government of India had started reaching out to the Indian diaspora, even before the restructuring of the economy, by asking them to buy bonds in India and participate in other saving schemes to ward off India's economic woes, particularly its balance-of-payment crisis. Two programs were launched in the 1970s—the Foreign Currency Non-Resident Account and the Non-Resident (External) Rupee Account—to attract funds in foreign currency from overseas Indian immigrant communities. In 1992, following a serious national debt crisis, the government issued India Development Bonds that could be bought exclusively by Indians living abroad. Furthermore, the Resurgent India Bonds were launched in 1998, in the backdrop of global sanctions on India for testing nuclear weapons, followed by the India Millennium Development Bond in 2000 (Kapur 2010; Bose 2008). These attempts by the Indian government to attract foreign currency in the forms of savings and bonds were modestly successful and marked a phase of increase in diasporic economic transnationalism. The process further intensified and took new forms in subsequent years, with the changed economic regime in India. The intensification was aided by the emergence of information technology and related fields as a priority area in the Indian economy and the concentration of a significant segment of Indian Americans in this field.

Comparing the Indian diaspora to its Chinese counterpart, Devesh Kapur points out that the Chinese diaspora has played a major role in creating a labor-intensive manufacturing export business from China in recent years, whereas the Indian diaspora is playing an important role in creating exports of tradable services such as software and IT-related products. The emergence of a vibrant Indian American technology professional and entrepreneurial community is an important part of this process. A strong presence of Indian Americans in the IT sector is evident in the fact that Chinese and Indian engineers and entrepreneurs were running 29 percent of Silicon Valley's technology businesses by the end of the IT business boom in the 1990s (Saxenian 2002). The boom in the U.S. IT sector in the 1990s and the subsequent skilled-labor shortage not only brought a large number of engineers and software professionals from India on H-1B and other kinds of visas, but also led to the growing numbers of cross-regional start-ups between Silicon Valley (and other parts of the United States with technology businesses) and India. Indian Americans have played a major role in such cross-national start-up ventures.

AnnaLee Saxenian cites example of technology start-ups and underlines the importance of immigrant and ethnic networks and cross-national connections for such businesses. For instance, Rakesh Mathur, who started three successful technology companies—Armedia, Junglee, and Stratify—after working for Intel in the United States for many years, used his network in India to structure his business model. He explained: "The key constraint to starting a business in Silicon Valley in the late 1990s was the shortage of software developers. I realized that I could go to India. All three of my start-ups had design centers in Bangalore but were registered as American technology companies" (Quoted in Saxenian 2005, 52). Similarly, Mahesh Veerina, who launched a technology start-up in Silicon Valley in 1993, hired programmers in India for one-quarter of the Silicon Valley rate, and his engineers noted that they were able to cut development time in half because the Indian team worked while the U.S. team slept. The firm had sixty-five employees in Santa Clara and twenty-five in India by 1998, and it required that every engineer spend at least a couple of weeks working in the other country (Saxenian 2005). South Asian ethnic networks such as The Indus Entrepreneurs (TIE), an organization of South Asian American entrepreneurs and professionals, have played a major role in facilitating the launch of start-up companies by South Asians by providing mentorship and creating networks among members (Upadhya 2004).

The trend of Indian American–led start-up companies in Silicon Valley with cross-national operations attracted venture capital specifically focused on investing money into start-ups that built on networks and led to an expertise spread across two countries. The initial attempt by major venture capital firms such as Draper International—a group established by a veteran Silicon Valley venture capitalist to invest in IT start-ups in India—was to find new dynamic companies in India for investment. However, the investors quickly found that it was more challenging to find viable start-ups in India that they could profitably invest in. There was a change in strategy on the part of investors as they started putting money in Silicon Valley–based companies in the United States with sizable operations in India. A new generation of cross-border investors with accumulated experience in both Silicon Valley and India emerged in the process, which promoted the strategy of asking cash-strapped Silicon Valley firms to set up engineering centers in India to make their businesses viable (Upadhya 2004).

Experts in the fields of business and technology argue that Indian American professionals and entrepreneurs, and those who returned to India after studying and working in the United States, have played a major role in initiating and building businesses that draw upon their cross-national expertise. There are no reliable figures on the extent of Non-Resident Indian (NRI) or Indian American investment in the technology sector in India, but experts estimate that at least half of the IT companies set up in Bangalore since 1999 had some NRI funding, and the majority of these investors were Indian American professionals and entrepreneurs. Underlining this trend, Carol Upadhya argues that the interests of Indian American technology professionals and investors led to a decisive shift in the structure of the IT industry in India. In the past, foreign capital entered the Indian IT sector mostly through direct investment by multinationals. Now, transnational capital is flowing into even smaller firms primarily through venture capital supported by Indian Americans (Upadhya 2004).

According to Saxenian, this new form of business transnationalism, involving immigrant communities, challenges the traditional idea of a "brain drain" in which the migration of skilled professionals from developing countries such as India or China to developed countries such as the United States is considered a permanent loss of skilled human resources for the developing countries. The new paradigm, which has been made possible by transnational investment and entrepreneurial engagement of immigrant communities, reflects more of a "brain circulation" or "brain bank" whereby immigrant communities contribute to the economic activities of their country of origin alongside their contribution to the host country (Saxenian 2005; Kapur 2010). Scholars point to the benefits of networks, resources, knowledge of both the countries, and an increasingly globalized economic system as important elements of the "brain circulation" thesis, rather than mere love for the home country. Aihwa Ong refers to this emerging modality among transnational immigrant communities as a "flexible citizenship," which allows the affluent diasporic populations to negotiate national boundaries and attachments to maximize their material and social gains (Ong 1999).

The IT sector remains one of the most important areas that continue to witness substantive economic transnationalism among Indian Americans. However, there are other spheres, such as real estate, the biotech industry, education, and health where diasporic business interests and transnational flows are becoming very important. The health sector in India, for example, has seen the interest of Indian Americans, given that there is a large number of physicians of Indian origin in the United States. A small number of these physicians have gone back to work in India, and some have started private hospital chains (the Apollo Hospitals chain is a prime example). The burgeoning trend of medical tourism in India—the phenomenon of patients from across the globe traveling to India for relatively cheaper surgeries and treatments—has made the market even more lucrative for large hospital chains, attracting both professionals and investment from overseas Indians.[2] The diasporic Indian medical and entrepreneurial community is also playing an important role in outsourcing some segments of laboratory and diagnostic testing to India. Indian diagnostic laboratories are approximately 70 to 80 percent less expensive than their U.S. counterparts (Kapur 2010). This trend has become an important part of emerging health-sector practices in the United States and Britain.

On the side of the Indian state, its policy toward the diaspora has changed dramatically. In fact, the government's policy toward the diaspora was characterized in the post-independence period as indifferent and disengaged (Lall 2001; Gupta 1992; Kerkhoff and Bal 2003). The migration of highly educated Indians, starting in the 1960s and 1970s, to the United States and other Western nations was seen primarily through the lens of the "brain drain" described above. However, the large-scale transformation of the Indian economy beginning in the late 1980s, as mentioned earlier, leading to the opening up of the economy for foreign investment and trade, accelerated the process of active engagement with the diaspora. The Indian diaspora was now seen as important for remittances as well as investment in the Indian economy (Kapur 2003). It is important to note that India is currently the largest recipient of remittances—approximately $71 billion in 2013—from Indian immigrants living abroad, surpassing other major migrant remittance-sending countries such as China, Mexico, and the Philippines.[3] Given the size of remittances and the increasing business engagement of the Indian diaspora, the policy toward diaspora has been changing fast to accommodate and encourage these trends.

One of the most important policy initiatives to attract the diasporic population to India pertains to allowing more rights—travel, work, investment, and owning property—for Indians who acquired citizenship in countries where they are currently settled. The first such initiative, termed the Person of Indian Origin (PIO) card, was introduced in 1999. It allowed noncitizens of Indian origin—those who held an Indian passport or had parents/grandparents/or great grandparents who were born or permanently resided in India—multiple entries without a visa for fifteen years. It also exempted them from registering with the government (a requirement for international visitors in India) for a stay of less than 180 days and enabled them to own and transfer immovable properties as well as gain rights for their children to attend educational institutions.[4] A more expansive provision called Overseas Citizens of India (OCI) was introduced in 2005 that granted greater rights to noncitizen Indians (or children and grandchildren of those who were eligible for citizenship of India after January 26, 1950). Often wrongly called dual citizenship, the OCI allows unrestricted entry into India, unlimited period of stay without registering with the government, and ability to work and own property. However, it does not allow for voting rights and eligibility to take up government jobs, as India stopped short of accepting dual-citizenship rights that had been granted by many migrant-sending countries (Sejerson 2008). The PIO and OCI cards were merged together in 2015 to simplify this process and all eligible persons are now being issued OCI cards only (Kelkar 2015).

The increased engagement of the Indian state with the diasporic population was also reflected in the formation of a separate Ministry of Overseas Indian Affairs in 2004. Furthermore, a high-profile annual conference focused on the Indian diaspora—called Pravasi Bharatiya Divas (PBD)—was initiated in 2003. It provides a shared platform for high-powered elected representatives and government officials, diasporic professionals and entrepreneurs, and Indian businesses, alongside nonprofit and cultural groups. The engagement with diaspora, particularly with entrepreneurs, professionals, and investors, has now reached a stage where different provinces in India are competing to attract investment and other kinds of involvement from Indians settled abroad. States such as Gujarat, Punjab, Andhra Pradesh (now Seemandhra and Telangana), and Karnataka are leading competitors, since a large number of Indian immigrants come from these states. Other states have also tried to come up with policies—lower land prices and lowered environmental, labor, and other kinds of regulations—that are attractive to diasporic investors.

The Indian American community has come to acquire a particularly important place for India not only due to the economic prowess of the community but also because of its increasing political influence in the United States. The signing of a civil nuclear deal between India and the United States in 2006 was a pivotal moment that illustrated the convergence of political interests of the Indian state and the stance adopted by powerful Indian American groups, signaling that diasporic nationalism could be a powerful mobilizing tool. In the following section I analyze this important moment in Indian American transnational political engagement to emphasize the centrality of economic and professional elites in espousing the cause of diasporic nationalism.

## The U.S.–India Civil Nuclear Deal: Dual Engagement and Elite Mobilization

The U.S.–India Civil Nuclear Deal, signed as an agreement between the United States and India on March 2, 2006, was aimed at carving out an exception for India from the U.S. laws limiting nuclear technology trade with countries that refused to sign the Nuclear Nonproliferation Treaty (NPT). The lobbying by Indian American groups in favor of this nuclear deal between the two countries suggests that there is no high wall between political activism concerning the country of origin—India—and involvement with the political process in the United States. An analysis of the lobbying campaign demonstrates the linkages between the two and underlines the need for a framework that goes beyond a strict nation-state paradigm for analyzing political involvements of immigrant communities. The analysis also suggests that this form of political engagement is limited in terms of who got mobilized from the community and that it engendered a process that relied on a selective elite within the Indian American community.

The changing foreign policy imperatives of the United States after the Cold War as well as its geopolitical considerations in Asia brought India and the United States closer together. The U.S.–India Civil Nuclear Deal was an indicator of the Bush administration's willingness to go beyond the established U.S. nuclear technology framework to achieve its foreign policy objectives (Levi and Ferguson 2006).[5] The U.S.–India Civil Nuclear deal in 2006 was in essence a formal approval of India's status as a nuclear power. There was an informal recognition of India as a nuclear power before this deal, but the existing U.S. policy disallowed any nuclear technology cooperation with India. The deal thus heralded a new era in the India–U.S. relationship.

The deal was also seen as a moment of reckoning and recognition for the Indian American community. The role of Indian American groups arose in the context of U.S. congressional approval of the deal, which was required to change the existing U.S. laws that banned civil nuclear trade with India. The Bush administration, breaking away from the established U.S. foreign policy paradigm, announced a negotiated framework for nuclear cooperation with India on July 18, 2005.[6] Congressional approval became very critical for moving this deal forward as there was a high possibility that it would be buried in congressional debate, given the strength of the nonproliferation lobby. A sizable number of Democrats in the Congress, along with a section of Republicans, were very suspicious of this move by the Bush administration, and they saw the deal as rewarding a state that had defied the NPT all along. It was the resistance at the level of Congress that made lobbying with its members a critical prerequisite for the success of the deal. The Indian American organizations, enthusiastic supporters of the nuclear deal, which they saw as a new turn in the Indo–U.S. relationship, took upon themselves to mobilize the community and its emerging financial and political prowess to lobby with Congress for passage of the nuclear deal.

The nuclear deal campaign by the Indian American community followed a longer tradition of involvement of different immigrant communities in U.S. foreign policy making. Cuban, Greek, and Jewish immigrant groups have been involved with a similar process in the past because of their deep linkages to their countries of origin and the possible impact of foreign policy on their communities. However, such involvements on the part of immigrant communities have always been seen through the prism of national loyalty and have often been considered an expression of loyalty to country of origin. Asian Americans in particular have been perceived as tools—knowingly or unknowingly—of foreign entities, due to their lobbying in favor of home countries on certain issues. However, for groups like Cubans and Jews, where foreign policy activism is considered natural and is often supported by the U.S. government for different historical and geopolitical reasons, questions of loyalty seldom arise (Watanbe 1999). The disparate reactions to transnational engagement of different immigrant groups suggest that such engagement is shaped by the differences in racial and ethnic origins of the groups and popular discourses around them, as well as the broader geopolitical considerations of the United States.

The concerns about extraterritorial loyalty seem deeply exaggerated when such lobbying efforts on behalf of home countries by different immigrant communities are analyzed closely. In fact, a closer look at some of the foreign policy campaigns by immigrant groups suggests that they are also about acquiring a place and recognition in domestic politics, and they become a convenient rallying point for getting involved in the U.S. political process and institutions (Karpathakis 1999).[7] The involvement of Indian American organizations with lobbying on the nuclear deal reflected this duality of engagement in their political activism, even while appearing to keep home country concerns at the center of their political practice. The Indian American lobbying on the nuclear deal, in fact, was broadly in consonance with both with the U.S. foreign policy establishment and the dominant nationalist position in India.

The Indian immigrant organizations with links and influence in Washington, D.C., have periodically tried to intervene in the past on foreign policy issues, with a moderate to low level of influence on the policy outcomes. They also created political influence through creating a network of support among members of Congress and other policy makers. One of the most significant campaigns by the Indian American groups before the nuclear deal was the intervention opposing the proposed sale of Airborne Early Warning Surveillance Systems (AWACKS) planes to Pakistan in 1987 (Motwani 2003). The success of the Indian American groups' campaign can be measured by the fact that they were called before the Senate Foreign Relations Subcommittee to testify on the issue.

Jagat Motwani, an Indian American community activist, testified to the Senate subcommittee on behalf of the National Federation of Indian Americans (NFIA) in 1987 to argue against the sale of AWACKS planes to Pakistan:

> I should add that a bomb in Pakistani hands is a source of concern, not only to India, but to other friendly countries around the world, including Israel, since it has been developed as an Islamic bomb. The events of the past 39 years attest to the fact that Pakistan has used U.S. supplied military equipment against no other country except India, although the aid was given for use as defense against communist invasion. Once Pakistan has these sophisticated military weapons, it may not hesitate to use them against India. (Motwani 2003, 282–83)

The nationalist rhetoric employed by Indian American groups was not only about parochial Indian nationalism, it was simultaneously accompanied by a growing desire and anxiety about creating a space within the U.S. political system for the Indian American community. Thomas Abraham, president of NFIA, remarked about the 1987 Indian American testimony at the Senate Foreign Relations Subcommittee hearing, "It is a historic moment for the Indian American community since we have been invited for the first time by the Senate Foreign Relations Subcommittee to present our views. It is recognition of our growing community in the U.S." (Motwani 2003, 284). Even though this campaign was limited to a specific foreign policy issue in Washington, D.C., the acknowledgment by Congress of Indian Americans as a legitimate voice on this issue was seen as a sign of the early recognition of the growing strength of the community in U.S. politics.

The U.S.–India Civil Nuclear Deal came approximately twenty years after the 1987 AWACKS planes campaign by Indian American groups. The Indian immigrant community had grown much bigger, and its desire to get a place in the U.S. political arena was even more pronounced. The high level of sophisticated lobbying by the Indian American organizations with the U.S. Congress and the foreign policy-making establishment on the U.S.–India Civil Nuclear Deal reflected the growing prowess of the community as well as the continuation of their dual interests — the interest in issues related to India as well as the urge to create a political space for the Indian American community in U.S. politics. Over the years they have been able to build linkages between these two interests.

Indian American groups were enthused and emboldened by the seeming possibility of a convergence of interests between the U.S. government and the Indian state. The issue galvanized Indian American organizations as never before, and it brought Democratic, Republican, and nonpartisan groups on the same platform. The U.S.–India Political Action Committee (USINPAC), Indian American Security Leadership Council (IASLC), U.S. India Friendship Council, U.S. India Business Council, and various other smaller groups and individuals of Indian American origin came together. At the end of April 2006, just before Congress was reconvened to start considering the Henry Hyde Act dealing with the nuclear deal, around 200 Indian American leaders from across the United States came to Washington, D.C., to lobby their Senate and House members for approval of the deal (Jones 2006).[8] The Indian American leaders also had a strategy meeting with White House senior staffers led by Karl Rove, the deputy chief of staff to President George W. Bush. Indian American groups were turning out to be important allies for the Bush administration, which was struggling to muster congressional support to get the bill passed.

The nuclear deal campaign also galvanized the established membership-based Indian American organizations such as the American Association of Physicians of Indian Origin (AAPI) and the Asian American Hotel Owners Association (AAHOA). AAPI, representing around 41,000 doctors and 10,000 medical students of Indian origin, and AAHOA, representing about 8,300 members, owning more than 20,000 small hotels and motels, contributed generously to the campaign and lobbied members of Congress from different areas. To express their support for the nuclear deal, these two organizations jointly held a luncheon in Washington, D.C., which was addressed by then Secretary of State Condoleezza Rice (Kumar 2006).

The importance of this issue for unifying disparate Indian American groups is reflected in the following comment made by an Indian American activist: "Our diaspora was always much more divided, but now we have the nuclear deal to unite us . . . I have been contacting my congressmen here in California, and I know many of my friends and colleagues are doing the same. This whole fight has brought out of the woodwork

Indian-Americans who were never involved in politics at all" (Sands 2006). The issue worked as a rallying point for Indian American groups and provided an opportunity for the groups to engage with U.S. political institutions on a specific issue. The lobbying campaign on the U.S.–India Nuclear Deal was important for the Indian American groups not only because they wanted to support India's interest on this issue but also because it was a test of their strength and maturity as far as their political influence in the U.S. was concerned. The *Washington Times*, in a write-up on this issue, reflected this sentiment among Indian American groups. The write-up noted: "The political clout of one of the county's wealthiest and best-educated minorities is being put to the test as the Bush administration faces a tough fight in the Congress to pass a major civil nuclear power agreement with India, one the administration officials say could cement ties with an emerging world power and redraw the strategic map of Asia" (Sands 2006). The Indian American groups saw this as an opportunity to demonstrate their political influence and acumen in affecting policy outcomes. "This is the chance to show that the community has matured and can translate that into political effectiveness," said Sanjay Puri, chairman, USINPAC (McIntire 2006).

If viewed through the lens of the traditional notions of political participation, this kind of political engagement on foreign policy issues concerning the home country could be dismissed as something external to the U.S. political process. However, a closer analysis suggests that the campaign reflected an engagement of immigrants with U.S. domestic political institutions, and it was not just about achieving a limited end concerning India but a part of the broader ongoing attempt to gain acceptance and recognition in U.S. politics. The issue of the U.S.–India Nuclear Deal suggests that even though lobbying and mobilization around the issues of the home country are not the most important modes of immigrant political participation, they do play a significant role in initiating and shaping the political engagement of the group.

While lobbying by Indian American groups on issues concerning the home country seems to be a significant step toward involvement with the domestic U.S. political process, this form of political engagement has limitations in terms of the scope of its mobilization. It engendered a process that relied on selective elite mobilization within the Indian American community. Despite the apparent diversity of the groups involved in the lobbying process, the efforts of the Indian American community

were spearheaded mostly by organizations that represented the professional and entrepreneurial sections of the community. The emphasis on
the fund-raising prowess of the community to muster support from
members of Congress for the nuclear deal was indicative of participation
being limited to the rich and professionally successful sections of the
community. A case in point is USINPAC, an Indian American organization that has been organizing fund-raisers for both Democratic and Republican politicians to mobilize bipartisan support for issues important
to the Indian American community. By emphasizing the fund-raising
ability of the Indian American community, USINPAC has been developing a political strategy that relies on a narrow segment of the community
that can make financial contributions to political parties and candidates.
USINPAC primarily utilized the strengths and influence emerging out
of this strategy to effectively mobilize support for the nuclear deal among
lawmakers in Washington, D.C. This mode of political participation
through lobbying has a very limited impact on the larger Indian immigrant community in terms of bringing them to participate in the domestic
political arena. Moreover, the interests of the professional, entrepreneurial, and financially successful segments coincide with the strong nationalistic orientation expected from this section of the diaspora by the
Indian state.

The strategic importance of the economic and professional elites in the
Indian American community was not missed by the government of India.
It was reflected in the report of a High Level Committee (HLC) on the
diaspora constituted by the government of India in 2000. The focus of
the report was on the entrepreneurs and professionals of Indian origin
living in the advanced industrial Western countries, particularly the
United States (Chaturvedi 2005). The report stated:

A section of financially powerful and politically well connected
Indo-Americans have emerged during the last decade. They have
effectively mobilized on issues ranging from the nuclear tests in
1998 to Kargil, playing a crucial role in generating a favorable
climate of opinion in [the U.S.] Congress and defeating anti-India
legislation there, and lobbied effectively on other issues of concern
to the Indian community. . . . For the first time India has a
constituency in the United States with real influence and status.
The Indian community in United States constitutes an invaluable

asset in strengthening India's relationship with the world's only superpower. Their receptiveness to India concerns will depend greatly on the quality of their interaction with the country of origin and their sensitivity to their concerns displayed in India. (High Level Committee on Indian Diaspora 2002, xx–xxi)

The focus on a financially successful and politically connected segment of Indian immigrants, and the call on them to represent the nation's interests, are remarkable in terms of who the Indian state considers important for advancing its geopolitical and economic interests.[9] The report was very emphatic about the centrality of this section and projected them as the ideal Indian immigrants who were to be courted to support India in its economic and political endeavors. The Indian American groups, responding partly to appeals by the Indian state, thus adopted the dominant nationalist paradigm. In fact, lobbying by these groups did not even reflect the debates that took place in India over the desirability of the nuclear deal. There was an ongoing intense debate in India over this issue, with powerful voices such as the Communist Party of India (Marxist) and other antinuclear groups that argued against the nuclear deal and asserted that the deal was tantamount to surrendering the sovereignty and independent foreign policy of India to the United States. There were others who considered India's entry into the group of legitimate nuclear power states a negative development for regional peace and security (Bidwai 2007).

The political mobilization strategy that was developed by Indian American groups reflected this approach of primarily relying on the professional and business elite within the community. It also used a nationalist framework to unify the diasporic community in the interest of the country of origin, which was made far easier by the seeming convergence of interest between the United States and India. The convergence between the interests of the home country (India) and the host country (United States) on this issue allowed the Indian American groups to espouse the cause of India without any fear of backlash in the United States. The dual attachments pushed their mobilization strategy in such a way that the common interest between the two countries created the most comfortable political space for the groups involved in the lobbying campaign. The example of lobbying by Indian American groups on the issue of the nuclear deal thus demonstrates the linkages between simultaneous involvement with the home country and the host country and suggests that the conventional understanding of a deep divide between the two is a flawed one. It was through mobilizations on the issue of the nuclear deal that Indian American groups demonstrated their influence with members of Congress and established themselves as an emerging immigrant community that wielded influence in the corridors of power. However, this moment of seeming diasporic political unity (despite its selective elite mobilizing) has not been replicated in other spheres of mobilization among Indian Americans. The notion of a unified diasporic mobilization is squarely challenged by fractures within the community along the lines of religious identity and by divergence over the treatment of minority communities in India and the issue of secularism.

### The Politics of Hate and the Multiplicity of Transnational Mobilizing

Lobbying in favor of the U.S.–India Nuclear Deal points to a moment in diasporic mobilizing marked by a dominant nationalist framework, as there was no significant contestation of this framework within the community.[10] However, heralding this mobilization as an occasion of recognition for the unified power of the Indian American community conceals other significant moments of political articulation that point to sharp internal cleavages and contestations within the community. In this section I present an analysis of Indian American diasporic political mobilizations in response to the emergence of a powerful Hindu nationalist politics in India to illustrate internal diasporic contestations. The emergence of Hindu majoritarian politics in India had strong reverberations in the Indian diaspora, and it was particularly pronounced in the United States. As discussed earlier, the Indian American community is majority Hindu, but sizable numbers of Muslims, Christians, and Sikhs are also a part of the community. The ascendance of *Hindutva* politics—the politics of Hindu nationalism—in the 1980s and 90s in India led to mobilizations and ruptures within the Indian American community too. These ruptures could be traced along ideological lines—a Hindu nation versus a secular and inclusive Indian state—and along religious lines, where minority groups such as Indian American Muslims and Christians mobilized in the United States to contest the ascendance of Hindu nationalist politics and violence against religious minorities in India. Both ruptures—ideological as well as religious—often overlapped and came together to contest *Hindutva* assertions, but they also diverged in terms of articulation and mobilization. The diasporic responses thus cannot be attributed primarily to ideological differences over the issue of secularism in India or broader questions around separation of state and religion, but they also represent fractures along lines of religious identity that were articulated by majority and minority religious communities.

## Emergence of Hindu Nationalism in India and Reverberations in the United States

The ascendance of Hindu nationalist politics in India in the last several decades has deeply influenced Indians in the diaspora, particularly in the United States. Hindu nationalist political mobilization in modern India began in a systematic manner in the British colonial period. Rashtriya Swayamsewak Sangh (RSS)—a well-known Hindu political formation that has functioned as the parent body for a number of organizations committed to the idea of a Hindu nation—came into existence in 1925 to advance the cause of Hindu unity, defense, and progress. Hindu nationalist politics was built on a conception that the Indian nation belonged only to Hindus; Muslims and Christians were considered primarily outsiders who needed to be disciplined and controlled. Hindu nationalism remained a small but significant stream in Indian politics until its resurgence in the 1980s with the Ayodhya Temple Movement, which called for the building of a temple of Lord Rama (a Hindu God) in Ayodhya, a town in north India, at the site of an old mosque (Babri Masjid), which was constructed in the sixteenth-century by a Muslim emperor (Basu et al. 1993).[11] The Bharatiya Janata Party (BJP), the political and electoral wing of the RSS, had a meteoric rise once it openly embraced the Ayodhya Temple Movement and turned that into a central plank of the party platform. As a result, the BJP rode the wave of majoritarian Hindu mobilization and saw many electoral victories leading to political power in different provinces, until it finally came to form the national government from 1998 to 2004 (a coalition government with the support of other political parties). After a gap of ten years, the BJP again succeeded in forming a government in 2014 with an absolute majority under the leadership of Narendra Modi, a controversial figure in Indian politics due to his role as chief minister of Gujarat during an anti-Muslim pogrom in 2002.

The ascendance of majoritarian Hindu nationalist mobilization in India triggered open hostility and violence against religious minorities. Two major incidents stand out in this context: (1) the demolition of Babri

Mosque in December 1992 by a Hindu mob led by some of the top leaders of the BJP and other Hindu nationalist groups and (2) the Gujarat pogrom against Muslims in 2002. The demolition of the old mosque shook the nation and led to religious riots marked by large-scale violence against Muslims. The incident was one of the most important developments in post-independence India in terms of creating a climate of deep insecurity for Muslims (Basu et al. 1993). This act was followed by the events of 2002 in Gujarat, a province in the western part of India, that witnessed organized violence against Muslims leading to the killing of approximately 2,000 Muslims and the rape and maiming of women and children in large numbers.[12] Many independent groups that investigated the ghastly incidents termed the killings a state-sponsored pogrom of Muslims that involved the ruling BJP, various Hindu nationalist affiliates, the local police departments, and, most importantly, then chief minister of Gujarat, Narendra Modi, who became the prime minister of India in May 2014. Besides these two major events, there were numerous incidents of targeted violence against Christian missionaries and converts to Christianity in states such as Orissa, Gujarat, Madhya Pradesh, and Jharkhand. The most infamous incident was the attack on Christian missionary Graham Staines and his two children in January 1999. They were burnt to death while sleeping in a station wagon in the Keonjhar district of Orissa. The convict was an activist of Bajrang Dal, a Hindu nationalist organization, and supposedly wanted to teach a lesson to Graham Staines for spreading Christianity among the local tribals.[13] In subsequent years, many churches were burnt, and missionaries were targeted as a part of the broader Hindu nationalist assertion (Human Rights Watch 1999).

The growth of *Hindutva* politics in India led to the emergence of Hindu nationalist and religious mobilizations among Indian American Hindus. Scholars have argued that the *Hindutva* framework found a particularly sympathetic terrain among the Hindu diasporic population in the United States. This is particularly because the message of Hindu nationalism, with its emphasis on Hindu pride and heritage, appeals to the group's experience of being a minority in the United States, facing negative perceptions of Hinduism, and feeling a level of marginalization in social, religious, and cultural arenas (Kurien 2007a; Mathew and Prashad 2000; Rajagopal 2000). As argued in chapter 3, the ideology and institutions of multiculturalism provide formal avenues to assert the process of seeking recognition through religious identity. In fact, the ideological and organizational expansion of Hindu nationalism among

Hindu Indian Americans took shape under these conditions in the United States. Moreover, a very deliberate strategy on the part of Hindu nationalist organizations in India to create diasporic *Hindutva* organiza-tions further strengthened this support.

The growth of Hindu nationalism in the diaspora has been enabled by a strong organizational network that *Hindutva* groups built over a period of time. One of the earliest *Hindutva* organizations in the United States, Vishwa Hindu Parishad of America (VHPA), was founded by four mem-bers of RSS in 1970 on the East Coast and formally incorporated in 1974. Founded as a nonprofit tax-exempt organization, VHPA, aligned closely with Hindu nationalist politics in India, claimed to be promoting Hinduism and pursuing cultural activities rather than political mobili-zations. Currently, the group has chapters in most states in the United States.[14] Hindu Swayamsewak Sangh (HSS), another important Hindu nationalist organization founded in 1989, has branches in several states in the United States and functions through organizing weekly camps—called *Shakhas*—focused on imparting Hindu values, martial skills, character building, and self-discipline. Organizations like the Hindu Student Council (HSC) and Hindu American Federation (HAF) came into exis-tence later in the 1990s, and they are seen as the second wave of *Hindutva* organizations in the United States that tend to focus on second-generation Hindu Indian Americans (Kurien 2007a; 2007b; Rajagopal 2000). The multi-faceted development of *Hindutva* organizations has thus allowed them to use different forms to reach out to diverse sections of the Hindu Ameri-can community. The *Hindutva* organizations witnessed a strong surge in support among Hindu Americans in the 1990s with the ascendance of Hindu nationalism in India. Indian American Hindus sympathetic to the cause of Hindu nationalists were buoyed by the Ayodhya Temple Movement and contributed money for the campaign and sent sanctified bricks from different cities in the United States to be used for building a temple in place of the old Babri mosque in Ayodhya (Rajagopal 2000).[15] The Hindu nationalists in India, in turn, took great pride in the support they were getting from diasporic Hindu populations, par-ticularly from Hindus in the United States and Britain, and they fo-cused on strengthening these supportive political, cultural, and religious networks.

There is a relative lack of scholarly work on the strength of Hindu nationalist organizations in the United States, even though a lot has been written on the emergence and modality of *Hindutva* politics in the United States (Mathew and Prashad 2000; Rajagopal 2000). However, the evidence does suggest that Hindu nationalist cultural and political organizations have gained substantial strength in the last two decades, and they have become an important cultural and political force in the Indian American community. Furthermore, the ascendance of Narendra Modi as prime minister of India in 2014 has allowed Hindu nationalist organizations to gather even more strength both in India as well as in the Indian diaspora. The emergence of Hindu nationalism in India and *Hindutva* mobilizations among Indian Americans, however, also created countermobilizations that underlined the fissures within the Indian American community.

### Countermobilization against Hindutva: *Debating Universal and Particular Identities*

The same series of events that mobilized a segment of the disaporic Hindu population—demolition of Babri Masjid, attacks on Christians, and the Gujarat pogrom against Muslims—triggered another set of reactions from within the Indian American community that demonstrated cleavages within the community not only on ideological lines but also religious ones. I will discuss in this section the countermobilization against Hindu nationalism in the United States and argue that such transnational diasporic mobilizations challenge the notion of a unified community and point to the internal cleavages and divergence of interests ignored by a monolithic construction of the community. I will also illustrate how minority groups within the Indian American community—Muslims and Christians in particular—responded to Hindu nationalist assertions by mobilizing themselves as religious groups as well as by aligning with secular and progressive groups. These groups collectively developed resources and networks to mobilize American political institutions—Congress, the State Department, and other policy institutions—to contest *Hindutva* politics while asserting their own place within the larger Indian American community.

One of the first well-documented mobilizations against Hindu nationalism in the United States was a campaign initiated by the group called Campaign to Stop Funding Hate (CSFH). It was one of the many initiatives that emerged from ongoing conversations in a group called Forum of Indian Leftists (FOIL), which was later renamed Forum for

Inqalabi Leftists to make it more inclusive of other South Asians who were of similar inclination.[16] CSFH came into existence after the Gujarat pogrom in 2002, and its stated purpose was to investigate funding from the United States, primarily from the Hindu Indian American community, to support *Hindutva* organizations that were involved in anti-Muslim and anti-Christians campaigns in different parts of India.[17] CSFH was initially supported by progressive academics and left-wing and secular individuals, including a large number of Hindus from the Indian American community, but very soon it started attracting the attention of the larger Muslim and Christian Indian American communities that were feeling under siege due to the increasing attacks on these groups in India as well as the United States by *Hindutva* formations.

CSFH systematically investigated the stories circulating in the media and community spaces that *Hindutva* organizations were mobilizing financial resources in the name of funding charity work in India to surreptitiously support organizations involved in violence against Muslims and Christians as a part of the Hindu nationalist project. The India Development and Relief Fund (IDRF), registered in Maryland as a tax-exempt charitable organization that prohibited it from providing aid to a partisan or sectarian group, was at the center of this campaign for diverting money collected from the Indian American community and U.S. corporations to *Hindutva* organizations in India. A report published by CSFH, titled *The Foreign Exchange of Hate*, chronicled how IDRF diverted money to organizations that were working under the guidance of RSS, the prime *Hindutva* organization in India, to propagate Hindu nationalist politics and target minority groups in the process (Sabrang Communications 2002).[18] According to the report, between 1994 and 2000, the total disbursement of IDRF was 3.2 million dollars, and approximately 75 percent of the money went to IDRF-designated organizations. The organizations affiliated with the RSS, with the implicit or explicit goal to propagate anti-Muslim and anti-Christian views in tribal and poor areas, got approximately 80 percent of the money that went to India.[19] This CSFH report became highly controversial since it implicated IDRF in promoting antiminority politics in India and established the linkages between Hindu nationalist organizations and the seemingly neutral and charity-oriented work of IDRF. The campaign led to decisions by corporations such as Cisco, Sun Microsystems, and Oracle to stop matching the donations of their employees to IDRF (Bank 2003).

Some scholars have characterized the anti-*Hindutva* mobilizations in the United States as an example of diasporic mobilizing that has moved away from particularism of identities to more universal and inclusive political ideals that are partly informed by a cosmopolitan outlook (Biswas 2010). It is important, however, to recognize that, even while universal political ideals such as secularism, inclusivity, and cosmopolitan outlook were important impulses behind the anti-*Hindutva* mobilizations in the United States, deployment of specific religious identities such as Indian Muslim and Christian continue to play an important role in mounting a resistance to *Hindutva* mobilization in the United States. The particular workings of the anti-*Hindutva* mobilization in the United States—as explained below—are thus a simultaneous product of an assertion of specific religious identities and an evocation of universal political ideals such as secularism and inclusivity.

The minority groups within the Indian American community—Muslims and Christians in particular—played a particularly pivotal role in building a countermobilization against Hindu nationalist politics in the United States (and India). The mainstream narrative of anti-*Hindutva* mobilization in the United States during the 1990s and later has mostly highlighted the central role of left-wing, progressive, and secular groups in creating an effective counter to Hindu nationalist mobilization (Biswas 2010). However, Muslim and Christian Indian American organizations have been at the forefront of this mobilization and created important resources and networks in the process. These minority groups were directly impacted by the rise of Hindu nationalism in India, and their reactions were to immediately ensure the safety and security of their families, communities, and faith in India. For example, the Indian American Christian community organized itself in the face of continued violence against Christians in India by Hindu nationalist organizations. The Federation of Indian American Christian Organizations (FIACONA) was formed in 2000 to bring together several Indian American Christian organizations under one banner. The focus of the group was evident from its website, which stated: "It is deeply concerned about the increasing threat to the secular and pluralistic nature of Indian society and about the state of religious freedom of Christians in India."[20]

Even though organizations representing particular Indian Christian denominations had existed in the United States for decades, they were primarily focused on building a religious and social space for their communities in a new land. The formation of FIACONA, however, was prompted directly by the rising Hindu nationalist attacks on Christians in India. In fact, the group chose the U.S. visit of India's prime minister, Atal Bihari Vajpayee, who represented the ascendance of Hindu nationalists in Indian politics, to announce their strength and determination to contest *Hindutva* politics. Indian American Christians held a peace vigil outside Capitol Hill to bring attention to the violence targeted at Christians in India while the Indian prime minister delivered his high-profile address to the U.S. Congress in 2000.[21] Since then, FIACONA has been at the forefront of several important mobilizations against religious violence targeted at Christians and Muslims in India, and it played a major role in lobbying the U.S. Congress to condemn the increased religious violence in India. Their efforts (along with other groups) led to the placing of India on a "watch list" for violence against minorities for three years in a row (2009–2011) by the United States Commission on International Religious Freedom (USCIRF), an independent body created by the U.S. government to monitor religious freedom at the international level.[22]

In its continuing effort to mobilize against attacks on Christians in India, FIACONA has especially reached out to Indian American tribals as well as Dalits—formerly termed "untouchables" in the Indian caste system—who are relatively new converts to Christianity in India. FIACONA, along with the Indian Christian Forum and the Gujarat Christian Federation of America, organized a major protest at the United Nations in August 2008 following a spate of attacks by Hindu nationalists on Christians and tribals in Orissa and other states.[23] The vigil at the UN was synchronized with the call by the Indian Catholic Church to close all its institutions in India for a day to protest the extremist violence against the Christian community, the clergy, and religious and charity institutions.[24]

The Gujarat pogrom against Muslims in 2002, in particular, was a turning point for a broad mobilization against Hindu nationalism in the United States as well as India. A significant number of Indian Muslims living in the United States have relatives, family members, and friends in India who have been directly affected by the violence against the community. A number of Indian American Muslim, Christian, and secular organizations came together to form the Coalition Against Genocide (CAG) in 2002, which focused on demanding accountability for the systematic killing and rape of Muslims by Hindu mobs with the alleged support of the ruling BJP and the state chief minister, Narendra Modi.[25] CAG worked closely with groups in India that demanded an investigation into the killings, particularly into the role of state government officials and top elected leaders. The group brought out reports and facilitated testimonies of survivors of violence at various international forums as well as before the U.S. Congress. USCIRF had a major hearing on the 2002 Gujarat pogrom (and its aftermath), where activists from India and the United States testified about the scale of violence against Muslims and Christians.[26] Different Indian American religious groups, alongside secular groups, have contested Hindu nationalist politics by reaching out to members of Congress and policy makers to highlight the violence and victimization faced by these groups in India. In fact, transnational engagements have propelled them to find allies and supporters in U.S. politics, and these communities have been very savvy about building these connections. Their experience supports the idea that there is no great wall between engagement with the politics of the home country and engaging with political structures and institutions in the United States.

Indian American Muslim organizations such as the American Federation of Muslims of Indian Origin (AFMI), Association of Indian Muslims of America, Indian American Muslim Council (IAMC), and Indian Muslim Relief and Charities were a major part of CAG and brought tremendous energy and resources to the group. AFMI, one of the oldest Indian American Muslim organizations, founded in 1989, has been focused primarily on charity work and creating dialogue with the political class in India on the issues important to Indian Muslims. The annual conventions of the organization have traditionally attracted important political figures from India and the United States, and such resources have become crucial in building a campaign against religious violence in India.[27] IAMC, a Washington, D.C.–based tax-exempt nonprofit organization with multiple local chapters, was established in August 2002 in direct response to the rising violence against Muslims in India. The group works on developing resources for strategic advocacy to promote pluralism and social justice in India and has been building widespread alliances against religious violence perpetrated by Hindu nationalists. It monitors the political developments in India very closely and raises issues pertaining to the security and safety of Muslims in India. It has made extensive efforts to mobilize within the Indian American Muslim community through meetings, annual conventions, and fund-raising dinners.[28]

One of the major mobilizations that brought all these groups together after the 2002 Gujarat pogrom was to prevent the alleged primary political actor of the pogrom, Narendra Modi, then chief minister of Gujarat, from visiting the United States. Modi symbolized the threatening resurgence of Hindu nationalism in India, and the mobilization against his visit to the United States was an attempt to question the legitimacy of *Hindutva* politics as well as highlight the role of individual BJP leaders in antiminority violence. The controversy erupted when Narendra Modi was invited by the Asian American Hotel Owners Association (AAHOA), an organization of hotel and motel owners primarily of Indian origin, to address their 2005 annual convention in Greater Fort Lauderdale, Florida.[29] He was simultaneously invited by a pro-*Hindutva* Indian American organization to speak at Madison Square Garden in New York City (Chatterji 2005).

A coalition of Indian American Muslims, Christians, and left-wing and secular organizations, under the aegis of CAG, decided to oppose Modi's visit and demanded that he should be denied entry into the United States because of his central role in the 2002 Gujarat pogrom that led to the killing and rape of thousands of Muslim men, women, and children. They launched a public campaign asking the U.S. State Department to deny him a visa to enter the United States (Chatterji 2005). The issue divided the Indian American community in unprecedented ways, and there emerged a parallel mobilization *for* granting a visitor visa to Modi. Amidst the spate of mobilizations and countermobilizations, on March 18, 2005, the U.S. State Department decided to deny a diplomatic visa to Narendra Modi under section 214(b) of the Immigration and Nationality Act (INA) invoked by the U.S. embassy in New Delhi, as this was not a diplomatic visit. His tourist and business visa was revoked under INA section 212(a) (2) (G), "as an official responsible for carrying out severe violations of religious freedom," under section 3 of the International Religious Freedom Act of 1998 (Chatterji 2005).

Lobbying by multiple Muslim, Christian, and secular organizations with members of Congress and other agencies played a major role in the denial of Modi's visa in 2005. Since some of these groups had already done extensive work to persuade USCIRF to designate India a "Country of Particular Concern" in 2003 and 2004 for violence against religious minorities, there existed a substantive network of support for the demands of anti-*Hindutva* groups in policy-making circles. In fact, due to a sustained campaign by these groups, the commission had held extensive hearings on religious violence, with a specific focus on different Indian states, before the visa controversy broke out (Chatterji 2005). After the denial of visa, AAHOA withdrew its invitation to Narendra Modi, but the Association for Indian Americans of North America (AIANA), a pro-*Hindutva* organization primarily of Indian immigrants of Gujarati descent, went ahead with its planned Madison Square Garden meeting and beamed in Narendra Modi via satellite.[30] There were animated protests outside the venue by CAG and other organizations, but inside there were speeches eulogizing Modi's achievements as the chief minister of Gujarat and decrying the high-handedness of the U.S. government in denying him a visa.[31]

The mobilization by Indian American Muslim, Christian, and secular and left-wing groups against Narendra Modi's U.S. visit in 2005 attracted an unusual combination of political and social forces. The demand for visa denial got legal traction because of the International Religious Freedom Act, which became a law in 1998 with massive support from Christian evangelical groups and lawmakers who were concerned about attacks on Christians across the globe. The law became an important tool for the campaign against Hindu nationalist-led religious violence in India against Muslims and Christians. In fact, Narendra Modi was the only person who had been denied a visa to the United States under the International Religious Freedom Act. The support for the denial of Modi's visa came from varied groups that included Indian American Muslim and Christian groups, left-wing and secular South Asian groups, and conservative Christian U.S. lawmakers from the Republican Party alongside lawmakers from the Democratic Party.[32] The campaign was a testimony to the determination and resources of Indian American Muslim and Christian groups, as well as left-wing and secular organizations, who built alliances with lawmakers and groups from across the political spectrum of U.S. politics.

The mobilization on both sides became even more intense leading up to the victory of the BJP in the 2014 general elections in India. Indian American Muslims, Christians, and secular groups once again foregrounded the issue of continued denial of justice for the victims of the

Gujarat pogrom. As a part of this intensified push, a vigil was organized in New York City on March 3, 2012, by several groups under the aegis of CAG to commemorate ten years since the Gujarat pogrom. The vigil attracted several hundred Indian Americans, and a significant part of the mobilization was done by Indian American Muslim groups such as IAMC and the Muslim Peace Coalition, with significant support from secular groups such as the South Asia Solidarity Initiative (Saad 2012). Continued lobbying and mobilizations by Indian American Muslim and Christian groups in particular led to a bipartisan press conference in Washington, D.C., on December 5, 2012, over the issue of the Gujarat pogrom and the Gujarat government's role in denial of justice to the victims. Congressional representatives Joe Pitts, Frank Wolf, Keith Ellison, and Trent Franks, with family members of the victims of Gujarat pogrom at their side, urged then secretary of state Hillary Clinton to deny a possible new visa application by Narendra Modi and ensure justice for the victims (Stancati 2012). Persistent lobbying and mobilization by Indian American Muslim and Christian groups alongside left-wing and progressive groups created sizable support for this campaign among members of Congress.

On the other side, Narendra Modi and his party, BJP, have supporters who mobilized and lobbied other members of Congress and the Obama administration to reverse its stance on granting a visa to Modi. Groups such as Indian Americans for Freedom—formerly known as the National Indian American Coalition—and the National Indian American Policy Institute have worked extensively in support of *Hindutva* organizations in India and in support of Narendra Modi (Prashad 2013).[33] The most recent intervention by these groups was organizing a visit by three Republican members of Congress to the state of Gujarat in March 2013. These members of Congress—Aaron Schock, Cynthia Lummis, and Cathy Rodgers—made a splash in the Indian media by praising Modi for his exemplary leadership, and they promised to work toward revoking the U.S. visa ban on him (Pandya 2013). The visit by the congressional delegation was followed by an address by Modi that was relayed in eighteen U.S. cities on June 13 to mark the founding day of Gujarat (Ghosh 2013). This major push was a reaction to a rebuff that Modi received from the Wharton School of Business at the University of Pennsylvania when his invitation to deliver a speech via video in a prestigious conference on India was canceled after a series of protests lodged by a group of faculty members. The controversy over this invitation led to mobilization on both sides and once again demonstrated the intensity of political divergence within the community (Bhowmick 2013).

The election of Narendra Modi as the prime minister of India in 2014 dramatically changed the stance of the U.S. government on the issue of his visa denial. On the invitation of President Barack Obama, Modi visited New York City and Washington, D.C., between September 26 and 30, 2014, marking the end of the travel ban that had been in effect since 2005. Besides his ceremonial address to the General Assembly of the United Nations and his official visit to the White House, he addressed a gathering of 18,000 enthusiastic Indian American supporters at Madison Square Garden in New York City. The Madison Square Garden event, sponsored by the Indian American Community Foundation, was led by Indian American Hindu nationalist organizations that were ardent supporters of Modi during the period of his travel ban to the United States. The largest turnout for the event was from the U.S. Gujarati community, which constitutes a large segment of the Indian American community. Narendra Modi hails from the same community, and he courted the Gujarati diasporic community assiduously during his tenure as chief minister of Gujarat. Svati Shah, analyzing the constellation of factors that created huge support for Modi among Indian Americans, described the crowd at Madison Square Garden:

The crowd of supporters on Sunday was very similar to the Gujaratis of my family's community in my youth—solidly lower middle class and aspiring to much more. Standing there, I could understand some of their fervor. This was the first time a sitting Indian prime minister descended from his ivory tower in Delhi to speak with a bunch of immigrants just barely holding on to their middle-class identities, employing a language of struggle and aspiration as no Indian prime minister had before. (2014)

The gathering, however, also attracted the support of Indian American professional elites and corporate leaders who were eager to build connections in order to explore the possibilities of investment in India under the new regime, which promises to be highly probusiness.

Given the history of polarization within the Indian American community over Narendra Modi, his visit evoked strong reactions from varied segments of the Indian American community. A day before Modi reached New York City from India, a U.S. federal court issued a summons asking him to respond within twenty-one days to allegations outlined in a civil suit. The case, filed by the American Justice Center on behalf of two victims of the 2002 Gujarat violence against Muslims, accused him of crimes against humanity, extrajudicial killings, and negligence under the Alien Tort Claims Act and Torture Victim Protection Act.[34] There was a concerted attempt on the part of those who had been raising questions about Narendra Modi's role in the 2002 violence in Gujarat to use all possible avenues to challenge him during his visit. A large protest was held outside Madison Square Garden while Narendra Modi addressed his supporters inside the arena. The protestors included a large number of Sikhs alongside Muslims, Christian, and secular progressive groups who, under the aegis of the newly formed Alliance for Justice and Accountability, demanded justice for the victims of the Gujarat pogrom and highlighted violence against religious minorities in India (Constable 2014). The presence of a large number of Sikhs at the protest, who linked the 1984 killing of Sikhs in Delhi to the 2002 Gujarat anti-Muslim violence, underlined the continued impunity in both cases.

Diasporic mobilizations and contestations around the issues of antiminority violence and Hindu nationalist politics in India continue to reflect that religious identities are important fissures within the community. Prema Kurien (2007b) explains this contestation in the United States in terms of a clash between a cluster of organizations that are created around Hindu religious identity and those that are secular and inclusive, evoking a broader South Asian panethnic identity. The analysis I presented in this chapter, however, suggests that both sides are equally invested in deploying particular religious identities as well as a nation-state-based identity, instead of a panethnic one. In fact, a considerable sensitivity exists among Indian American Muslims and Christians on the issue of Indian identity because of a particular kind of dominant framework in India that casts Muslims and Christians as outsiders. For instance, there exists a strong discourse in India about the presumed loyalty of Indian Muslims to Pakistan. Similarly, in Hindu nationalist discourse, Indian Christians are portrayed as loyal to religious authorities outside India that are alien to Hindu Indian culture. Given this discourse, the Indian American Muslim and Christian groups deliberately foreground their *Indian* Muslim and *Indian* Christian identities and heritage and deliberately eschew a broader Muslim, Christian, or even South Asian identity that can be used to question their attachment and loyalty to the homeland. Thus, the transnational engagements of the Indian American community with respect to *Hindutva* politics cannot be framed without reference to the internal religious cleavages that define the contours of the community.

## Conclusion

This chapter has illustrated the emerging forms of Indian American transnational engagement in the economic as well as political arenas. The business and professional elites among Indian Americans have used the newer modes of business globalization and economic regimes both in India and the United States to create new professional and business opportunities, and this segment of the community has a sustained interest in negotiating with the economic policies and political regimes on both sides. This form of transnationalism is distinctive and suggests the specificity of diasporic engagements that are shaped by occupational and class resources. Diasporic discourses often deploy a framework that foregrounds the idea of a unified "nation outside the nation." This nationalist discourse works to mask all internal differentiations and project a unified political community. The mobilization among Indian Americans in support of the U.S.–India Nuclear Deal was an attempt to create that seamless unity. However, the history of transnational political mobilizing among Indian Americans points to the foregrounding of identities such as class, religion, caste, gender, and sexuality that often challenge the nationalist framework of a unified community. My analysis of political mobilizations in the community in response to Hindu nationalism and religious violence in India illustrates the internal cleavages along the lines of religious identity that have become more pronounced within the Indian American community with the resurgence of *Hindutva* politics in India. This analysis points to the importance of internal differentiations and suggests that neither a unifying identity based on a diasporic nationalist framework nor an ethnic identity (Indian American) that has developed in the U.S. racial context provides an adequate framework to understand the political mobilization of Indian Americans. Diasporic mobilizations need to be situated in the specificities of internal cleavages within the community.

The Indian American experience also suggests that immigrant political participation cannot be neatly divided into involvement with host country and home country issues. Instead, many instances of pure home country political concerns have pushed the group into greater engagement with the political institutions and power centers in the United States. Both the U.S.–India Civil Nuclear Deal and mobilizations in the United States for or against Hindu nationalist politics in India have propelled community groups to find allies and supporters in the legislative and policy-making branches of the government. Such needs have often mobilized the community groups to reach out to legislators and other state institutions at different levels to gain recognition in U.S. politics thereby questioning the divide between engagement with home and host countries.

# Conclusion

# Negotiating Identities and Crafting Political Solidarities

"Exclusion of Hindus from America Due to British Influence," published in 1916, is the first-known pamphlet documenting discrimination against South Asians (termed "Hindus" at the time) in the United States. It was authored by Ram Chandra Bharadwaj, president of the San Francisco-based Ghadar Party.[1] It is just one more reminder of the long history of discrimination that immigrants and minorities have faced in the United States, and how South Asians have been an integral part of that history. The role of ethnoracial identities in democratic participation has been an enduring and intractable issue for American democracy, and immigrant and minority communities have always negotiated these identities while striving to find a place in social and political arenas.

History has demonstrated that ethnoracial identities have not only been barriers to political inclusion, but they have also served as an important resource to overcome resistance to inclusion. Racial and ethnic solidarity has been an important part of the story that explains the inclusion of previously disenfranchised minorities as well as new immigrant groups. Political mobilizations shaped by ethnoracial solidarity have thus been central to African American inclusion as well as to the incorporation of European immigrants in the earlier part of the twentieth century. Moreover, scholarship on the contemporary experiences of Latino, Asian, and Caribbean immigrant groups seems to indicate that solidarity based on common ethnoracial identities should lead to greater political efficacy and leverage for these groups. *Desis Divided* challenges the centrality of an ethnoracial solidarity approach for understanding immigrant and minority political mobilization and inclusion, and proposes an approach to contemporary racial and ethnic politics that underlines the importance of internal group cleavages. The internal differentiations, in turn, produce distinctive mobilizations within an ethnoracial group, leading to multiple paths of political empowerment for different subgroups and thereby defying a unified group experience as suggested by the dominant models of political incorporation. Furthermore, this book also underlines the importance of religious identities, not only in producing differential racialization experiences for South Asians but also distinctive responses to racialization.

I have drawn upon the works of race and immigration scholars such as Cathy Cohen (1999) and Cristina Beltran (2010) alongside intersectionality scholars such as Kimberlé Crenshaw (1991) and Ange-Marie Hancock (2007) who critically engage with the issue of unified ethnoracial solidarity and point to the challenges and limitations of creating a political agenda that could unify groups such as African Americans and Latinos. The starting point for these scholars is the recognition of group commonalities based not only on ethnicity, race, nation of origin, and language, among other attributes, but solidarities produced through shared racialized experiences derived from their particular placing in the U.S. racial hierarchy. The process of racialization takes specific form for each group, producing essentialized traits ranging from inferiority, criminality, dependence, and laziness to perpetual foreignness, passivity, being threatening, being a terrorist, as well as traits associated with the model minority construction. Both Beltran and Cohen, however, highlight the internal dynamics of racialized groups and argue that the attempts to produce a unified group politics—a political agenda that brings the group together—need to be interrogated, since the power hierarchies within groups are reproduced in the process, resulting in the marginalization of certain interests, ideologies, and histories.

Cohen, for instance, underlines the complicated and distinct nature of power in black communities and points to ways in which "consensus" issues that are supposed to unify the African American community for political mobilization end up marginalizing the concerns of the poor, women, and gays and lesbians who do not fit the notion of "respectability" within the community. Here the emphasis on intersectional identities and the situated nature of experiences explored by intersectionality scholars also becomes important. For Cohen, the focus is on internally marginalized groups and agendas that get undermined in a unified group mobilization approach, and her prescriptive suggestion seems to be a reworking of a unified black political agenda so that it is inclusive of these marginalized concerns. Beltran's analysis, distinct from Cohen since she is not invested in restructuring a unified group agenda, takes a poststructural view and argues that rather than attempting to uncover a unitary core (language, mestizaje, racism, etc.) that legitimizes a unified Latino politics, Latino scholars and advocates should embrace the instability and incompleteness of the category "Latino." In her framework, Latino community contains and engages with multiple political possibilities, and it is a site of permanent contestation. For Beltran, dreams of unity suppress the possibility of multiple political visions emerging from situated identities within the broader Latino category, and, in the process, transformative political visions are not allowed to bloom.

The approach adopted in this book advances the framework provided by these scholars by underscoring the impact of internal differentiation and contestation, specifically on the group political incorporation process. Building on these insights, the analysis presented in this book emphasizes the differentiated nature of ethnic mobilization among South Asians rather than a lack of it. The focus of this work is not so much on internal marginalization—as suggested by Cohen—but the specificities of ethnoracial mobilization produced by internal cleavages that challenge the attempts to create unified mobilization. In other words, the analytical focus is not on the issues and conditions that could produce an inclusive group agenda but to emphasize the differentiated nature of ethnoracial mobilization. The specificity of ethnoracial mobilization, informed and shaped by the internal cleavages within the community, tends to produce distinct forms of political engagements, relies on different resources to gain visibility, uses varied mobilizational strategies, and generates particular alliances. For instance, ethnic mobilization produced by occupation- and class-based organizations representing Indian American physicians (AAPI), Silicon valley entrepreneurs (TIE), taxi workers (NYTWA and LATWA), and domestic workers (Andolan and Awaz) are extremely different in terms of their concerns, demands, mobilization tactics, and alliance-building strategies. The analytical task, therefore, is not to brush the internal cleavages and contestations aside while analyzing political moments and mobilizations that claim to produce a unified community.

The point of foregrounding internal distinctions among South Asians is not to argue that ethnoracial identity has no importance for understanding South Asian political incorporation. It is rather to emphasize that ethnoracial identity is deployed by particular segments of the South Asian population to produce very specific kinds of mobilizing and organizational infrastructures. The larger implication of this study is to reconsider ethnoracial solidarity as *the* most important step to overcome the social and political marginalization of immigrant and minority communities in U.S. politics. It is the differentiated nature of ethnoracial mobilizing, contingent on internal cleavages, that makes the task of group political incorporation more challenging and demands more situated and specific analysis of inclusions and exclusions. In a racially stratified society such as the United States, ethnoracial solidarity is seen not only as a way of asserting ethnic pride but also of producing mobilization to address marginalization and underrepresentation. From this perspective, the absence of ethnoracial solidarity—that is able to unify the community—could be seen as a major weakness of South Asian Americans, something to bemoan. However, the analysis presented in this book argues that often what is presented as South Asian American or Indian/Pakistani/Bangladeshi American mobilization only represents a specific segment of the population. Thus, ethnoracial solidarity politics are created around narrow sets of issues that fail to engage with diverse realities of the community. A more situated analysis of different segments of South Asian Americans, however, points to the assertions and mobilizations that speak to the diversity of interests and aspirations within the community and points to different experiences of inclusions and exclusions. Such analysis also underlines the efficacy of cross-racial groups and alliances that emerge from the specific situations of South Asian Americans working as taxi drivers, construction workers, and domestic workers, who mostly gain the visibility and resources to encounter marginalization of different kinds through such alliances.

One of the dominant forms of mobilization among South Asian Americans, termed selective elite mobilization, is made possible by a particular class composition of the community, which includes a large number of highly educated middle-class and affluent professionals as well as entrepreneurs who have made their mark in different professions. Furthermore, the emergence of political entrepreneurs within the South Asian community, who bring together affluent segments of the community for political fund-raisers, enables and strengthens the process of selective elite mobilization. It is useful at this point to recall the three prominent trends that the book discussed to emphasize the trend of selective elite mobilization—representation from white-majority districts (or districts with a negligible South Asian population), prominence of campaign fund-raising as a strategy for gaining political power, and the importance of lobbying on the issues concerning home country. These trends produce a unique mode of mobilization that precludes large segments of South Asians from getting drawn into the political process.

The trend of South Asian political aspirants contesting primarily from white-majority districts, with a few notable exceptions, has resulted in instances of South Asian candidates succeeding in the electoral arena without mobilizing the broader South Asian American community. These candidates primarily deploy a deracialized campaign strategy, invoking the discourse of being a model minority and postracial politics. As noted earlier, this trend is in contrast with the political strategy of a sizable number of African American and Latino candidates, who engage in mobilization of their own ethnoracial communities, primarily due to the nature of their electorate that is comprised of a significant number of co-ethnics. For most South Asian candidates, the only notable form of co-ethnic mobilization has been to reach out to affluent South Asians across the nation for campaign contributions. The analysis presented in the book suggests that the trend of contesting from white-majority districts—accompanied with a deracialized campaign strategy—will continue to be a significant part of the South Asian attempt to enter into electoral politics and gain political representation. However, there are a few exceptions in California and New York that could produce electoral representation of South Asians by following the traditional ethnic mobilization path—having a large-scale co-ethnic mobilization. Such electoral districts are likely to see not only greater co-ethnic (Indian/Pakistani/Bangladeshi) mobilization but also increased deployment of South Asian panethnicity. One future direction in which further research could be pursued is based on a preliminary observation that South Asians have found it more challenging to find space in "majority-minority" districts (particularly in the Democratic Party) due to the highly competitive nature of minority politics.[2]

Political entrepreneurs in the South Asian community, particularly among Indian Americans, have projected the ability to make campaign contributions as one of the major strengths of the community. A relatively high number of South Asian fund-raisers—"bundlers" in electoral politics parlance—have further encouraged the trend of elite mobilization. The discourse of Indian Americans being an affluent community and their ability to make campaign contributions was one of the important attractions for members of Congress who engaged and supported the community on the issue of the nuclear deal. The political support and networks created through selective elite mobilization have also enabled the nominations and appointments of a significant number of Indian Americans to important political, policy, and judicial positions. The appointments by the Obama administration, as discussed in chapter 4, have been particularly notable in this regard. Of course, the presence of a large number of high-performing professionals from the community in different fields, including finance, business, technology, medicine, law, policy, as well as the nonprofit sector, helps in this particular mode of inclusion. The trend of nomination and appointment of South Asians is expected to continue as an important part of their inclusion in the arenas of politics and policy making.

Selective elite mobilization stands in stark contrast with the efforts by social justice–oriented groups that have worked toward mobilizing the fast-growing low-income and working-class segments of the community. The South Asian community is witnessing a fairly robust growth of organizations and campaigns that are specifically focused on the needs of these sectors, which were previously ignored by traditional community organizations. It is mostly the nonprofit and labor advocacy groups that are bringing the low-income and working-class sectors into the political process through advocacy campaigns, voter registration, candidate forums, and other kinds of activities oriented toward larger civic and political engagement. Operating under the constraints of the nonprofit sector, a large number of these groups practice a service-oriented model that provides ESL classes, skill development, legal and other kinds of support against domestic violence, health clinics, immigration and naturalization workshops, and resources to find affordable housing. These groups rely on funding from different nonprofit sources and mostly operate on shoestring budgets.

The work among low-income South Asians has generated debates about the approach and priorities of these organizations. There are some South Asian groups, also inhabiting the larger world of the nonprofit sector, that emphasize political organizing and focus on movement building, developing leadership from the rank and file, and building organizations that could be self-sustaining. In fact, the issue of political organizing versus service delivery has been contentious not only among South Asians but among other low-income segments also. It relates to the question of a larger perspective—relief versus social transformation—and also to the availability of resources. There are notable examples of groups, such as NYTWA, that have been able to build organizations primarily through membership contributions and other kinds of support without taking the nonprofit path. NYTWA has not only been able to emerge as an important labor organization in New York City but has also initiated sustained work in other cities to create similar organizations. Other groups, such as DRUM, have prioritized political organizing among low-income South Asians and deemphasized a service delivery approach. Most South Asian organizations, however, practice a combination of the two approaches, and the issue of which approach to emphasize remains a challenging one.

A highly notable aspect of the ongoing work among the low-income and working-class segment of the South Asian American community is the organizations' heavy emphasis on panethnic identity as well as multiracial coalition building. South Asian identity is deployed by almost all nonprofit organizations working among these communities. It helps them reach out to a larger segment of the population, become politically and organizationally efficacious, and position them as serving a wider community for the purposes of funding. In fact, this is the sphere where a South Asian identity has gotten the widest possible deployment. The emergence of the National Coalition of South Asian Organizations (NCSAO) under the leadership of SAALT has further strengthened this nascent trend.

A related and highly significant trend among low-income and working-class-oriented South Asian organizations is the distinct move in the direction of multiracial organizing. The examples of organizing among taxi drivers, and domestic, construction, and restaurant workers suggest that the concerns about resources, political efficacy, and working and living conditions have moved these organizations toward multiracial organizing. For instance, the work among South Asian domestic workers under the leadership of Awaaz and Andolan achieved some significant milestones in terms of highlighting the issue of Desi domestic workers and gaining important victories in some individual disputes, but these two organizations have gradually oriented themselves more toward the larger multiracial organization of domestic workers that includes Caribbean, Latino, and other racial groups. They also became a part of the National Alliance for Domestic Workers and played an important role in a legislative campaign that led to the passage of New York State Domestic Bill of Rights. The move toward multiracial organizing is motivated by the need to create organizations that can be effective in representing domestic workers, but it has also been caused by the difficulty in sustaining organizations focused on a smaller ethnic group.

The South Asian taxi workers' organizations, both in New York and Los Angeles, have been multiracial from their inception, and the decision of NYTWA to become a national organization is a testimony to this approach. There is a similar trend among restaurant workers that is reflected in the work of Restaurant Opportunities Centers United (ROC). In the field of advocacy work, SAALT has been working not only with Asian American groups but others as well on issues such as hate crime, racial discrimination, and immigration reform. The deployment of South Asian panethnicity and increased efforts to develop multiracial organizing and coalition building are defining the current mobilizing efforts among low-income and working-class South Asians. These are relatively fledgling trends, but they are extremely important for defining the contours of future South Asian American political mobilization.

The patterns of political mobilizations identified under the broad rubrics of elite mobilization and social justice–oriented organizing among South Asians underline the challenges of a unified ethnic or panethnic mobilization. Besides class- and occupation-based mobilization divergence, the religious diversity within the South Asian communities has produced a remarkable series of organizational developments and resource building, not only in terms of creating places of worship and networks supporting them, but also in response to racialization in the United States as well as political developments in the countries of origin. Religious identities have not only produced differential racialization experiences for South Asians but also distinct responses to racialization. For instance, Sikh and Muslim mobilizations in the context of post-9/11 racial backlash and government surveillance have been very different than the Hindu response. My analysis of racial targeting of South Asians in the post-9/11 United States emphasizes how exclusive religious identities shaped the responses of South Asian communities against racialization, thereby challenging the existing understanding that hostility against a racially lumped group leads to greater group cohesiveness and reactive panethnic solidarity. Trends in recent years have clearly demonstrated that there is a sustained mobilization against racial targeting and surveillance along the lines of religious identity. For instance, South

Asian Muslims have developed alliances with other Muslim groups to build effective resistance to such incidents. Sikh Americans have also responded in similar ways by building strong organizations around Sikh identity, and the post-2001 period has seen remarkable organizing within the community in terms of creating new organizations and developing campaigns to reach out and educate law enforcement agencies and policy makers. Notwithstanding the campaigns undertaken by groups such as SAALT, SAN, and DRUM to build a strong panethnic South Asian response, the salience of religious mobilization—or relative silence in the case of Hindu American groups—suggests that political identity formation, interest articulation, alliance building, and organizational developments among South Asians have been deeply impacted by religious identities.

One of the notable developments that illustrate this dynamic is the formation of the Hindu American Political Action Committee (HAPAC), which contributes money to Hindu political candidates in the United States or to candidates who are willing to support the Hindu cause. HAPAC is a relatively small and new entity, but it has some of the same donors and supporters who are actively involved with the Hindu American Foundation (HAF), a well-established organization that has been criticized for its alleged closeness to Hindu nationalist politics in India. Both HAF and HAPAC are keen to push political mobilization around Hindu religious identity while engaging with the larger Indian American community.[3]

The religious-identity-inspired mobilizations, as discussed in chapter 6, have surfaced more acutely in the arena of transnational political mobilizing. My analysis of political mobilizations in the Indian American community on the issue of Hindu nationalism and religious violence in India emphasizes the internal cleavages along the lines of religious identity that have become more pronounced within the community in the United States with the resurgence of *Hindutva* politics in India. The contestation among different Indian American groups on the issues of Hindu nationalist politics continues to shape their engagements with the political process in the United States. The congressional election in the 17th district of California, an Asian American majority district that includes a significant number of Indian Americans, is a highly pertinent example in this context. Mike Honda, the incumbent Asian American Democratic

Congressman, was challenged in a 2014 primary and the general election by Ro Khanna, an upcoming Indian American Democrat who ultimately lost the contest.

The election holds relevance for the future direction of South Asian political mobilization because of the importance that *Hindutva* political themes assumed in the campaign. It became an issue because of Mike Honda's support as a congressman for visa denial to Narendra Modi, the Hindu nationalist leader and current prime minister of India. Ro Khanna attacked Mike Honda's support of a continued visa ban as an attempt to enhance his appeal to Hindu Indian American voters. The race became even more contentious when Ro Khanna was forced to moderate his own position in the face of opposition by Muslim groups—particularly Indian American Muslims—who were angry with him for wanting to revoke the visa ban. On the other side, Mike Honda faced opposition from those Indian American groups supportive of Modi, and had to concede that he would look into the matter and reconsider his position on the visa ban.[4] The whole controversy on this issue suggests how the religious divide and mobilizations around Hindu nationalist politics in India impacts South Asian American political mobilization. This dynamic is likely to become more pronounced with the victory of Modi and the Hindu nationalist BJP in the 2014 general elections in India. The mobilization around transnational issues within the Indian American community, deeply affected by religious identity in the context of Hindu nationalist politics in India, will continue to reflect this divide and influence the South Asian political mobilization in the U.S. domestic context as well. The salience of religious identities both in the context of U.S. racialization as well as transnational context points to the challenges of ethnoracial mobilizations that claim to unify the community.

*Desis Divided* has primarily been focused on the challenges of a unified group solidarity. However, it is important to acknowledge the ongoing attempts at producing political framings, organizations, and mobilizations that jostle for the mantle of representing the unified community. As noted earlier, there are multiple kinds of ethnoracial mobilizations among Indian/Pakistani/ Bangladeshi or South Asian Americans, and each emerges from specific segments and experiences of these groups. Organizations such as USINPAC, PAKPAC, and SAALT do claim to represent Indian, Pakistani, and South Asian Americans, respectively, and at different points there are attempts by these groups to produce political framings and issues that could represent moments of unified mobilization. USINPAC, an Indian American lobby group, focuses on the political framing of increased representation of Indian Americans in Washington and works closely with professional, business, and political elites from India. It presented the mobilization around the U.S.–India Civil Nuclear Deal as a unifying moment that underscored the strength of the Indian American community. In contrast, SAALT is an advocacy organization that relies on a political framing that highlights South Asian identity and foregrounds the issues of low-income South Asians alongside racial discrimination, hate crime, sexuality, and unfair immigration policies. These are just two examples of extremely different political framings that attempt to produce community mobilizations with distinct and contrasting visions. They reflect the presence of multiple visions and conceptions of the community. Instead of looking for a core or single framing that could unify the community, we should acknowledge the contested nature of politics produced by South Asian communities. The contestation is reflective not only of internal cleavages such as class, religion, nation, and sexuality but also of ideological orientations and aspirations. While the focus here may be on South Asian Americans, the balancing of cleavages with a notion of unified community has important implications for Asian Americans as a whole, as well as for other racial and ethnic groups.

The journey for immigrant and minority inclusion is a multifaceted one that produces distinct challenges and possibilities for different segments of these groups. This book, above all, is a reminder that the only way ahead for South Asian social and political incorporation—or for that matter, inclusion of other Asian Americans and minorities—is to recognize the significance of particular and situated intersectional identities that go beyond unifying ethnoracial identities. It highlights the ways in which distinctive groups within an ethnoracial community mobilize and negotiate with the community to counter the racialized hierarchies of American democracy in their quest for equality and inclusion.

# Acknowledgments

The journey of writing this book has been circuitous. I came to this topic in graduate school as part of an attempt to make sense of the new world that I encountered after moving to the United States from India, and this work came to encapsulate my growing interests in the issues of race, immigration, marginality, and privilege.

I want to thank my mentors and advisors in graduate school who witnessed this project from its inception. Janelle Wong has been central to this book, and the initial ideas of this project were triggered by many conversations we have had both inside and outside the classroom. She was there every step of the way to provide me with the intellectual support and encouragement to take this project forward. Ann Crigler has been a source of constant support since I started graduate school at the University of Southern California (USC), Los Angeles. Her insights, critical engagement, and willingness to engage with this work have been valuable for me. Jeb Barnes, Judith Grant, the late Michael Preston, Ricardo Ramirez, Alison Renteln, and Marita Sturken at USC helped me develop as a scholar and researcher. I am thankful to the USC College of Letters, Arts, and Sciences for awarding me a postdoctoral appointment that allowed me to make progress on this book. Jane Junn was an ideal postdoctoral mentor who kept me focused on the book project. I am also thankful to Ange-Marie Hancock for her support and engagement with my work. Archana Agarwal, Art Auerbach, Charles Lee, Jillian Medeiros, Sangha Padhy, Seda Unsar, Linda Veazey, and Raechelle Mascrenhas are friends from graduate school who continue to be a source of support.

I am grateful to Karthick Ramakrishnan for his intellectual engagement with my work and constant encouragement to finish this project. Arudra Burra, Ruchi Chaturvedi, Kavita Datla, Vinay Lal, Biju Mathew, Ali Mir, Vijay Prashad, and Linda Vo read this work at different stages and provided valuable suggestions that helped me move the project forward. John Mollenkopf has been very supportive of my work, and he enabled my semester-long visiting position at the CUNY Graduate Center. Phil Kasinitz, Richard Alba, and Anny Bakalian welcomed me to the Graduate Center and also provided the opportunity to present my research. The Center for Global Islamic Studies and the Department of Political Science at Lehigh University awarded me the Mellon Postdoctoral Fellowship, which allowed me to finish the first draft of the book manuscript. I am thankful to Rick Matthews and Rob Rozehnal at Lehigh University for welcoming and introducing me to the institution. I am also grateful to Saladin Ambar, Nandini Deo, Vera Fenell, and Janet Laible for their company and conversations at Lehigh University. Colleagues at Drew University have been highly encouraging, and I want to thank Jason Jordan, Catherine Keyser, Deb Liebowitz, Pat McGuinn, Hans Morsink, Phil Mundo, and Carlos Yordan for their support. Lydia Feldmen at the department has been especially helpful. I also want to thank the dean of the college, Chris Taylor, for institutional support.

Family and friends spread across cities and continents have kept me going despite insurmountable odds. Even though it has been challenging to maintain close relationships in the face of constant mobility and distance, I am grateful for their continued warmth, love, and care. I want to thank my parents, Chandrakali Devi and Rangnath Mishra, who always wanted me to excel and make them proud but were also willing to embrace my trajectory of life choices that were different from theirs. I wish my mother were still around to see the result of my years of hard work. My sisters, Pramila and Dharmshila Dubey, and sister-in-law, Ratna Manjri Mishra, have always ensured that our every trip back to India is memorable and fun. My brother, Badri N. Mishra, and brothers-in-law, Shree Bhagwan and Dinesh Dubey, have been a crucial part of the family support system. My nieces and nephews have been an important part of our lives, and the memory of playing and having fun with them as toddlers and teenagers is not too distant. Now they are all grown up and make me extremely happy by their warmth, sensitivity, and resilience. I am thankful to my nieces, Abha, Neha, Madhu, Shalini, Saloni, and nephews, Abhishek, Animesh, and Rahul, for who they are. I am also thankful for their spouses, Amar, Amitabh, Rakesh, Chhavi, and Sushma, whom I am getting to know slowly.

My in-laws, Bidyut and Manoranjan Mohanty, have always been a source of inspiration. Their love and support have been an important part of this journey. The family in Los Angeles—my brother-in-law, Berkeley Sanjay, and sister-in-law, Brinda Vasisht—has been most closely involved with the trials and tribulations of graduate school and after. They provided much needed space and comforts outside school, and they remain a constant source of strength and affection. My nieces in Los Angeles, Raeva and Adya, have given us some of the most fun-filled times, and they always open a different world to us. Rickie, Mita, and Minnie Patnaik in Los Angeles have also been a crucial part of our lives in this period.

I am truly grateful to friends, both in India and the United States, who have been anchors in my life. I am indebted to the warmth, care, and creativity of my friends with whom I started exploring the world of politics and social transformation. The political and moral compass that we developed together continues to shape my worldview today. Amit Bhattacharya, Naveen Chander, Yogendra Dutt, Subhash Gatade, Ravindra Goel, Kamlesh Kumar, Sanjeev Kumar, Kishore Jha, Jinee Lokaneeta, Ritu Mishra, Vipin Negi, Shiv Shankar Prashad, Anjali Sinha, Kanchan Sinha, Ravi Sinha, Roopali Sinha, and many others were an integral part of this journey. Kishore Jha continues to be an amazing source of strength, and he personifies incredible generosity that is rare to find. Amit Bhattacharya and Amiti Sen have ensured over the years that Delhi feels unchanged and comforting to us when we visit, despite the rapid changes it has experienced. I also thank Shahana Bhattcharya, Suman Bisht, Alok Dash, Avinash Jha, Biswajit Mohanty, Rinku Pegu, Kumar Rohit, Itishree Sahoo, and Babita Varma for their friendship. Ashok Prashad, Ramaa Vasudevan, N. Jacob, and Madhvi Zutshi are cherished friends who continue to be a source of warmth over the years. Janaki Abraham and Vikram Vyas have always been there with their incredible generosity and warmth, and they provided me comfort when I needed it the most. I am thankful to Pratiksha Baxi, who has not let distance affect our friendship and warmth. Upendra and Prema Baxi, Anand Chakravarti, Uma Chakravarti, Mark Juergensmeyer, Nivedita Menon, Ashok Nagpal, Aditya Nigam, and Rabi Sahoo have been a great source of personal support and inspiration through these years. The ability to reach out to Honey Oberoi for both insightful conversations and laughter makes ours a precious friendship.

I made new friends and reconnected with old ones after moving to the East Coast. I am thankful to Deepankar Basu, Sharmadip Basu, Daniel Bender, Varuni Bhatia, Paula Chakravartty, Kavita Datla, Robindra Deb,

Shakti Jaisingh, Sonia Joseph, Humayun Kabir, Vidya Kalaramadam, Anjali Kamat, Sangeeta Kamat, Tausif Khan, Biju Mathew, Ali Mir, Raza Mir, Teju Nagaraja, Murli Natarajan, Rupal Oza, Prachi Patankar, Nayma Qayum, Sekhar Ramakrishnan, Ash Rao, Svati Shah, Jayeeta Sharma, Prachee Sinha, Priyanka Srivastava, Abha Sur, Sue Susman, Saadia Toor, and Zoya Vallari for their friendship and support. I am also thankful to the South Asia Solidarity Initiative for the space it has created for meaningful activism and thinking.

Arudra Burra has been a wonderful friend and source of support during my postdoctoral appointment in Los Angeles. I am grateful to Ruchi Chaturvedi for numerous conversations on politics and academia and for introducing me to the exciting aspects of New York City. Maliha Safri has been an incredible friend over the years, witnessing the ups and downs, and has remained a steadfast source of strength.

This book would not have been possible without the active support of friends and family members who provided contacts in the South Asian community for research interviews both in Los Angeles and New York. I thank Robin Khundkar, Nishanth Balaji, Berkeley Sanjay, Biju Mathew, Saurav Sen, Hamid Khan, and Manju Kulkarni for pointing me to the right people. I also express my heartfelt thanks to all those who took time from their busy lives to sit down and go through the lengthy interview process for this project. Pieter Martin at the University of Minnesota Press has been incredibly supportive and helped me navigate the review process and take this manuscript to a new level. I am also thankful to the two anonymous reviewers who engaged with my work and provided generous comments to make it better.

I am incredibly thankful to Robert Brown and Damaris Carriero for their care and support over the years. Paul Martin, Tse-Ling Fong, and Jacob Korula have also helped me.

Jinee Lokaneeta has been an immense source of strength. I am greatly thankful for her love, care, and companionship through this journey. This book would not have been possible without her support and gentle prodding. She made it possible for me to feel differently about every problem that seemed insurmountable. She read through several drafts of this book and talked through many of the ideas that I have developed here.

# Notes

## Introduction

1. Not a formal Census category, "South Asian" represents individuals with ancestry from Bangladesh, Bhutan, India, Nepal, Pakistan, Sri Lanka, and the Maldives, as well as members of the South Asian diaspora who originally settled in the Caribbean, Africa, Canada, Europe, and other parts of the world.

2. "Study Confirms Most NYC Cab Drivers are Foreign Born." 2004. USA Today.com. http://usatoday30.usatoday.com/travel/news/2004-07-07-nyc-cabbies_x.htm.

3. In a large number of cases, female (or male, in some cases) migrants come as "dependents" with their spouses on professional visas such as H-1B. Their stay in the country is not only dependent on the visa of their spouses, but they are also not allowed to work as per the visa regulations until they become permanent residents or acquire a different visa, both of which are challenging and difficult. However, changes in immigration laws introduced in 2015 have created exception for the spouses of certain categories of H-1B visa holders by allowing them to be eligible for work authorization (Lakshman 2015).

4. The term ethnoracial comes from the acknowledgment that the binary between race and ethnicity is not able to capture the identity of many of the groups in the United States that combine both ethnic and racial characteristics. Ethnorace is a social group whose members are defined by a combination of culture, descent, and visible physical characteristics. I use the term ethnoracial through the book to underline this dynamic interplay of race and ethnicity in characterizing groups such as South Asians.

## 1. South Asian Americans and Immigration Regimes

1. Historians differ on exact numbers, and it is not clear whether this figure is a cumulative number or the number arriving in one particular year. There is some debate as to whether or not this number includes the South Asians who migrated to Canada (Ramnath 2011).

2. The Asiatic Exclusion League issued warnings about the new "menace" from India as they denounced Indians as "dirty" and "diseased" competitors of white labor (Takaki 1998). The racialization of "Hindoos" as dirty and undesirable was followed by a crackdown on South Asians who were seeking entry into the United States. Responding to the extreme exclusionist pressures, immigration officials denied entry to approximately 3,453 Asian Indians between 1908 and 1920 on the grounds that they would likely become public charges (Takaki 1998, 297).

3. The farmers used Punjabi laborers to keep the wages down and paid them approximately twenty-five to fifty cents less per day than the Japanese workers (Takaki 1998, 302).

4. New Orleans was a major tourist destination and a thriving market for Oriental goods that these peddlers were able to supply (Bald 2013).

5. The group attempted to organize an armed rebellion in India with the help of volunteers from North America and other places who boarded ships for India with plans to procure arms on the way. Upon reaching India in 1914, many of them were detained immediately, and others escaped to different parts of the country. This attempt was a high point of the early organizing of the Ghadar group, and they faced severe crackdowns across the globe before they could regroup (Ramnath 2011).

6. The law was extended by Congress in 1870 to make "aliens of African nativity and persons of African descents" eligible for citizenship (Haney-López 2006).

7. In the *U.S. v. Balsara* (1910) and *Ajkoy Kumar Majumdar* (1913) decisions, the courts held that Asian Indians were Caucasians entitled to be considered "white persons" and hence eligible for citizenship. In a similar ruling, *Dow v. United States* (1915), Syrians were deemed eligible for citizenship on the same ground (Haney-López 2006).

8. Vaishno Das Bagai, an immigrant from India who arrived in 1915 with his family and acquired citizenship, took his life after learning that the government had nullified his citizenship (Takaki 1998).

9. A very small number of South Asian women—in comparison to the male immigrants from South Asia—were able to emigrate to the United States in this period, and it became almost impossible for women to migrate after the 1917 Asiatic Barred Zone Act.

10. In Northern California between 1913 and 1946, 47 percent of wives of Indian immigrants were Mexican. In Central California and Southern California, the numbers were 76 and 92 percent, respectively (Takaki 1998, 310–11).

11. Karen Leonard's book *Making Ethnic Choices: California's Punjabi Mexican Americans* was the most important work on this question that brought this part of South Asian American history to wider knowledge. The work also intro-

duced the world of Punjabi pioneers who created a community in the United States.

12. The 1965 Immigration and Naturalization Act was the single most important piece of legislation for South Asians seeking to enter the United States. The proposal, initiated by presidents Kennedy and Johnson, led to the reversal of a half-century-old policy of discrimination against Asian immigrants. The act led to the abolition of the national origin quota and was replaced by a quota for areas outside the Western hemisphere of 170,000 immigrants, within which a maximum of 20,000 visas could be allocated to the people of a single country in a given year. Also, the special restrictions regarding Asians were removed; the act prohibited the exclusion of any immigrant on the basis of race, sex, or nationality. The act also established new criteria for the issuing of visas: familial, financial, and occupational (Tichenor 2002).

13. Novels such as *The Namesake* (2004) by Jhumpa Lahiri, later turned into a film by Mira Nair, capture the lives of these early second wave professional immigrants who struggled to maintain connections with the home country and made enormous efforts to create a community of co-ethnics in the United States despite their small numbers and geographic dispersal.

14. Silicon Valley in northern California witnessed the start-up of a number of technology companies in this period by South Asian immigrants who came to the United States as professionals in different periods (Saxenian 2002).

15. A steady and progressively increasing number of students from South Asia (India in particular) have been coming to the United States for higher education for several decades. They are the second largest group of international students and a large majority of them come for graduate level education (Institute of International Education 2015).

16. The Patels of Gujarat mainly descended from the urban and rural areas of the southern districts of the state. Gujaratis, like other Hindu Indian communities, are composed of numerous castes and subcastes. Leva Kanbis, also referred to as Leva Patels, are particularly well represented in the U.S. motel industry. Patels were traditional leaders within rural communities in Gujarat who collected land revenue for the king. They are a subgroup of the Vaishna caste, the dominant caste in Gujarat, and are considered to be an upwardly mobile and powerful group (Dhingra 2012, 26–27).

17. It is estimated that at least 66,000 Indo-Caribbean live in the United States. This estimate is based on an analysis of American Community Survey data from 2005 to 2009 that provide information about the ancestry of Indian Americans (SAALT 2012). However, Indo-Caribbean organizations dispute this number and argue that there is an undercounting of the population, as many fail to self-report their ancestry.

18. Caste permeates the society of Indians living abroad. Some of the prominent examples of caste associations in the United States are the Rajput Association of North America, Brahman Samaj of North America, and Leuva Patidar Samaj of USA. In fact, large meetings are held with the purpose of getting young people from the same caste together and Patidar Samaj is known for organizing such events (Gaag 2005). Caste also shapes the larger ethnic and linguistic associations whereby a particular caste starts dominating an association. For instance, if we look at the associational dynamics of the Telugu-speaking immigrants from India, the Telugu Association of North America is dominated by the members of the Kamma caste while the American Telugu Association is dominated by the rival Reddy caste (Leonard 2005a).

19. The Dalit diaspora across the globe has been involved in organizing against caste oppression and discrimination. International groups and diasporic Dalit networks have organized conferences and campaigns at the global level to bring attention to this issue. Some of the important diasporic initiatives were a 1998 conference in Vancouver, Canada; a conference in London in 2000; and participation in the World Racism Conference in Durban in 2001. A conference in Washington, D.C., in March 2015, advocating for a binding resolution from the U.S. Congress against caste-based discrimination and a close involvement of the United Nations, suggests the growing strength of this movement (see Kumar 2003).

20. For a systematic analysis of the Pakistani American community, please refer to Adil Najam's book titled *Portrait of a Giving Community: Philanthropy by the Pakistani-American Diaspora* (2006).

21. The figures from Immigration and Naturalization Services indicate that the number of Pakistani immigrants increased considerably after 1968 when the new law came into effect. For instance, in 1965, the number of Pakistani admitted as immigrants was only 187, increasing to 1,528 in 1970, and 4,625 in 1980. This growth trajectory has by and large continued unabated (Najam 2006, 49–50).

22. Between 1995 and 2001, the number of Pakistani immigrants increased approximately 70 percent, from 9,774 in 1995 to 16,488 in 2001. A significant proportion of them came through Diversity Visas (Leonard 1997).

23. In the year 2001, 16,393 Pakistanis were granted permanent residency, but the numbers dropped to 13,694 and 9,415 in 2002 and 2003, respectively. However, the number climbed up to 17,418 in 2006 (U.S. Department of Homeland Security 2007).

24. There was an annual immigration quota of one hundred people in this period for countries such as India and Pakistan. A very small number of Pakistanis came in this period, and included some from East Pakistan, which became Bangladesh in 1971 (Najam 2006).

25. According to INS figures, a modest number of 1,649 Bangladeshis were admitted in 1987, but the figures jump between 1990 and 2000, ranging from 3,000 to 10,000 people per year (Baluja 2003).

26. The Bangladeshi community has the second-highest poverty rate among Asian Americans and Pacific Islanders after Hmong Americans.

27. The U.S. Census asks individuals to self-report their race/ethnicity. The only South Asian option printed on the 2010 Census form for the race/ethnicity was "Asian Indian." Individuals from Bangladesh, Bhutan, Nepal, Pakistan, Sri Lanka, and the Indian diaspora coming from other places than India found that their ethnicity was not specifically delineated on the form. South Asians other than Indians had to choose between "Asian Indian" or writing in another ethnicity under the "Other Asian" category. Many non-Indian South Asians may have possibly checked off "Asian Indian" upon seeing it as the only South Asian option printed on the form, leading to a likely inflation of the Indian population and undercount of the other South Asian populations (SAALT 2012).

28. According to the 2010 Census, there are 59,490 Nepalese and 45,381 Sri Lankans in the United States (SAALT 2012).

29. The Association of Indians in America (AIA) spearheaded the campaign to get an exact counting of Indian immigrants in the U.S. Census in order to assert their presence. The group also decided that Indian immigrants should not continue to be classified as "White" in the Census, given the past history of discrimination as well as the continued discrimination against members of the Indian American community. The campaign, started in the 1970s, led to the classification of Indian immigrants as "Asian Indians" in the 1980 Census, and eventually as part of the "Asian American and Pacific Islander" category from 1990 onward (Das Gupta 2006).

30. The involvement of South Asians with Asian American organizations has gradually increased in recent years. Deepa Iyer, the former director of South Asian Americans Leading Together (SAALT), chaired the National Council of Asian Pacific Americans, a coalition of thirty-one Asian Pacific American organizations, as recently as 2013, and managed to build strong linkages between South Asian community organizations and their Asian American counterparts. Another related example reflecting the change is an increased focus on South Asian American themes in academic bodies such as the Asian American Studies Association, which has traditionally focused on other Asian American and Pacific Islander communities.

31. According to the Department of Homeland Security figures, there were approximately 270,000 undocumented immigrants from the Philippines in 2011 (see Hoefer, Rytina, and Baker 2012).

32. The first wave was comprised of relatively well-educated Vietnamese, followed by waves of migration from rural areas, which were caused by the

deepening of the crisis caused by the war. Between 1979 and 1980, almost 90,000 Vietnamese arrived in the United States, and the numbers kept increasing. Furthermore, a family reunification quota of 20,000 per year was negotiated with Vietnam in 1982 (Takaki 1998).

33. Between 1975 and 1986, the U.S. government provided 5 billion dollars to a refugee assistance program that helped settle Vietnamese and other South East Asian refugees (Rumbaut 1995).

## 2. Political Incorporation and New Immigrants

1. This approach to studying political incorporation has been dominant among scholars since it provides concrete ways to measure incorporation. A recent monograph titled *Newcomers, Outsiders, and Insiders: Immigrants and American Racial Politics in the Early Twenty-First Century* employs four measures—political participation, representation, influence through membership in governing coalition, and adoption of policies favoring minority groups—to assess the state of minority political incorporation at the beginning of the twenty-first century (Schmidt et al. 2009).

2. *Newcomers, Outsiders, and Insiders* is focused on political incorporation experiences of Blacks, Latinos, and Asian Americans and proposes the following models of political incorporation: individual assimilation, pluralism, biracial hierarchy, and multiracial hierarchy. Both assimilation and pluralism suggest that racial barriers have been sufficiently diminished in the United States and they will not prevent racial minorities from achieving incorporation into the political and governmental structures as equal members. However, biracial and multiracial hierarchy models depict relatively rigid structures and social formations and relatively enduring and rigid constraints on the efforts of racial minority groups for greater political influence. Both these frameworks are fully captured in the pluralist and minority group models in a parsimonious manner with clear demarcations (Schmidt et al. 2009).

3. The stigmatization and exclusion from whiteness of Eastern and Southern European immigrants—who were racialized as undesirable and inferior—has also been a part of the European ethnic experience. Their long and torturous journey to whiteness and subsequent political inclusion spoke clearly of the socially contested and changing meanings of racial categories and the power of whiteness to define and attribute meanings and values to groups in relation to itself (Roediger 2005; Jacobson 1998).

4. Robert Park and Ernest W. Burgess of the Chicago School framed the issue of immigrants in the United States at the turn of the twentieth century as a question of assimilation. Park's "race relations cycle"—with four different stages termed as contact, conflict, accommodation, and assimilation—was the most

NOTES TO CHAPTER 3 · **229**

influential paradigm to analyze immigrant incorporation. The emphasis was not on the study of differences but on the necessity of assimilation. Migrants were viewed as "people who have abandoned the political allegiance of the old country and are gradually acquiring the culture of the new" (Park and Burgess 1969, 734).

5. The critics of the pluralist model underline the centrality of race in minority political incorporation experience and argue that contemporary nonwhite immigrants will not replicate the experience of European immigrants as far as overcoming racial barriers is concerned (Pinderhughes 1987; Hero 1992).

6. "Latinidad" refers to the sociohistorical process through which various Latin American national-origin groups are understood as sharing a sense of collective identity and cultural consciousness (Beltran 2010).

## 3. Race, Religion, and Communities

1. See http://articles.latimes.com/2011/apr/11/local/la-me-0411-sikhs-20110411.

2. Kamal Haasan is a well-known film actor and director from India. He was famously stopped at Toronto airport while traveling to the United States in 2002. It was believed that he was stopped because of his Muslim-sounding last name.

3. Interview, Long Island, N.Y., 2007.

4. There are varied estimates of the number of Hindus in the United States. According to Harvard's Pluralism Project, there are 1.3 million Hindus in the United States. This figure is based on the 2004 World Almanac. The American Religious Identification Survey (2008) estimates the number at closer to 1.2 million. However, the Religious Landscape Study conducted in 2015 by Pew Research Center estimated that Hindus constitute approximately 0.7 percent of the U.S. population. The approximate number is close to 2.25 million (http://www .pewresearch.org/fact-tank/2015/05/12/5-key-findings-u-s-religious-landscape/).

5. The Sikh community in the United States is primarily of Indian descent. According to one estimate there are 250,000 Sikhs in the United States (http:// pluralism.org/resources/statistics/tradition.php#Sikhism). Sikh Coalition estimates the total Sikh population in the United States to be close to 500,000. However, it does not cite any source for this estimation.

6. There are different estimates about the Muslim population of the United States. The American Religious Identification Survey (2008) estimated their number close to 1.3 million. However, the 2015 Religious Landscape Study estimates the number of Muslims to be 0.9 percent of the total U.S. population, which brings the Muslim population close to 2.9 million.

7. Organizations such as South Asian Network (SAN), Desis Rising Up and Moving (DRUM), Sakhi, Manavi, South Asian Americans Leading Together (SAALT), and numerous others—who identify themselves as South Asian

American as opposed to Indian, Pakistani, or Bangladeshi—are the dominant trend among service-oriented nonprofit organizations. The logic of procuring funding may be one of the reasons why these organizations initially adopted a broader panethnic category to demonstrate a wider constituency. Notwithstanding the practical politics of funding, there has also been an attempt to craft solidarity among South Asian communities faced with similar issues and there is a strong committment to a broader panethnic identity.

8. These are mostly professional organizations aimed at bringing together people of South Asian descent. The 1980s and 1990s saw the emergence of these organizations, and they have played a major role in popularizing the category of South Asian among the elite of the community as well as the policy makers outside the community. The formation of left activist groups such as *Youth Solidarity Summer* (YSS) in New York, *Friends of South Asia* (FOSA) in the Bay area, and *South Asia Solidarity Initiative* in New York City (all these over the last fifteen years) also reflect the importance of this category for political engagement both in the United States and South Asia.

9. See http://www.dailymail.co.uk/news/article-1394081/Rais-Bhuiyan-blind ed-eye-Mark-Anthony-Stroman-post-9–11-hate-crime-fights-change-attackers -death-sentence.html.

10. As discussed earlier in this volume, in the early twentieth century racial naturalization laws were applied to all nonwhite immigrants, and the issue ultimately reached the Supreme Court in 1923 (*Bhagat Singh Thind v. U.S.*). The court ruled that immigrants from India were not eligible for citizenship because they were not white. Ian Haney-López (2006) discusses these cases carefully and links them to the construction of "Whiteness" in legal discourse. Finally, the Luce-Celler Act, signed by President Harry Truman on July 2, 1946, granted naturalization rights to Filipino and Indian immigrants. The act ended the discriminatory legal barrier to citizenship for these two Asian immigrant groups.

11. Interview, Los Angeles, Calif., 6 March 2006.

12. Interview, New York, N.Y., 14 March 2007.

13. Interview, New York, N.Y., 7 February 2007.

14. Interview, New York, N.Y., 10 February 2007.

15. The *New York Times* reported in May 2014 that the NYPD regularly recruits informants from the Muslim community by using controversial tactics. They interview Muslims who are arrested as part of its routing law enforcement practice. Muslims detained for minor violations are either enticed or coerced through various means to become a part of the NYPD's network of Muslim informants who gather information about the community. For details, see Goldstein 2014.

16. The Los Angeles Police Department (LAPD) under the leadership of William Bratton started a program, termed as Muslim mapping, that aimed to collect varied kinds of information including places of worship, residential

patterns, restaurants, cultural centers, and other kinds of spaces inhabited by the Muslim community. It was scrapped in 2007 after strong objections by the local Muslim communities and civil liberties group terming this practice as thinly disguised racial profiling practice (see MacFarquhar 2007). The local FBI also engaged in surveillance of Muslim community leaders who were part of Multi Cultural Advisory Council created by FBI to build communication and trust between law enforcement agencies and the community. The dispute over surveillance led to a case (*FBI v. Islamic Shura Council of Southern California*) that revealed a systematic surveillance of Muslim community leaders by FBI (see Reza 2006; Mishra and Lokaneeta 2012). FBI engaged in similar practices in Northern California whereby community groups, places of worship, and other Muslim spaces became target of routine surveillance (see La Ganga 2012).

17. Interview, New York, N.Y., 3 March 2007.

18. Interview, New York, N.Y., 15 March 2007.

19. Interview, New York, N.Y., 12 February 2007.

20. See http://www.sikhcoalition.org/advisories/2013/victory-10-months-after -oak-creek-fbi-group-votes-to-track-sikh-hate-crimes.

21. Interview, Los Angeles, Calif., 25 July 2006.

22. Report published by Stanford, Peace Innovation Lab, and SALDEF titled "Turban Myth: The Opportunities and Challenges of Reframing Sikh American Identity in Post-9/11 America." See http://online.wsj.com/public/resources/docu ments/TurbanMyths.pdf.

23. A number of scholars have looked at media, specifically film, television, and video games, to assess how Arab- and Islamic-appearing characters are portrayed. An analysis by J. G. Shaheen (2009) shows that, out of 1,000 films that have Arab and Muslim characters (from the years 1896 to 2000), twelve were "positive" depictions, fifty-two were "even-handed," and the rest of the 900 or so were "negative." A comprehensive review of Arab representation in video games confirms the continuation of stereotypical representations in first-person shooter games such as *War in the Gulf* (Empire, 1993), *Delta Force* (NovaLogic, 1998), *Conflict: Desert Storm* (SCi Games, 2002), *Full Spectrum Warrior* (THQ, 2004), *Kuma/War* (Kuma Reality Games, 2004), and *Conflict: Global Terror* (SCi Games, 2005). The stereotypes and accompanying simplistic narratives reinforce the dark turbaned "other" as the enemy (Sisler 2008).

24. Asian Indians were targeted across California and Washington, and Sikhs were one of the prime targets of these attacks. Their turbans were particularly singled out in the process (Mazumdar 2003).

25. Sukhbir Channa, who was fired by Disney World over its dress code policy, which did not allow employees to grow beards or wear turbans, filed a lawsuit against the company. See http://www.washingtontimes.com/news/2008/jun/18 /mickey-has-the-look-donald-has-the-look-even-jafar/?page=all.

26. See http://www.nytimes.com/2004/07/29/nyregion/two-sikhs-win-back
-jobs-lost-by-wearing-turbans.html.

27. See http://articles.latimes.com/2014/apr/13/nation/la-na-military-sikhs
-20140414.

28. See http://www.sikhcoalition.org/stay-informed/sikh-coalition-advisories
/146.

29. Interview, Long Island, N.Y., 13 November 2006.

30. The emergence of *Hindutva* right wing politics in India in the last three decades has strengthened the politics of a religious divide, and anti-Muslim politics has become a part of the mainstream social and political discourse there. The *Hindutva* right wing forces have also built strong support among Hindu diasporic communities, particularly among those based in the United States (Mathew and Prashad 2000). The ongoing regional rivalry between India and Pakistan further contributes to the politics of a religious divide.

31. Interview, New York, N.Y., 15 January 2007.

32. The *bindi* is a dot-shaped ornament worn on the forehead, primarily by Hindu women.

33. It is important to note that the *bindi* has been marked in different ways both by the community as well as outsiders. In the post-9/11 period, *bindis* were thought to have the symbolic potential of differentiating Hindus from Muslims. However, there is another history of the *bindi* in the United States that marked it as symbolizing the outsider and racial other. In the late 1980s, there were numerous incidents of hate violence in New Jersey against Indian women who sported *bindis* and traditional Indian dress. A group known as "Dotbusters" (the dot referring to *bindi*) came into existence in that period, and it claimed to be against Indian immigrants settling in the New Jersey and New York area. Many of the attacks on Indian immigrants in that period were attributed to this group, and an Indian immigrant, Navroj Mody, was killed in one of the hate attacks that took place in Jersey City in 1987 (Marriott 1987).

34. The other kind of response, according to Kurien, was rooted in the idea of a broader South Asian identity. The two responses had different implications, and they presented two different visions of community mobilization (Kurien 2003).

35. A New Jersey suburb with a predominantly Indian Hindu immigrant population.

36. Interview, New York, N.Y., 18 February 2007.

37. The Council on American-Islamic Relations (CAIR) is one of the leading civil rights organizations active among American Muslims on issues of racial profiling and hate crimes against Muslims. The Sikh Coalition and Sikh American Legal Defense and Education Fund (SALDEF) are some of the leading Sikh civil rights organizations.

38. Interview, Los Angeles, Calif., 15 March 2006.

39. Deepa Iyer referred to the initial support by some Asian American groups—particularly Japanese Americans—in the wake of the 9/11 hate crime attacks, but pointed to the perception that post-9/11 targeting of Muslims, Arabs, and South Asians was not seen as a central Asian American issue (Iyer 2011).

40. Prema Kurien, in her work on Hindu Americans, underlines this emerging trend, where Hindu organizations in the United States have started occupying multicultural spaces as the community's representatives. In fact, multicultural institutions in the United States have been used by Hindu groups to promote politics primarily based on a Hindu religious identity, despite the diversity of religious faith among Indian immigrants (Kurien 2007a).

41. Another such act that got wide publicity in the Indian American community was the opening of the U.S. Senate session with Hindu Prayer in 2007. A priest was invited to perform Hindu prayer before the Senate opened its proceedings on July 12, 2007. It was a gesture on the part of the U.S. Senate to recognize the importance of Hinduism in the United States. In fact, the Hindu prayer in the Senate became controversial because of the protest staged by a Christian right wing group (Senate Prayer 2007).

42. Excerpt of a letter from 146 South Asia–related scholars to the California Board of Education (on file with the author).

43. The following websites detail the philosophy and goals of these organizations:

American Hindus against Defamation (http://www.hindunet.org/anti_defa mation/); Hindu American Foundation (http://www.hinduamericanfoundation .org/).

## 4. Mapping the Modes of Mobilization

1. PNAAPS uses the category "South Asian," which includes Indian and Pakistani participants, whereas NAAS includes only Indian Americans. NAAS, however, is nationally representative and an improvement over PNAAPS, which relied on samples from only five metropolitan areas.

2. It is important to note that this comparison is only among Asian American groups, which already suffer from lower levels of political participation in comparison to other ethnoracial groups.

3. Interview, New York, N.Y., 10 February 2007.

4. Interview, New York, N.Y., 3 March 2007.

5. Interview, New York, N.Y., 3 March 2007.

6. Recent works on other minority groups such as Latino and Caribbean immigrants in New York City also point to this trend (Jones-Correa 1998; Rogers 2006; Wong 2006).

7. Interview, New York, N.Y., 12 March 2007.

8. Interview, New York, N.Y., 6 November 2006.

9. Interview, Los Angeles, Calif., 7 July 2006.

10. See http://www.nyc.gov/html/dc/downloads/pdf/2013_01_14_testimony_taking_our_seat.pdf.

11. Sayu Bhojwani's dissertation work on South Asian political incorporation in New York City analyzes the creation of a South Asian "opportunity district"—a district with a sizable South Asian population that could enhance the chances of a South Asian candidate—for the New York State Assembly during the redistricting process. She argues that class cleavages in the district and among South Asians create challenging problems for such a district, which stretches from Bellerose, one of the more affluent areas of the city, with an annual median household income of $137,334, to Richmond Hill, with a median household income of $56,693. The schools in these two areas are very different, with Richmond Hill residents extremely dissatisfied with the condition of the local school while the Bellerose school performs very well. Bhojwani points to the frustration of political aspirants in creating a South Asian mobilization given the economic diversity among South Asians and the differences in their concerns in these two areas (Bhojwani 2014, 112–13).

12. Interview, New York, N.Y., 7 February 2007.

13. Interview, Northern New Jersey, 10 February 2007.

14. See http://www.nytimes.com/2010/01/27/nyregion/27maloney.html.

15. See http://india.blogs.nytimes.com/2012/11/08/for-indian-american-candidates-a-disappointing-election-day/?_php=true&_type=blogs&_r=0.

16. Although there are some examples of crossover candidates among African American and Latino groups, this has not been the dominant trend.

17. The term "postracial" has been used widely in recent times to broadly convey the phenomena of moving beyond race. Paul Gilroy was the first to characterize the current moment as postracial in his book *Against Race: Imaging Political Culture beyond the Color Line* (2002). Gilroy's use of the term referred to postracial humanism to underline the need to go beyond race. Others have used the term to communicate a particular understanding of race politics that claims to transcend race. Michael Omi and Howard Winant (1994) refer to the politics of colorblindness as a conservative reaction to affirmative action and race-based organizing. Postracial has been defined by some scholars as an extension of colorblind politics and a neoliberal response to the progressive politics of racial equality (Wise 2013; Haney-López 2010).

18. See www.rediff.com/news/2007/jun/15clinton.htm.

19. This line of criticism of Hillary Clinton's campaign by the Obama campaign was reminiscent of the controversy over contributions by Asian Americans

to Bill Clinton's presidential campaign in 1996. The controversy centered around the presumption that contributions by Asian Americans represented the interests of Asian capital in the Pacific Rim, and that tainted offshore Asian money was coming through Asian Americans to buy political influence in the United States.

20. See www.newser.com/story/3248/obama-sorry-for-hillary-memo.html.

21. Interview, Los Angeles, Calif., 5 July 2006.

22. Interview, Los Angeles, Calif., 23 June 2006.

23. Center for Responsive Politics. See https://www.opensecrets.org/pres12/bundlers.php.

24. Interview, Los Angeles, Calif., 22 June 2006.

25. The book was Mearsheimer and Walt's *The Israel Lobby and U.S. Foreign Policy* (2007).

26. See http://indiatribune.com/get-involved-call-to-young-indian-americans-gala-fundraiser-for-nikki-haley-in-chicago/.

27. The Telugu Association of North America (TANA) is an example of an ethnocultural organization. TANA, an association of immigrants who have connections to Andhra Pradesh in India, organizes yearly conferences where high-profile speakers and performers both from India and the United States are invited. For instance, the 2007 annual conference was organized in Washington, D.C., where the main speaker was former president Bill Clinton. The event also had a number of cultural and political figures from Andhra Pradesh, India. TANA is composed of a number of local level Telugu associations active all over the United States. Similar organizations of Gujaratis, Bengalis, Marathis, Oriyas, and others are active in the United States.

28. As mentioned earlier, it is also important in this context to note the persistence of caste identity among Indian Americans. The issue of caste is often glossed over, but its persistence is reflected in myriad ways in many of these ethnic organizations. Even though broader ethnocultural and linguistic identities are more prominent in South Asian communities, and most of the organizations are formed on the basis of these identities, caste remains an important social category. The importance of caste in the social lives of Indian immigrants is particularly reflected in the existence of caste-based organizations in the United States. Indian immigrants have traditionally belonged to the "upper castes," and it is only in recent years that immigrants from oppressed castes and erstwhile "untouchable" and "backward castes" have started registering a presence in the United States. Organizations of oppressed castes working toward the elimination of caste oppression in India are also being formed in the United States as a result of the increased presence of the oppressed castes here.

29. See http://aapiusa.org/.

30. See http://www.appna.org/.

31. A group of Indian hotel and motel owners formed an association in Tennessee—the Midsouth Indemnity Association—in 1985 to support their businesses. It was later renamed the Indo American Hospitality Association when it expanded into other parts of the United States. They joined forces with the AAHOA in 1994 and the two became one organization to better represent their constituents (Dhingra 2012).

32. See http://www.aahoa.com/AM/Template.cfm?Section=About_Us.

33. AAHOA was one of the important groups that lobbied in favor of the U.S.–India Nuclear Deal and reached out to members of Congress for their support on this issue. The group has also played an important role in supporting Narendra Modi, the prime minister of India, who is accused of involvement in the massacre of Muslims in Gurjarat.

34. See www.pakpac.net/.

35. See http://pakistanrelations.org/pages/Congressional%20Pakistan%20Caucus.html.

36. A report titled "Workers Rights are Human Rights: South Asian Immigrant Workers in New York City" was published by DRUM and Urban Justice Center in 2012. Available at http://www.drumnyc.org/wp-content/themes/wpaid/images/wc-report.pdf.

37. See https://nytwa.org/.

38. For a longer discussion of this debate, see Ananya Bhattacharjee (1997), Margaret Abraham (2000), and Linta Varghese (2006).

39. See http://www.proxsa.org/resources/ghadar/v5n1/kaur.htm.

40. Andolan has taken up cases that involve abuse and exploitation by UN diplomats. One of the most publicized cases was of Shamela Begum, a Bangladeshi woman who was contracted to work for a diplomat from Bahrain and came to the United States in 1998 on a special visa issued to domestic workers of UN diplomats. After her arrival in New York, Begum's employer confiscated her passport, and she was forbidden to leave the apartment alone. For nine months, she worked seven days a week and was paid a meager $100 per month. With the support of Andolan, ultimately Begum's case was settled out of court and she received compensation. There were other similar cases that led Andolan to start a campaign against diplomatic immunity in the case of exploitation and abuse of domestic workers (Sengupta 2000).

41. See http://southasiannetwork.org/units-programs/cru-civil-rights-unit/.

42. See http://southasiannetwork.org/2011/05/16/22-workers-on-pioneer-blvd-awarded-95000/.

43. See http://www.drumnyc.org/wp-content/themes/wpaid/images/wc-report.pdf.

44. See http://www.indolink.com/displayArticleS.php?id=061107042937.

45. See http://saalt.org/the-coalition/meet-the-ncso/.

## 5. Transnationalism and Political Participation

1. The PNAAPS included a total of 1,218 adults of Chinese, Korean, Vietnamese, Japanese, Filipino, and South Asian (Indians and Pakistanis) descent residing in the Los Angeles, New York, Honolulu, San Francisco, and Chicago metropolitan areas who were randomly selected for this survey and interviewed by phone between November 16, 2000, and January 28, 2001. The NAAS included a total of 5,159 Asian Americans of six major national-origin groups. It was a national sample conducted between August and October of 2008. Both surveys are available through the Inter-University Consortium for Political and Social Research available at http://www.icpsr.umich.edu/icpsrweb/ICPSR/.

2. The questions relevant for this analysis that these two surveys investigated include the extent to which Asian immigrants have adapted to U.S. society and culture; the forms of ethnic and panethnic identity and consciousness that Asian Americans express; the views that Asian Americans hold about the U.S. political system; and the participatory habits, political habits, and partisanship of Asians in the U.S. political system. The survey also measured ethnic in-group feelings, national and transnational attachments that Asian Americans form, and patterns of adaptation and acculturation they exhibit over time in the United States.

3. To analyze the data on South Asian immigrants in comparison to other Asian Americans, a dummy variable was created by dividing the sample into two categories—South Asians and Other Asians. Similarly, dummy variables were created for each of the indicators of transnational attachment and political participation in the United States. The three different measures of transnational attachment used for this analysis from the PNAAPS were (1) frequency of contact—either by phone, mail, or in person—with people in respondents' country of origin; (2) attention to news in the country of origin; and (3) participation in political activities related to the country of origin. The NAAS used a fourth measure—sending money to the home country—as one of the important indicators of transnational attachment. The U.S. political participation measures used for this analysis were (1) the rate of voting among registered voters, (2) participation beyond voting, (3) interest in politics, (4) familiarity with the presidential election, (5) membership in ethnic organizations, (6) citizenship, and (7) willingness to acquire citizenship.

4. The dummy variables created for the transnational attachment category of "frequency of contact with the country of origin" included (1) those who maintained a high level of contact—once a week or more, two or three times a month, or at least once a month—and (2) those who maintained a low level of contact—once a year or less.

5. The difference is significant at a .01 level of significance.

6. In fact, a number of long-distance companies such as Vonage use South Asian subjects in their advertisements, referring to their propensity to call home frequently.

7. The five-year cut-off point is due to the provision of five years of permanent stay in the United States to be eligible for naturalization.

8. The multivariate regression analysis shows that the relationship between South Asians and political participation is statistically significant at the .10 level. However, it is important to note that the positive relationship between the two variables is not very strong, given the level of significance.

9. Interview, Los Angeles, Calif., 17 April 2006.

10. Interview, Los Angeles, Calif., 20 June 2006.

11. Interview, Los Angeles, Calif., 13 June 2006.

12. Interview, Costa Mesa, Calif., 14 July 2006.

13. Interview, Irvine, Calif., 7 June 2006.

14. Interview, New York, N.Y., 6 February 2007.

15. Interview, New York, N.Y., 12 March 2007.

## 6. Diasporic Nationalism and Fragments Within

1. Economic liberalization in India started in the 1990s and changed the orientation of the Indian economy in very important ways. The reforms included opening up international trade and investment, deregulation of what had been derided as the "license-permit Raj"—an economy with heavy state regulation—and privatization of public-sector companies, among other policy initiatives. Reforms were also introduced in the area of labor and trade union rights, making it easier to hire and fire. The engagement with diaspora also reached a different level with these reforms, which intensified the mobility of goods and capital across borders.

2. Hospitals are able to pay lucrative salaries to their doctors due to a booming business aided by medical tourism. A trend of reverse migration of physicians from the West is being noted in this context. See http://www.ndtv.com/article/diaspora/reverse-brain-drain-indian-doctors-come-home-to-medical-tourism-hub-540153.

3. India has been among the top remittance-receiving countries for the last six years. Despite having a smaller diasporic population than China, one of the reasons India gets more remittances is the fact that the economic condition of a large number of families sending migrants remains precarious, inviting more money from those family members living abroad. See http://www.hindustantimes.com/business-news/sectorsbpos/remittances-exceed-india-s-it-export-earnings-world-bank/article1-1130639.aspx. See also Chishti (2007).

4. The card, however, disallowed anyone from availing themselves of these facilities if the person had been a citizen of Afghanistan, Bangladesh, Bhutan, China, Nepal, Pakistan, or Sri Lanka.

5. There has been vocal opposition to the U.S.–India Civil Nuclear Deal in India. The opposition in India can be broadly divided into two kinds. The first kind was from the opposition party of the time, the Bharatiya Janata Party (BJP), which argued that India was compromising its nuclear program by accepting the U.S. terms and conditions. The second kind of opposition was from the Left, which has different strands. Notwithstanding the differences, there is a strong consensus within the Left that, by aligning with the United States, India is abandoning its independent foreign policy and starting to toe the line of U.S. hegemonic policies. There is also a strong anti-nuclear lobby within the Left that does not want India to pursue nuclear ambitions—either civil or military—with or without U.S. support. The coalition government of the time led by the Indian National Congress Party—which was supported by the Left parties from outside—faced a major battle on the question of the nuclear deal, as Left parties withdrew their support of the government after the deal was finalized (Bidwai 2007).

6. After the explosion of its first atomic bomb in 1974, India was considered to be following its nuclear ambitions outside the framework developed by the Western nuclear powers led by the United States. India never signed the NPT and continued its nuclear program without U.S. approval, which remained a source of contention between the two countries.

7. Anna Karpathakis's (1999) work on Greek immigrants in New York City argued along similar lines that concern with the home country's issues led to greater engagement in the U.S. political process.

8. The Henry J. Hyde U.S.–India Peaceful Atomic Energy Cooperation Act (2006) details the provisions of the U.S.–India Civil Nuclear Deal.

9. Paula Chakravarrty (2006) writes about the H-1B workers and the IT sector as inhabiting "white collar nationalisms" both in India and the United States.

10. The nuclear deal was criticized by individuals and groups within the Indian American community on different grounds, primarily by those opposed to nuclear proliferation and also by some who believed that by signing this agreement India was compromising its political sovereignty. However, there was very little mobilization within the Indian American community to oppose the deal.

11. The Ayodhya Temple Movement, initiated by Vishwa Hindu Parishad (VHP) and Bajrang Dal, among others, claimed that the mosque was built by erasing the temple, which existed there to mark the birthplace of Lord Rama. The archaeological evidence for this claim could never be verified, but the movement for the temple decided to take the issue to the streets and whip up religious passions on all sides (Basu et al. 1993).

12. The exact death count from this religious conflict is still in dispute, as many independent groups that investigated the riots came up with figures that were higher than those reported officially. The government told Parliament that

790 Muslims and 254 Hindus were killed, 223 more people were reported missing, and another 2,500 injured (http://news.bbc.co.uk/2/hi/south_asia/4536199.stm).

13. See http://www.hindustantimes.com/India-news/NewDelhi/Killer-Dara -wanted-to-teach-Staines-a-lesson-Supreme-Court/Article1-653205.aspx.

14. See http://www.vhp-america.org/.

15. *Hindutva* organizations in India began in 1989 to collect and consecrate bricks—the Ram Shilas—to lay the foundation of the Ram Janamsthan Mandir in Ayodhya. VHP and RSS cadres took several hundred thousand Ram Shilas, made of local earth in different places, to scattered villages and towns. The bricks were wrapped in saffron cloth, worshipped for several days, consecrated by priests and village elders, and carried in processions throughout the country. Almost 200,000 villages sent bricks, 300,000 pujas of the Ram Shilas were performed, and altogether about 100 million people attended the various processions that carried the bricks to and from Ayodhya (Chandhoke 2000). The process of brick sanctification was carried out by *Hindutva* organizations in many U.S. cities as well.

16. See http://netivism2.blogspot.com/2007/04/biju-mathew-interview-tran script.html.

17. See http://www.coalitionagainstgenocide.org/reports/2002/fxhate.20nov 2002.idrf.pdf.

18. The report was contested by IDRF, which came out with a counter-report titled *A Factual Response to the Hate Attack on the India Development and Relief Fund (IDRF)* in which it defended RSS, VHP, and other *Hindutva* organizations rather than distancing itself from those organizations. IDRF also launched a petition titled "Let India Develop" that appealed to corporations to rescind their decision to stop matching contributions that their employees made to IDRF (for details, see http://www.letindiadevelop.org/thereport/).

19. The report enumerated the names of organizations that received funding and provided evidence for the linkages between these organizations and RSS. It also provided details on the activities these organizations were involved in and traced their ideological and structural linkages to *Hindutva* organizations. Many of these organizations were working among segments of tribal populations that had converted to Christianity, and they were also reportedly involved in the "reconversion" of Adivasi Christians to Hinduism, along with creating very hostile conditions for Christian missionaries working in the area.

20. See http://www.fiacona.org/.

21. "Vajpayee Urges Indo-U.S. Concert Against Terror," 2000, *Statesman*, September 15.

22. See http://www.persecution.org/2011/05/14/indian-americans support -usirf-report-on-religious-freedom/.

23. See http://inwww.rediff.com/news/report/orissa/20080830.htm.

24. See http://articles.timesofindia.indiatimes.com/2008–08–30/indians-abroad/27913083_1_indian-american-christian-organisations-orissa-christian-community.

25. See http://www.countercurrents.org/guj-cag220205.htm.

26. See http://www.coalitionagainstgenocide.org/reports/2002/uscirf.10jun2002.transcript.pdf.

27. See http://www.afmi.org/index.asp. The 2012 annual convention of the organization was held in Brampton, Canada, and was attended by hundreds of delegates. A prominent parliamentarian and Dalit leader of India, Ram Vilas Paswan, was the keynote speaker.

28. See http://iamc.com/.

29. As discussed in chapter 4, the small hotel and motel industry in the United States has a sizable number of Indian American owners. AAHOA represents this segment of the industry. A large number of these owners and managers are Hindus from the state of Gujarat, and historically they have come from trading communities and found ways to start small businesses in the United States. *Hindutva* organizations in the United States have traditionally found strong support in this community.

30. See http://timesofindia.indiatimes.com/india/Modi-has-a-way-to-beat-US-ban/articleshow/1056484.cms.

31. Congressman Frank Pallone and New Jersey assemblyman Upendra Chivukula were among speakers who decried the U.S. government for denying a visa to Modi (http://www.rediff.com/news/2005/mar/21sld1.htm).

32. The campaign for the denial of a visa to Narendra Modi was criticized for taking support from Christian conservatives in the United States, and some termed this as bias against Hinduism. However, it was clear from the way the campaign evolved that groups mobilizing against religious violence in India found a very important opening in the International Religious Freedom Act, and they used the infrastructure created by the law to build support for congressional hearings against religious violence in India as well as a ban on Narendra Modi from traveling to the United States. The support of Christian conservative groups in the United States became an important part of the campaign. My conversations with people involved in the campaign suggest that activists on the left were uncomfortable with this alliance, but they had to rely on support that came from different quarters (Mann 2014; Shah 2014).

33. These two organizations are run by the same group of people, who are primarily based in Chicago. Shalabh "Shalli" Kumar, a Chicago-based entrepreneur, is one of the important persons behind these groups, and it is widely believed that he and his groups work in close association with *Hindutva* organizations in the United States. Many of the functionaries of these groups are also associated with the Republican Party (Prashad 2013).

34. The lawsuit did not have any practical bearing on Narendra Modi's visit, since a visiting head of state has immunity from any such legal challenge. However, the lawsuit did indicate the willingness of the affected communities and individuals to challenge Narendra Modi's legitimacy at a time when the U.S. political establishment had decided to reverse its stance toward him (Mandhana 2014).

## Conclusion

1. See http://www.saada.org/item/20100916–121.

2. A number of interviewees spoke about the challenges of negotiating with other minority groups, particularly in majority-minority districts. They suggest that older coalitions and leaders are so well entrenched in those districts that new and aspiring minority groups have difficulty finding space for themselves.

3. See http://www.americanbazaaronline.com/2014/06/02/hindu-american -pac-puts-list-us-house-representative-members-supports/.

4. See http://pando.com/2014/05/29/ruh-ro-how-the-valleys-favorite-politician -may-be-foiled-by-a-hindu-supremacist-banned-from-the-us/.

# Bibliography

Abdulrahim, Raja. 2010. "Little Bangladesh Must Grow into Its Name." *Los Angeles Times*, November 28.

Abraham, Margaret. 2000. *Speaking the Unspeakable: Marital Violence among South Asian Immigrants in the United States*. New Brunswick, N.J.: Rutgers University Press.

Ahmad, Muneer. 2002. "Homeland Insecurities: Racial Violence the Day after September 11." *Social Text* 20(3): 101–15.

———. 2004. "A Rage Shared by Law: Post-September 11 Racial Violence as Crimes of Passion." *California Law Review* 92(5): 1259–1330.

Aizenmann, Nurith, and Edward Walsh. 2003. "Immigrants Fear Deportation after Registration." *Washington Post*, July 28.

Akram, Susan, and Martiza Karmley. 2005. "Immigration and Constitutional Consequences of Post-9/11 Policies Involving Arabs and Muslims in the United States: Is Alienage a Distinction without Difference?" *U.C. Davis Law Review* 38: 609–99.

Alba, Richard. 2005. "Bright vs. Blurred Boundaries: Second-Generation Assimilation and Exclusion in France, Germany, and the United States." *Ethnic and Racial Studies* 28(1): 20–49.

Alba, Richard, and Victor Nee. 1997. "Rethinking Assimilation Theory for a New Era of Immigration." *International Migration Review* 31: 826–75.

———. 2003. *Remaking the American Mainstream: Assimilation and Contemporary Immigration*. Cambridge, Mass.: Harvard University Press.

American-Arab ADC and Penn State University. 2009. *NSEERS: Consequences of America's Efforts to Secure its Borders*. Washington, D.C.: American-Arab Anti-Discrimination Committee and Penn State University's Dickinson School of Law Center for Immigrants' Rights.

American Civil Liberties Union. 2004a. *America's Disappeared*. New York.

———. 2004b. *How Deporting Immigrants After 9/11 Tore Families Apart and Shattered Communities*. New York.

Andersen, Kristi. 1979. *The Creation of a Democratic Majority, 1928–1936*. Chicago: University of Chicago Press.

Anderson, Benedict. 1992. "The New World Disorders." *New Left Review* 1(193): 4–11.

APIA Vote and Asian Americans Advancing Justice. 2014. "Left, Right, or Center? Asian American Voters in 2014." http://www.apiavote.org/sites/default /files/APV-AAJC-LeftRightCenter-oct7FINAL.pdf.

Appiah, Anthony K. 1994. "Identity, Authenticity, Survival: Multicultural Societies and Social Reproduction." In *Multiculturalism: Examining the Politics of Recognition,* edited by Amy Gutmann, 75–86. Princeton, N.J.: Princeton University Press.

Bagai, Leona B. 1967. *The East Indians and Pakistanis in America.* Minneapolis, Minn.: Lerner Publications.

Bakalian, Anny, and Mehdi Bozorgmehr. 2009. *Backlash 9/11: Middle Eastern and Muslim Americans Respond.* Berkeley: University of California Press.

Bald, Vivek. 2013. *Bengali Harlem and the Lost Histories of South Asian America.* Cambridge, Mass.: Harvard University Press.

Baluja, Kaari F. 2003. *Gender Roles at Home and Abroad: The Adaptation of Bangladeshi Immigrants.* New York: LFB Scholarly Publishing.

Banerjee, Neela. 2007. "In Jews, Indian-Americans See a Role Model for Activism." *New York Times,* October 2.

Bank, David. 2003. "Companies Face Quandaries Over Matching-Gift Programs." *Wall Street Journal,* February 18.

Baretto, Matt. 2010. *Ethnic Cues: The Role of Shared Ethnicity in Latino Political Participation.* Ann Arbor: University of Michigan Press.

Barker, Lucius J. 1988. *Our Time Has Come: A Delegate's Diary of Jesse Jackson's 1984 Presidential Campaign.* Urbana: University of Illinois Press.

Basch, L., N. Schiller, and S. Blanc. 1994. *Nations Unbound: Transnational Projects, Postcolonial Predicaments and Deterritorialized Nation-States.* Amsterdam: Gordon and Beach Publishers.

Basu, Tapan, Pradip Datta, Sumit Sarkar, Tanika Sarkar, and Sambuddha Sen. 1993. *Khaki Shorts Saffron Flags.* New Delhi: Orient Longman.

Baubock, R. 2003. "Towards a Political Theory of Migrant Transnationalism." *International Migration Review* 37(3): 700–23.

Beltran, Cristina. 2010. *The Trouble with Unity: Latino Politics and the Creation of Identity.* New York: Oxford University Press.

Berger, Joseph. 2008. "A Place Where Indians, Now New Jerseyans, Thrive." *New York Times,* April 27.

Bhattacharjee, Ananya. 1992. "The Habit of Ex-Nomination: Nation, Woman, and the Indian Immigrant Bourgeoisie." *Public Culture* 5(1): 19–44.

———. 1997. "A Slippery Path: Organizing Resistance to Violence against Women." In *Dragon Ladies: Asian American Feminists Breathe Fire,* edited by Sonia Shah, 29–45. Boston: South End Press.

Bhojwani, Sayu V. 2014. "Coming of Age in Multiracial America: South Asian Political Incorporation." Ph.D. Diss., Columbia University.

Bhowmick, Nilanjana. 2013. "Why Wharton Canceled Narendra Modi's Speech." *Time,* March 5. http://world.time.com/2013/03/05/why-wharton-canceled -narendra-modis-speech/.

Bidwai, Praful. 2007. "Political Fallout of India-U.S. Nuclear Deal Turns Severe." *IPS.* http://ipsnews.net/news.asp?idnews=38926.

Biswas, Bidisha. 2010. "Negotiating the Nation: Diaspora Contestations about Hindu Nationalism in India." *Nations and Nationalism* 16(4): 696–714.

Bonilla-Silva, Eduardo. 2004. "From Bi-Racial to Triracial: Towards a New System of Racial Stratification in the USA." *Ethnic and Racial Studies* 27(6): 931–50.

Bose, Pablo S. 2008. "Home and Away: Diasporas, Developments, and Displacements in a Globalising World." *Journal of Intercultural Studies* 29(1): 111–31.

Bosniak, Linda. 2000. "Citizenship Denationalized." *Indiana Journal of Global Studies* 7(2): 447–510.

———. 2001. "Denationalizing Citizenship." In *Citizenship Today: Global Perspectives and Practices,* edited by T. Alexander Aleinikoff and Douglas Klusmeyer. Washington, D.C.: Carnegie Endowment for International Peace.

Braziel, Jana Evans, and Anita Mannur. 2003. *Theorizing Diaspora: A Reader.* Hoboken, N.J.: Wiley-Blackwell.

Browning, Rufus P., Dale Rogers Marshall, and David H. Tabb, eds. 1997. *Racial Politics in American Cities,* 2nd ed. New York: Longman.

———. 2003. *Racial Politics in American Cities,* 3rd ed. New York: Longman.

Carby, Hazel. 1992. "The Multicultural Wars." *Radical History Review* 54: 7–18.

Center for Human Rights and Global Justice (NYU School of Law). 2007. *Americans on Hold: Profiling, Citizenship, and the "War on Terror."* http:// www.chrgj.org/docs/AOH/AmericansonHoldReport.pdf.

Chakravartty, Paula. 2006. "White Collar Nationalisms." *Social Semiotics* 16(1): 39–55.

Chan, Sucheng. 1991. *Asian Americans: An Interpretive History.* Boston: Twayne.

Chandhoke, Neera. 2000. "The Tragedy of Ayodhya." *Frontline,* June 24–July 7.

Chang, Edward. 1988. "Korean Community Politics in Los Angeles: The Impact of the Kwangju Uprising." *Amerasia* 14(1): 51–67.

Chatterji, Angana. 2005. "How We Made U.S. Deny Visa to Modi." *Asian Age,* March 22.

Chaturvedi, S. 2005. "Diaspora in India's Geopolitical Vision: Linkages, Categories, and Contestations." *Asian Affairs: An American Review* 32(3): 141–68.

Chavez, Linda. 1991. *Out of the Barrio: Toward a New Politics of Hispanic Assimilation.* New York: Basic Books.

Chishti, Muzzafar. 2007. *The Phenomenal Rise in Remittances to India: A Closer Look.* Washington, D.C.: Migration Policy Institute.

Chishti, Muzzafar, and Faye Hipsman. 2015. *In Historic Shift, New Migration Flows from Mexico Fall Below Those from China and India.* Washington, D.C.: Migration Policy Institute.

Chishti, Muzzafar et al. 2003. *America's Challenge: Domestic Security, Civil Liberties, and National Unity after September 11.* Washington, D.C.: Migration Policy Institute.

Cho, Wendy K. Tam. 1999. "Naturalization, Socialization, Participation: Immigrants and (Non-) Voting." *Journal of Politics* 61(4): 1140–55.

Cho, Wendy K. Tam, and Suneet P. Lad. 2004. "Subcontinental Divide: Asian Indians and Asian American Politics." *American Politics Research* 32(6): 239–63.

Cigler, Allan, and Brudett Loomis, eds. 1986. *Interest Group Politics,* 2nd ed. Washington, D.C.: CQ Press.

Clough, M. 1994. "Grass-roots Policy Making: Say Good Bye to the 'Wise Men.'" *Foreign Affairs* 73(1): 2–7.

Cohen, Cathy. 1999. *The Boundaries of Blackness: AIDS and the Breakdown of Black Politics.* Chicago: University of Chicago Press.

Constable, Pamela. 2014. "New Indian leader Draws Cheers, Criticism from Diaspora as He Arrives in the U.S." *Washington Post,* September 28.

Conway, M. Margaret. 2001. "Political Participation in American Elections; Who Decides What." In *America's Choice,* edited by William J. Crotty. New York: Westview.

Cornell, Stephen, and Douglass Hartmann. 1998. *Ethnicity and Race: Making Identities in a Changing World.* Thousand Oaks, Calif.: Pine Forge.

Cornwell, Elmer E. 1960. "Party Absorption of Ethnic Groups: The Case of Providence, Rhode Island." *Social Forces* 38: 205–10.

Coser, Lewis A. 1956. *The Function of Social Conflict.* Glencoe, Ill.: Free Press.

Council on American-Islamic Relations. 2012. "Poll: 85 Percent of Muslim Voters Picked President Obama." http://www.cair.com/press-center/press-releases/11664-poll-85-percent-of-muslim-voters-picked-president-obama.html.

Creating Law Enforcement Accountability and Responsibility. 2013. *Mapping Muslims: NYPD Spying and Its Impact on American Muslims.* CUNY School of Law, MACLC, and AALDEF.

Crenshaw, Kimberlé W. 1991. "Mapping the Margins: Intersectionality, Identity Politics, and Violence against Women of Color." *Stanford Law Review* 43(6): 1241–99.

Dahl, Robert A. 1961. *Who Governs? Democracy and Power in an American City.* New Haven, Conn.: Yale University Press.

———. 1982. *Dilemmas of Pluralist Democracy.* New Haven, Conn.: Yale University Press.

Das Gupta, Monisha. 2006. *Unruly Immigrants: Rights, Activism, and Transnational South Asian Politics in the United States.* Durham, N.C.: Duke University Press.

Davé, Shilpa, Pawan Dhingra, and Sunaina Maira, et al. 2000. "De-Privileging Positions: Indian Americans, South Asian Americans, and the Politics of Asian American Studies." *Journal of Asian American Studies* 3(1): 67–100.

Davis, Angela. 1996. "Gender, Class, and Multiculturalism: Rethinking 'Race' Politics." In *Mapping Multiculturalism,* edited by Avery Gordon and Christopher Newfield, 40–48. Minneapolis: University of Minnesota Press.

Dawson, Michael. 1994. *Behind the Mule: Race and Class in African American Politics.* Chicago: University of Chicago Press.

DeSipio, Louis. 2003. *Immigrant Politics at Home and Abroad: How Latino Immigrants Engage the Politics of Their Home Communities and the United States.* Claremont, Calif.: Tomás Rivera Policy Institute.

———. 2006. "Do Home-Country Political Ties Limit Latino Immigrant Pursuit of U.S. Civic Engagement and Citizenship?" In *Transforming Politics, Transforming America: The Political and Civic Incorporation of Immigrants in the United States,* edited by Taeku Lee, Karthick Ramakrishnan, and Ricardo Ramírez, 106–26. Charlottesville: University of Virginia Press.

Dhingra, Pawan. 2012. *Life behind the Lobby: Indian American Motel Owners and the American Dream.* Stanford, Calif.: Stanford University Press.

D'Souza, Dinesh. 1995. *The End of Racism: The Principles for a Multiracial Society.* New York: Free Press Paperbacks.

Elliott, Andrea. 2003. "In Brooklyn, 9/11 Damage Continues." *New York Times,* June 7.

Erie, Steven P. 1988. *Rainbow's End.* Berkeley: University of California Press.

Espiritu, Yen Le. 1992. *Asian American Panethnicity: Bridging Institutions and Identities.* Philadelphia: Temple University Press.

Faist, Thomas. 2000. "Transnationalization in International Migration: Implications for the Study of Citizenship and Culture." *Ethnic and Racial Studies* 23(2): 189–222.

Fisher, Maxine. 1980. *The Indians of New York City: An Historical Overview.* New Delhi: Heritage Publishing.

Foner, Nancy. 2000. *From Ellis Island to JFK: New York's Two Great Waves of Immigration*. New Haven, Conn.: Yale University Press.

Friedman, Thomas L. 2007. *The World Is Flat: A Brief History of the Twenty-First Century*, 3rd ed. New York: Picador.

Gagg, Nikki. 2005. "Caste Out." *New Internationalist* 380. http://newint.org/features/2005/07/01/casteout/.

Gamm, Gerald H. 1989. *The Making of New Deal Democrats: Voting Behavior and Realignment in Boston, 1920–40*. Chicago: University of Chicago Press.

Gans, Herbert J. 1979. "Symbolic Ethnicity: The Future of Ethnic Groups and Culture in America." *Ethnic and Racial Studies* 2(1): 1–20.

Ghosh, Palash. 2013. "A New Bronx Tale: Bangladeshis Growing Presence In The Borough Creates Hope And Conflict." *International Business Times*, April 19.

Ghosh, Shamik. 2013. "Narendra Modi's 'Virtual' U.S. Tour: Hard Sells Gujarat, Slams Centre." *NDTV*, May 13. http://www.ndtv.com/article/india/narendra-modi-s-virtual-us-tour-hard-sells-gujarat-slams-centre-366102.

Gilroy, Paul. 1993. *The Black Atlantic: Modernity and Double Consciousness*. London: Verso.

———. 2002. *Against Race: Imagining Political Culture beyond the Color Line*. Cambridge, Mass.: Harvard University Press.

Glazer, Nathan. 1983. *Ethnic Dilemmas: 1964–1982*. Cambridge, Mass.: Harvard University Press.

Glazer, Nathan, and Daniel P. Moynihan. 1970. *Beyond the Melting Pot: The Negroes, Puerto Ricans, Jews, Italians, and Irish of New York City*, 2nd ed. Cambridge, Mass.: MIT Press.

Goldman, Adam, and Matt Apuzo. 2012. "NYPD: Muslim Spying Led to No Leads, Terror Cases." *Associated Press*, August 12. http://www.ap.org/Content/AP-In-The-News/2012/NYPD-Muslim-spying-led-to-no-leads-terror-cases.

Goldring, Luin. 1996. "Gendered Memory: Constructions of Rurality among Mexican Transnational Migrants." In *Creating the Countryside: The Politics of Rural and Environmental Discourse*, edited by E. M. DuPuis and Peter Vendergeest, 301–29. Philadelphia: Temple University Press.

Goldstein, Joseph. 2014. "New York Police Recruit Muslims to Be Informers." *New York Times*, May 10.

Goodstein, Laurie, and Gustav Niebuhr. 2001. "After the Attacks: Retaliation; Attacks and Harassment of Arab-Americans increase." *New York Times*, September 14.

Gopinath, Gayatri. 2005. *Impossible Desires: Queer Diasporas and South Asian Public Cultures*. Calcutta: Seagull Books.

Gordon, Milton, M. 1964. *Assimilation in American Life: The Role of Race, Religion, and National Origins*. New York: Oxford University Press.

Graham, Pamela M. 1997. "Reimagining the Nation and Defining the District: Dominican Migration and Transnational Politics." In *Caribbean Circuits: New Directions in the Study of Caribbean Migration*, edited by Patricia Pessar, 91–126. New York: Center for Migration Studies.

———. 2001. "Political Incorporation and Reincorporation: Simultaneity in the Dominican Migrant Experience." In *Migration, Transnationalization, and Race in a Changing New York*, edited by Hector Cordeero-Guzman, Robert C. Smith, and Ramon Grossfuguel, 87–108. Philadelphia: Temple University Press.

Guarnizo, Luis Eduardo. 1997. "The Emergence of a Transnational Social Formation and the Mirage of Return Migration among Dominican Transmigrants." *Identities* 4(2): 281–322.

Guarnizo, Luis Eduardo, and Alejandro Portes. 1991. "Tropical Capitalists: U.S.-bound Immigration and Small Enterprise Development in the Dominican Republic." In *Migration, Remittances and Small Business Development*, edited by Sergio Diaz-Briquets and Sidney Weintraub, 37–59. Boulder, Colo.: Westview.

Guarnizo, Luis Eduardo, Alejandro Portes, and William Haller. 2003. "Assimilation and Transnationalism: Determinants of Transnational Political Action among Contemporary Migrants." *American Journal of Sociology* 108(6): 1211–48.

Guarnizo, Luis Eduardo, and Michael Peter Smith. 1998. "The Location of Transnationalism." In *Transnationalsim from Below*, edited by Michael Peter Smith and Luis Eduardo Guarnizo, 3–34. New Brunswick, N.J.: Transaction.

Gupta, Akhil. 1992. "The Song of the Non-Aligned World: Transnational Identities and the Reinscription of Space in Late Capitalism." *Cultural Anthropology* 7(1): 63–77.

Gutmann, Amy. 1994. "Introduction." In *Multiculturalism: Examining The Politics of Recognition*, edited by Amy Gutmann, 3–24. Princeton, N.J.: Princeton University Press.

Hall, Stuart. 1990. "Cultural Identity and Diaspora." In *Identity: Community, Culture, and Difference*, edited by Jonathan Rutherford, 222–37. London: Lawrence and Wishart.

Han, June. 2006. *"We are Americans Too": A Comparative Study of the Effects of 9/11 on South Asian Communities*. Discrimination and National Security Initiative Report. Cambridge, Mass.: Pluralism Project, Harvard University.

Hancock, Ange-Marie. 2007. "When Multiplication Doesn't Equal Quick Addition: Examining Intersectionality As a Research Paradigm." *Perspectives on Politics* 5(1): 63–79.

Handlin, Oscar. 1951. *The Uprooted: The Epic Story of the Great Migrations That Made the American People.* Boston: Little, Brown.

Haney-López, Ian. 2006. *White By Law: The Legal Construction of Race.* New York: New York University Press.

———. 2010. "Post-Racial Racism: Racial Stratification and Mass Incarceration in the Age of Obama." *California Law Review* 98(3): 1023–74.

Hero, Rodney. 1992. *Latinos and the U.S. Political System: Two-Tiered Pluralism.* Philadelphia: Temple University Press.

High Level Committee on Indian Diaspora. 2002. *Report of the High Level Committee on Indian Diaspora (Executive Summary).* http://www.indiandiaspora.nic.in/contents.htm.

*The Hindoo Question in California.* 1908. *Proceedings of the Asiatic Exclusion League.* San Francisco, Calif., February.

Hing, Bill Ong. 1993. *Making and Remaking Asian America through Immigration Policy.* Stanford, Calif.: Stanford University Press.

Hochschild, Jennifer. 1981. *What Is Fair? American Belief about Distributive Justice.* Cambridge, Mass.: Harvard University Press.

Hochschild, Jennifer, and John Mollenkopf, eds. 2009a. *Bringing Outsiders In: Transatlantic Perspectives on Immigrant Political Incorporation.* Ithaca, N.Y.: Cornell University Press.

———. 2009b. "Modeling Immigrant Political Incorporation." In *Bringing Outsiders In: Transatlantic Perspectives on Immigrant Political Incorporation,* edited by Jennifer Hochschild and John Mollenkopf, 15–32. Ithaca, N.Y.: Cornell University Press.

Hoefer, Michael, Nancy Rytina, and Bryan Baker. 2012. *Estimates of the Unauthorized Immigrant Population Residing in the United States: January 2011.* U.S. Department of Homeland Security. https://www.dhs.gov/sites/default/files/publications/ois_ill_pe_2011.pdf.

*Human Rights Watch.* 1999. *"Politics by Other Means: Attacks against Christians in India."* Vol. 11(6C).

Huntington, Samuel. 1997. "The Erosion of American National Interests." *Foreign Affairs* 76(5): 28–49.

———. 2004. *Who Are We? The Challenges to America's National Identity.* New York: Simon and Schuster.

Institute of International Education. 2015. "Open Doors Data." http://www.iie.org/Research-and-Publications/Open-Doors/Data/International-Students/All-Places-of-Origin/2012-14.

Iyer, Deepa. 2011. "Forum: What Did September 11 Do to the Concept of 'Asian America'?" *Asian American Literary Review* 2(1.5): 144–69.

Jacobson, Matthew Frye. 1995. *Special Sorrows: The Diasporic Imagination of Irish, Polish, and Jewish Immigrants in the United States.* Cambridge, Mass.: Harvard University Press.

———. 1998. *Whiteness of a Different Color: European Immigrants and the Alchemy of Race.* Cambridge, Mass.: Harvard University Press.

Jensen, Joan M. 1988. *Passage from India: Asian Immigrants in North America.* New Haven, Conn.: Yale University Press.

Jones, J. 2006. "Indo-American Lobby for Nuclear Deal." *Inside Bay Area,* July 10.

Jones-Correa, Michael. 1998. *Between Two Nations: The Political Predicament of Latinos in New York City.* Ithaca, N.Y.: Cornell University Press.

Joshi, Khyati. 2006. *New Roots in America's Sacred Ground: Religion, Race and Ethnicity.* New Brunswick, N.J.: Rutgers University Press.

Junn, Jane. 1999. "Participation in a Liberal Democracy: The Political Assimilation of Immigrants and Ethnic Minorities in the United States." *American Behavioral Scientist* 42(9): 1417–38.

Kalita, S. Mitra. 2014. "The New Smithsonian Exhibit on Indian Americans Is Great—If Only It Were 1985." *Quartz.* http://qz.com/181481/the-new-smithsonian-exhibit-on-indian-americans-is-great-if-only-it-were-1985/.

Kamdar, Mira. 2007. "Forget the Israel Lobby: The Hill's Next Big Player Is Made in India." *Washington Post,* September 30.

Kapur, Devesh. 2003. "Indian Diaspora As Strategic Asset." *Economic and Political Weekly* 38(5): 445–48.

———. 2010. *Diaspora, Development, and Democracy: The Domestic Impact of International Migration from India.* Princeton, N.J.: Princeton University Press.

Karpathakis, Anna. 1999. "Home Society Politics and Immigrant Political Incorporation: The Case of Greek Immigrants in New York City." *International Migration Review* 33(1): 55–79.

Kelkar, Kamala. 2015. "Entry to India: How to Switch from PIO to OCI." *Wall Street Journal (India Real Time Blog),* March 16.

Kerkhoff, Kathinka S., and Ellen Bal. 2003. "'Eternal Call of the Ganga': Reconnecting with People of Indian Origin in Surinam." *Economic and Political Weekly* 38(38): 4008–21.

Kershaw, Sarah. 2001. "Queens to Detroit: A Bangladeshi Passage." *New York Times,* March 8.

Kibria, Nazli. 1998. "The Racial Gap: South Asian American Racial Identity and the Asian American Movement." In *A Part, Yet Apart,* edited by Lavina Dhingra-Shankar and Rajini Srikanth, 69–78. Philadelphia: Temple University Press.

———. 2007. "South Asia: Pakistan, Bangladesh, Sri Lanka, Nepal." In *The New Americans: A Guide to Immigration Since 1965,* edited by Mary C. Waters and Reed Ueda, 612–23. Cambridge, Mass.: Harvard University Press.

———. 2011. *Muslims in Motion: Islam and National Identity in the Bangladeshi Diaspora.* New Brunswick, N.J.: Rutgers University Press.

Kim, Claire J. 1999. "The Racial Triangulation of Asian Americans." *Politics and Society* 27(1): 105–38.

———. 2004. "Imagining Race and Nation in Multicultural America." *Ethnic and Racial Studies* 27(6): 987–1005.

Kim, Claire J., and Taeku Lee. 2001. "Interracial Politics: Asian Americans and Other Communities of Color." *PS: Political Science and Politics* 34(3): 631–37.

Kitano, Harry H. L., and Roger Daniels. 1995. *Asian Americans: Emerging Minorities*, 2nd ed. Englewood Cliffs, N.J.: Prentice Hall.

Koshy, Susan. 1998. "Category Crisis: South Asian Americans and Questions of Race and Ethnicity." *Diaspora: A Journal of Transnational Studies* 7(3): 285–320.

Kramer, Sarah K. 2011. "NYC Has No South Asian Elected Officials. Why?" *WNYC Radio.* May 24. http://www.wnyc.org/articles/its-free-country/2011/may/24/why-no-south-asian-elected-official-nys/.

Kumar, Arun. 2006. "Indian American Physicians and Hoteliers Lobby for N-Deal." *India eNews,* July 10. http://www.dnaindia.com/world/report-indian-americans-lobby-for-n-deal-1040724.

Kumar, Vivek. 2003. "Dalit Movement and Dalit International Conferences." *Economic and Political Weekly* 38(27): 2799.

———. 2004. "Understanding Dalit Diaspora." *Economic and Political Weekly* 39(1): 114–16.

Kurien, Prema. 2003. "To Be or Not To Be South Asian: Contemporary Indian American Politics." *Journal of Asian American Studies* 6(3): 261–88.

———. 2006. "Multiculturalism and 'American' Religion: The Case of Hindu Indian American." *Social Forces* 85(2): 723–41.

———. 2007a. *A Place at the Multicultural Table: The Development of an American Hinduism.* New Brunswick, N.J.: Rutgers University Press.

———. 2007b. "Who Speaks for Indian Americans? Religion, Ethnicity, and Political Formation." *American Quarterly* 59(3): 759–83.

Kymlicka, Will. 1995. *Multicultural Citizenship.* Oxford: Oxford University Press.

Kymlicka, Will, and Wayne Norman. 1994. "Return of the Citizen: A Survey of Recent Work on Citizenship Theory." *Ethics* 104(2): 352–81.

La Ganga, Maria L. 2012. "FBI documents reveal profiling of N. California Muslims." *Los Angeles Times,* March 28.

Lahiri, Jhumpa. 2004. *The Namesake.* New York: Mariner Books.

Lai, James, and Don T. Nakanishi. 2007. *National Asian Pacific American Almanac, 2007–2008,* 13th ed. Los Angeles, Calif.: UCLA Asian American Studies Center Press.

Lai, James, Wendy K. Tom Cho, Thomas P. Kim, and Okiyashi Takeda. 2001. "Asian Pacific American Campaigns, Elections, and Elected Officials." *PS: Political Science and Politics* 34(3): 611–17.

Lakshman, Narayan. 2013. "South Asian LGBTQ Groups Protest Section 377 Decision." *The Hindu,* December 17.

———. 2015. "Work Permits for Spouses of H-1B Visa Holders." *The Hindu,* February 26.

Lal, Prerna. 2014. "'Beyond Bollywood' but Perhaps Not Beyond the White Gaze." *Race Files.* http://www.racefiles.com/2014/03/19/beyond-bollywood -but-perhaps-not-beyond-the-white-gaze/.

Lal, Vinay. 1996. "Sikh Kirpans in California Schools: The Social Construction of Symbols, Legal Pluralism, and the Politics of Diversity." *Amerasia Journal* 22(1): 57–89.

———. 2008. *The Other Indians: A Political and Cultural History of South Asians in America.* Los Angeles, Calif.: Asian American Studies Center Press, UCLA.

Lall, M. 2001. *India's Missed Opportunity: India's Relationship with Non Resident Indians.* Aldershot, U.K.: Ashgate.

Landolt, Patricia. 2001. "Salvadoran Economic Transnationalism: Embedded Strategies for Household Maintenance and Immigrant Incorporation." *Global Networks,* July 1.

Leavitt, Jacqueline, and Gary Blasi. 2009. "The Los Angeles Taxi Workers Alliance." UCTC Research Paper 893. University of California Transportation Center, UC Berkeley. http://www.uctc.net/research/papers/893.pdf.

Lee, Taeku. 2014. "2014 Midterms: Patterns and Paradoxes in Voting Among Asian Americans." *Brookings.* http://www.brookings.edu/blogs/fixgov/posts /2014/10/29-2014-midterms-asian-american-voting-patterns-lee.

Lee, Taeku, and S. Karthick Ramakrishnan. 2012. "Asian Americans Turn Democratic." *Los Angeles Times,* November 23.

Leonard, Karen Isaksen. 1992. *Making Ethnic Choices: California's Punjabi Mexican Americans.* Philadelphia: Temple University Press.

———. 1997. *The South Asian Americans.* Westport, Conn.: Greenwood Press.

———. 2005a. "Asian Indian Americans." In *Multiculturalism in the United States: A Comparative Guide to Acculturation and Ethnicity,* edited by John D. Buenker and Lorman Ratner, 65–78. Santa Barbara, Calif.: Greenwood Publishing Group.

———. 2005b. "American Muslims and Authority: Competing Discourses in a Non-Muslim State." *Journal of American Ethnic History* 25(1): 5–30.

Levi, Michael, and Charles Ferguson. 2006. *U.S.–India Nuclear Cooperation: A Strategy for Moving Forward.* Council Special Report No. 16. New York: Council on Foreign Relations, June.

Levitt, Peggy. 2001. *The Transnational Villagers.* Berkeley: University of California Press.

Lichtblau, Eric. 2008. "Inquiry Targeted 2,000 Foreign Muslims in 2004." *New York Times,* October 30.

Lien, Pei-te. 2001. *The Making of Asian Americans through Political Participation.* Philadelphia: Temple University Press.

Lien, Pei-te, M. Margaret Conway, and Janelle Wong. 2004. *The Politics of Asian Americans: Diversity and Community.* New York: Routledge.

Light, Ivan, and Edna Bonacich. 1988. *Immigrant Entrepreneurs: Koreans in Los Angeles, 1965–1982.* Berkeley: University of California Press.

Lindblom, Charles. 1980. *The Policy-Making Process,* 2nd ed. Englewood Cliffs, N.J.: Prentice-Hall.

MacFarquhar, Neil. 2007. "Protest Greets Police Plan to Map Muslim Angelenos." *New York Times,* November 9.

Mandhana, Niharika. 2014. "U.S. Rights Group Files Lawsuit against Narendra Modi." *Wall Street Journal,* September 26.

Mann, James. 2014 "Why Narendra Modi Was Banned from the U.S." *Wall Street Journal,* May 12.

Marriott, Michel. 1987. "In Jersey City, Indians Protest Violence." *New York Times,* October 12.

Masouka, Natalie. 2006. "Together They Become One: Examining the Predictors of Panethnic Group Consciousness Among Asian Americans and Latinos." *Social Science Quarterly* 87(5): 993–1011.

Mastuda, Mary. 1993. "We Will Not Be Used." *UCLA Asian American Pacific Islands Law Journal* 1: 79–84.

Mathew, Biju. 2005. *Taxi: Cabs and Capitalism in New York City.* New York: New Press.

Mathew, Biju, and Vijay Prashad. 2000. "The Protean Form of Yankee Hindutva." *Ethnic and Racial Studies* 3(3): 516–34.

Mazumdar, Sucheta. 1989. "Race and Racism: South Asians in the United States." In *Frontiers of Asian American Studies,* edited by Gail Nomura et al., 25–38. Washington: Washington State University Press.

———. 2003. "The Politics of Religion and National Origin: Rediscovering Hindu Indian Identity in the United States." In *Antinomies of Modernity: Essays on Race, Orient, and Nation,* edited by Vasant Kaiwar and Sucheta Mazumdar, 223–60. Durham, N.C.: Duke University Press.

McIntire, M. 2006. "Indian-Americans Test Their Clout on Atom Pact." *New York Times,* June 5.

Mearsheimer, John, and Stephen M. Walt. 2007. *The Israel Lobby and U.S. Foreign Policy.* New York: Farrar, Straus and Giroux.

Mehra, Achal. 2008. "The Indian American Bundlers." *Little India,* January.

Min, Pyong Gap. 1995. "Korean Americans." In *Asian Americans: Contemporary Trends and Issues,* edited by Pyong Gap Min, 199–231. Thousand Oaks, Calif.: Sage Publications.

Ministry of Overseas Indian Affairs. 2007. *Compendium on Policies, Incentives and Investment Opportunities for Overseas Indians.* New Delhi.

Minnite, Lorraine C. 2009. "Lost in Translation? A Critical Reappraisal of the Concept of Immigrant Political Incorporation." In *Bringing Outsiders In: Transatlantic Perspectives on Immigrant Political Incorporation,* edited by Jennifer Hochschild and John Mollenkopf, 48–59. Ithaca, N.Y.: Cornell University Press.

Mishra, Sangay. 2009. "The Limits of Transnational Mobilization: The Indian American Lobby Groups and the India-U.S. Civil Nuclear Deal." In *The Transnational Politics of Asian Americans,* edited by Christian Collet and Pei-te Lien, 107–18. Philadelphia: Temple University Press.

———. 2012. "Oak Creek: Legacies of Racism and the Road Ahead." *Hyphen: Asian America Unabridged.* http://www.hyphenmagazine.com/blog/archive/2012/08/oak-creek-legacies-racism-and-road-ahead.

Mishra, Sangay, and Jinee Lokaneeta. 2012. "Suspicion and Trust in Community/Policing: A Study of Muslims in Post-9/11 United States." APSA Annual Meeting Paper. http://papers.ssrn.com/sol3/papers.cfm?abstract_id=2107938.

Mohanty, Chandra Talpade. 1993. "On Race and Voice: Challenges for Liberal Education in the 1990s." In *Beyond a Dream Deferred: Multicultural Education and the Politics of Excellence,* edited by Becky Thompson and Sangeeta Tyagi, 41–65. Minneapolis: University of Minnesota Press.

Mollenkopf, John, David Olson, and Tim Ross. 2001. "Immigrant Political Participation in New York and Los Angeles." In *Governing Cities,* edited by Michael Jones-Correa, 17–70. New York: The Russell Sage Foundation.

Moore, Joan, and Harry P. Pachon. 1985. *Hispanics in the United States.* Englewood Cliffs, N.J.: Prentice-Hall.

Motwani, Jagat. 2003. *America and India: In a "Give and Take" Relationship: Social-Psychology of Asian Indian Immigrants.* New York: Center for Asian, African and Caribbean Studies.

Mukhi, Sunita. 2011. "Forum: What Did September 11 Do to the Concept of 'Asian America'?" *Asian American Literary Review* 2(1.5): 144–69.

Murti, Lata. 2012. "Who Benefits from the White Coat: Gender Differences in Occupational Citizenship among Asian-Indian Doctors." *Ethnic and Racial Studies* 35(12): 2035–53.

Nagel, Joane. 1986. "The Political Construction of Ethnicity." In *Competitive Ethnic Relations,* edited by Susan Olzak and Joane Nagel, 93–112. San Diego: Academic Press.

Najam, Adil. 2006. *Portrait of a Giving Community: Philanthropy by the Pakistani-American Diaspora.* Cambridge, Mass.: Global Equity Initiative, Asia Center, Harvard University.

Nakanishi, Don T. 1991. "The Next Swing Vote? Asian Pacific Americans and California Politics." In *Racial and Ethnic Politics in California,* edited by

Bryan O. Jackson and Michael Preston, 25–54. Berkeley: Institute of Governmental Studies Press, University of California.

Nanda, Tanmaya Kumar. 2001. "Sikhs Become Target of Ire in New York." *Rediff News*, September 12.

National Asian American Survey. 2008. http://www.icpsr.umich.edu/icpsr web/RCMD/studies/31481.

———. 2012. "National Voter Turnout in Federal Elections: 1960–2008." http://www.infoplease.com/ipa/A0781453.html.

National Coalition for Asian Pacific American Community Development. 2013. *Spotlight: Asian American and Pacific Islander Poverty*. Washington, D.C.

Newhouse, John. 2009. "Diplomacy, Inc.: The Influence of Lobbies on U.S. Foreign Policy." *Foreign Affairs*, May/June.

Newland, Kathleen, and Hiroyuki Tanaka. 2010. *Mobilizing Diaspora Entrepreneurship for Development*. Washington, D.C.: Migration Policy Institute.

New York City Commission on Human Rights. 2003. *Discrimination Against Muslims, Arabs, and South Asians in New York City Since 9/11*. New York City Commission on Human Rights. http://www.nyc.gov/html/cchr/pdf/sur _report.pdf.

"Obama Camp Attacks Hillary's Indian links." 2007. *India Abroad*. www.rediff .com/news/2007/jun/15clinton.htm.

"Obama Sorry for Hillary Memo." 2007. *Newser*. www.newser.com/story/3248 /obama-sorry-for-hillary-memo.html.

Office of the Inspector General. 2003. *The September 11 Detainees: A Review of the Treatment of Aliens Held on Immigration Charges in Connection with the Investigation of the September 11 Attacks*. Washington, D.C.: Office of the Inspector General, U.S. Department of Justice.

Okamoto, Dina G. 2006. "Institutional Panethnicity: Boundary Formation in Asian American Organizing." *Social Forces* 85(1): 1–25.

Okihiro, Gary. 1994. *Margins and Mainstreams: Asians in American History and Culture*. Seattle: University of Washington Press.

Omi, Michael, and Howard Winant. 1994. *Racial Formation in the United States: From the 1960s to the 1990s*. New York: Routledge.

Ong, Aihwa. 1999. *Flexible Citizenship: The Cultural Logics of Transnationality*. Durham, N.C.: Duke University Press.

Ostergaad-Nielsen, Eva. 2003. "The Politics of Migrants' Transnational Political Practices." *International Migration Review* 37(3): 760–86.

Padilla, Felix M. 1985. *Latino Ethnic Consciousness: The Case of Mexican Americans and Puerto Ricans in Chicago*. Notre Dame, Ind.: Notre Dame University Press.

Pandya, Haresh. 2013. "American Republicans Visit Modi in Gujarat." *New York Times,* March 28.

Park, Jerry. 2008. "Second Generation Asian American Pan-Ethnic Identity: Pluralized Meanings of Racial Labels." *Sociological Perspectives* 51(3): 541–61.

Park, Robert E., and Ernest W. Burgess. 1969. *Introduction to the Science of Sociology.* Chicago: University of Chicago Press.

Passel, J. 2005 "Unauthorized Migrants: Numbers and Characteristics." *Pew Hispanic Center.* http://pewhispanic.org/files/reports/46.pdf.

Perlmann, J., and R. Waldinger. 1997. "Second Generation Decline? Children of Immigrants, Past and Present: A Reconsideration." *International Migration Review* 31(4): 893–922.

Pew Research Center. 2012a. *The Rise of Asian Americans.* Pew Research Center. http://www.pewsocialtrends.org.

———. 2012b. *Asian Americans: A Mosaic of Faiths.* Pew Research Center. http://www.pewforum.org/2012/07/19/asian-americans-a-mosaic-of-faiths -overview.

———. 2015. *Unauthorized Immigrants: Who They Are and What the Public Thinks.* Pew Research Center. http://www.pewresearch.org/key-data-points /immigration/.

Pilot National Asian American Political Survey 2000–2001. http://www.icpsr .umich.edu/icpsrweb/RCMD/studies/3832.

Pinderhughes, Diane. 1987. *Race and Ethnicity in Chicago Politics: A Reexamination of Pluralist Theory.* Urbana: University of Illinois Press.

Portes, Alejandro. 1984. "The Rise of Ethnicity: Determinants of Ethnic Perception among Cuban Exiles in Miami." *American Sociological Review* 49(3): 383–97.

Portes, Alejandro, Luis Guarnizo, and Patricia Landholt. 1999. "The Study of Transnationalism: Pitfalls and Promise of an Emergent Field." *Ethnic and Racial Studies* 22(2): 217–37.

Portes, Alejandro, and Ruben G. Rumbaut. 2001. *Legacies: The Story of the Immigrant Second Generation.* Berkeley, Calif.: University of California Press.

———. 1996. *Immigrant America: A Portrait,* 2nd ed. Berkeley: University of California Press.

Portes, Alejandro, and Alex Stepick. 1993. *City on the Edge: The Transformation of Miami.* Berkeley: University of California Press.

Portes, Alejandro, and Min Zhou. 1993. "The New Second Generation: Segmented Assimilation and Its Variants." *Annals of the American Academy of Political and Social Science* 530: 74–96.

Prashad, Vijay. 1998. "Crafting Solidarities." In *A Part, Yet Apart: South Asians in Asian America,* edited by Lavina Dhingra Shankar and Rajini Srikanth, 105–26. Philadelphia: Temple University Press.

———. 2000. *Karma of Brown Folk*. Minneapolis: University of Minnesota Press.

———. 2005. "How Hindus Became Jews: American Racism after 9/11." *The South Asian Quarterly* 104(3): 583–606.

———. 2012. *Uncle Swami: South Asians in America Today*. New York: New Press.

———. 2013. "Yankee Hindutva." *Frontline*, May 3.

Rahman, Shafiqur. 2011. *The Bangladeshi Diaspora in the United States after 9/11: From Obscurity to High Visibility*. El Paso, Tx.: LFB Scholarly Publishing.

Railey, Kimberly. 2015. "Indian-American Donors Rally to Elect More Indian-Americans to Congress." *National Journal*, April 19.

Rajagopal, Arvind. 2000. "Hindu Nationalism in the U.S.: Changing Configuration of Political Practice." *Ethnic and Racial Studies* 23(3): 467–96.

Ramakrishnan, S. Karthick. 2005. *Democracy in Immigrant America: Changing Demographics and Political Participation*. Stanford, Calif.: Stanford University Press.

———. 2013. "Incorporation versus Assimilation: The Need for Conceptual Difference." In *Outsiders No More: Models of Immigrant Political Incorporation*, edited by Jennifer Hochschild, Jacqueline Chattopadhya, Caludine Gay, and Michael Jones-Correa, 27–42. New York: Oxford University Press.

Ramakrishnan, S. Karthick, Jane Junn, Taeku Lee, and Janelle Wong. 2012. National Asian American Survey, 2008 [Computer file]. ICPSR 31481-v2. Ann Arbor, Mich.: Inter-university Consortium for Political and Social Research [distributor], 2012–07–19. doi:10.3886/ICPSR31481.v2.

Ramirez, Ricardo, and Luis Fraga. 2008. "Continuity and Change: Latino Political Incorporation in California Since 1990." In *Racial and Ethnic Politics in California*, vol. 3, edited by Bruce Cain, Jamie Regalado, and Sandra Bass, 61–93. Berkeley, Calif.: Berkeley Public Policy Press.

Ramnath, Maia. 2011. *Haj to Utopia: How the Ghadar Movement Charted Global Radicalism and Attempted to Overthrow the British Empire*. Berkeley: University of California Press.

Rana, Junaid. 2011. *Terrifying Muslims: Race and Labor in the South Asian Diaspora*. Durham, N.C.: Duke University Press.

Reza, H. G. 2006. "On Behalf of Muslims, ACLU Seeks Surveillance Data." *Los Angeles Times*, May 16.

Rodriguez, Gregory. 1998. "Minority Leader." *The New Republic*, October 19.

Roediger, David R. 2005. *Working Towards Whiteness: How America's Immigrants Became White: The Strange Journey from Ellis Island to the Suburbs*. New York: Basic Books.

Rogers, Reuel. 2006. *Afro-Caribbean Immigrants and the Politics of Incorporation: Ethnicity, Exception, or Exit.* New York: Cambridge University Press.

Rosenstone, Steven J., and John Mark Hansen. 1993. *Mobilization, Participation, and Democracy in America.* New York: Macmillan.

Rumbaut, Ruben G. 1995. "Vietnamese, Laotian, and Cambodian Americans." In *Asian Americans: Contemporary Trends and Issues,* edited by Pyong Gap Min. Thousand Oaks, Calif.: Sage Publications.

SAALT. 2001. "American Backlash: Terrorists Bring War Home In More Ways Than One." http://saalt.electricembers.net/wp-content/uploads/2012/09/American-Backlash-Terrorist-Bring-War-Home-in-More-Ways-Than-One.pdf.

———. 2012. *A Demographic Snapshot of South Asians in the United States.* South Asian Americans Leading Together and Asian American Federation, SAALT.org.

———. 2015. "Meet the NCSO." South Asian Americans Leading Together. http://saalt.org/the-coalition/meet-the-ncso/.

Saad, Shaik. 2012. "NY Rally and Vigil on Gujarat Riots 10th Anniversary." *Muslim Observer,* March 8.

Sabrang Communications. 2002. "The Foreign Exchange of Hate: IDRF and the American Funding of Hindutva." Mumbai, India: Sabrang Communications.

Sands, D. 2006. "Nuclear Pact Unifies Indian Americans: Well-to-Do Minority 'Galvanized' by Opportunity for Improved Ties." *Washington Times,* April 9.

Saxenian, AnnaLee. 2002. *Local and Global Networks of Immigrant Professionals in Silicon Valley.* San Francisco, Calif.: Public Policy Institute of California.

———. 2005. "From Brain Drain to Brain Circulation: Transnational Communities and Regional Upgrading in India and China." *Studies in Comparative International Development* 40(2): 35–61.

Schiller, N., L. Basch, and C. Blanc-Szanton. 1992. *Towards a Transnational Perspective on Migration: Race, Class, Ethnicity, and Nationalism Reconsidered.* New York: New York Academy of Sciences.

Schlesinger, Arthur M., Jr. 1992. *The Disuniting of America: Reflections on a Multicultural Society.* New York: W. W. Norton.

Schmidt, Ronald, Sr., Rodney L. Hero, Andrew L. Aoki, Yuvette M. Alex-Assensoh, eds. 2009. *Newcomers, Outsiders, and Insiders: Immigrant and American Racial Politics in the Early Twenty-First Century.* Ann Arbor: University of Michigan Press.

Sejersen, Tanja B. 2008. "'I Vow To Thee My Countries': The Expansion of Dual Citizenship in the 21st Century." *International Migration Review* 42(3): 523–49.

"Senate Prayer led by Hindu Elicits Protest." 2007. *Washington Post,* July 13.

Sengupta, Somini. 2000. "Settlement Reached in Maid's Suit against Diplomat." *New York Times,* July 15.

———. 2001. "Arabs and Muslims Steer through an Unsettling Scrutiny." *New York Times,* September 13.

Shah, Svati. 2014. "Who Was Protesting Modi's Madison Square Garden Speech Anyway?" *The Caravan,* October 17.

Shaheen, Jack. 2009. *Reel Bad Arabs: How Hollywood Vilifies a People.* Northampton, Mass.: Olive Branch Press.

Shain, Y. 1999. *Marketing the American Creed Abroad: Diasporas in the U.S. and Their Homelands.* New York: Cambridge University Press.

Shankar, Lavina Dhingra, and Rajini Srikanth, eds. 1998. *A Part, Yet Apart: South Asians in Asian America.* Philadelphia: Temple University Press.

Shefter, Martin. 1986. "Political Incorporation and the Exclusion of the Left: Party Politics and Social Forces in the New York City." *Studies in American Political Development* 1/Spring: 50–90.

Shukla, Aseem. 2009. "Obama Lights White House Diwali Lamp." *Washington Post,* October 15.

Shukla, Sandhya. 2003. *India Abroad: Diasporic Cultures of Postwar America and England.* Princeton, N.J.: Princeton University Press.

Singh, Amardeep (for Human Rights Watch). 2002. *"We Are Not The Enemy": Hate Crimes Against Arabs, Muslims, and those Perceived to be Arab or Muslim after September 11.* New York: Human Rights Watch Publications.

Singh, Sonny. 2011. "Healing the Trauma of Post-9/11 Racism One Story (and Melody) at a Time." *Left Turn,* September 11. http://www.leftturn.org/Sonny-Sept11-testimony.

Sisler, Vit. 2008. "Digital Arabs: Representation in Video Games." *European Journal of Cultural Studies* 11(2): 203–20.

Skerry, Peter. 1993. *Mexican Americans: An Ambivalent Minority.* Cambridge, Mass.: Harvard University Press.

Skocpol, Theda. 1999. "How Americans Became Civic." In *Civic Engagement in American Democracy,* edited by Theda Skocpol and Morris P. Fiorina, 27–80. Washington, D.C.: Brookings Institution Press, Russell Sage Foundation.

Smith, Michael P. 1994. "Can You Imagine? Transnational Migration and the Globalization of Grassroots Politics." *Social Text* 39(Summer): 15–33.

Smith, Neil. 2005. "Neo-Critical Geography, or the Flat Pluralist World of Business Class." *Antipode* 37(5): 887–99.

Smith, Robert. 2003. "Migrant Membership as an Instituted Process: Transnationalism, the State and the Extraterritorial Conduct of Mexican Politics." *International Migration Review* 37(2): 297–343.

Smith, Robert, and Eduardo L. Guarnizo. 1998. *Transnationalism from Below: Communities Identities Unbound*. New Brunswick, N.J.: Transaction.

Smith, Tony. 2000. *Foreign Attachments: The Power of Ethnic Groups in the Making of American Foreign Policy*. Cambridge, Mass.: Harvard University Press.

Sonenshein, Raphael J. 1993. *Politics in Black and White: Race and Power in Los Angeles*. Princeton, N.J.: Princeton University Press.

Soundarrajan, Thenmozhi. 2012. "The Black Indians: Growing up Dalit in the US, Finding Your Roots, Fighting for Your Identity." *Outlook,* August 20.

Soysal, Yasemin Nuhoglu. 1994. *Limits of Citizenship: Migrants and Postnational Membership in Europe*. Chicago: University of Chicago Press.

Srinivasan, Ragini. 2014. "True Stories: An Exhibition on Indian Americans Strives to Present the Community's Story on Its Own Terms." *The Caravan,* May.

Stancati, Margherita. 2012. "U.S. Legislators Say No to Modi." *Wall Street Journal,* December 5.

Stevanovic, Natacha. 2012. *Remittances and Moral Economies of Bangladeshi New York Immigrants in Light of the Economic Crisis*. PhD Dissertation, Columbia University.

Suárez-Orozco, Carola, and Marcelo Suárez-Orozco. 2001. *Children of Immigration*. Cambridge, Mass.: Harvard University Press.

Swarns, Rachel. 2003. "More Than 13,000 May Face Deportation." *New York Times,* June 7.

Takaki, Ronald. 1998. *Strangers from a Different Shore: A History of Asian Americans*. Boston: Little, Brown.

Tate, Katherine. 1994. *From Protest to Politics: The New Black Voters in American Elections*. Cambridge, Mass.: Harvard University Press.

Taylor, Charles. 1994. "The Politics of Recognition." In *Multiculturalism: Examining the Politics of Recognition,* edited by Amy Gutmann, 25–74. Princeton, N.J.: Princeton University Press.

Tichenor, Daniel. 2002. *Dividing Lines: The Politics of Immigration Control in America*. Princeton, N.J.: Princeton University Press.

Toyota, Tritia. 2010. *Envisioning America: New Chinese Americans and the Politics of Belonging*. Palo Alto, Calif.: Stanford University Press.

Tuan, Mia. 1998. *Forever Foreigners or Honorary Whites? The Asian Ethnic Experience Today*. New Brunswick, N.J.: Rutgers University Press.

Tung, Larry. 2011. "A Decade after 9/11, Little Pakistan Bounces Back." *Gotham Gazette,* September 9.

Uhlaner, Carole J., Bruce Cain, and D. Roderick Kiewiet. 1989. "Political Participation of Ethnic Minorities in the 1980s." *Political Behavior* 11(3): 195–231.

Upadhya, Carol. 2004. "A New Transnational Capitalist Class? Capital Flows, Business Networks and Entrepreneurs in the Indian Software Industry." *Economic and Political Weekly* 39(48): 5141–51.

U.S. Census Bureau. 2006. "American Community Survey, 2006." http://www.census.gov/prod/2006pubs/acs.

———. 2007. "American Community Survey, 2007." http://www.census.gov/prod/2007pubs/acs-05.pdf.

———. 2009–2011. "2009–2011 American Community Survey." https://catalog.data.gov/dataset/2009-2011-american-community-survey-3-year-estimates-summary-file.

———. 2010. "American Community Survey." http://factfinder2.census.gov/faces/tableservices/jsf/pages/productview.xhtml?pid=DEC_00_SF1_QTP7&prodType=table.

———. 2012. "Asian American Heritage Month: May 2012." Profile America: Facts For Features. http://www.census.gov/newsroom/releases/archives/facts_for_features_special_editions/cb12-ff09.html.

U.S. Department of Homeland Security. 2006. *Estimates of the Unauthorized Immigrant Population Residing in the United States.* Washington, D.C.: U.S. Department of Homeland Security, Office of Immigration Statistics.

———. 2007. *Yearbook of Immigration Statistics: 2006.* Washington, D.C.: U.S. Department of Homeland Security, Office of Immigration Statistics.

Vaidyanathan, Siddhartha. 2011. "For Sikhs in New York, a Decade of Progress Since 9/11 Backlash." *Wall Street Journal,* September 9.

Varadarajan, Tunku. 1999. "A Patel Motel Cartel?" *New York Times,* July 4.

Varghese, Linta. 2006. "Constructing a Worker Identity: Class, Experience, and Organizing in Workers' *Awaaz.*" *Cultural Dynamics* 18(2): 189–211.

Venugopal, Arun. 2010. "South Asian LGBT Community Marches in India Day Parade." *WNYC News,* August 16.

Verba, Sidney, and Norman H. Nie. 1972. *Participation in America: Political Democracy and Social Equality.* New York: Harper and Row.

Verba, Sidney, Kay Lehman Schlozman, and Henry E. Brady. 1995. *Voice and Equality: Civic Voluntarism in American Politics.* Cambridge, Mass.: Harvard University Press.

Vertovec, S. 1999. "Conceiving and Researching Transnationalism." *Ethnic and Racial Studies* 22(2): 447–62.

Visweswaran, Kamala. 1997. "Diaspora by Design: Flexible Citizenship and South Asians in U.S. Racial Formation." *Diaspora* 6(1): 5–29.

Vitello, Paul. 2007. "Mayor Symbolizes Indian-Americans' Rise." *New York Times,* August 1.

Volpp, Leti. 2002. "Citizen and Terrorists." *UCLA Law Review* 49: 1575–1600.

Waldinger, Roger. 2001. *Strangers at the Gate: New Immigrants in Urban America*. Berkeley: University of California Press.

Walters, Ronald W. 1988. *Black Presidential Politics in America: A Strategic Approach*. Albany: State University of New York Press.

Watanabe, Paul. 1999. "Asian American Activism and U.S. Foreign Policy." In *Across the Pacific: Asian Americans and Globalization*, edited by Evelyn Hu-Dehart. Philadelphia: Temple University Press.

Waters, Mary. 1999. *Black Identities: West Indian Immigrant Dreams and American Realities*. Cambridge, Mass.: Harvard University Press.

Wattenberg, Martin P. 1994. *The Decline of American Political Parties, 1952–1992*. Cambridge, Mass.: Harvard University Press.

———. 2001. *The Rise of Candidate-Centered Politics*. Cambridge, Mass.: Harvard University Press.

Wise, Tim. 2013. *Colorblind: The Rise of Post-Racial Politics and the Retreat from Racial Equity*. San Francisco, Calif.: City Lights Books.

Wolf, Susan. 1994. "Comments." In *Multiculturalism: Examining the Politics of Recognition*, edited by Amy Gutmann, 75–86. Princeton, N.J.: Princeton University Press.

Wong, Janelle. 2002. "Thinking about Immigrant Political Incorporation." Paper presented at Workshop on Immigrant Political Incorporation, Mobilization, and Participation. Maxwell School of Syracuse University, December 6.

———. 2006. *Democracy's Promise: Immigrants and American Civic Institutions*. Ann Arbor: University of Michigan Press.

Wong, Janelle, S. Karthick Ramakrishnan, Taeku Lee, and Jane Junn. 2011. *Asian American Political Participation: Emerging Constituents and their Political Identities*. New York: Russell Sage Foundation.

Wuthnow, Robert. 2005. *America and the Challenges of Religious Diversity*. Princeton, N.J.: Princeton University Press.

Young, Iris Marion. 1990. *Justice and the Politics of Difference*. Princeton, N.J.: Princeton University Press.

Zhou, Min. 1997. "Segmented Assimilation: Issues, Controversies, and Recent Research on the New Second Generation." *International Migration Review* 31(4): 825–58.

———. 2004. "The Role of the Enclave Economy in Immigrant Adaptation and Community Building: The Case of New York's Chinatown." In *Immigrant and Minority Entrepreneurship: Building American Communities*, edited by John Sibley Butler and George Kozmetsky, 37–60. Westport, Conn.: Praeger.

# Index

AABEA. *See* American Association of
Bangladeshi Engineers and
Architects

AAHOA. *See* Asian American Hotel
Owners Association

AALDEF. *See* Asian American Legal
Defense and Educational Fund

AAPI. *See* American Association of
Physicians of Indian Origin

Abraham, Thomas, 186

Absconder Apprehension Initiative,
86, 87

Adhikar, 140

African Americans, 6; boycotts of
Korean businesses, 44; civil rights
movement, 27, 52; intermarriage,
22; Latinos and, 61–62, 66;
Muslims, 78; political incorporation
of, 9, 52, 53, 58–59, 60–61, 67–68,
208; political representation, 124;
South Asian connections to, 22–23

agricultural worker provision, 6, 27,
29, 32–33, 47

AHAD. *See* American Hindus against
Defamation

Ahmad, Muneer, 81

AIA. *See* Associations of Indians in
America

AIANA. *See* Association for Indian
Americans of North America

AIPAC. *See* American Israel Public
Affairs Committee

Airborne Early Warning Surveillance
Systems (AWACKS), 185–86

Alam, Nahar, 146

Alba, Richard, 58–59

Alien Tort Claims Act (1789), 204

Alikhan, Arif, 105

al Qaeda, 85–86

American Association of Bangladeshi
Engineers and Architects
(AABEA), 136

American Association of Physicians
of Indian Origin (AAPI), 11, 35,
187

American Federation of Muslims of
Indian Origin (AMFI), 199

American Hindus against Defamation
(AHAD), 103

American Israel Public Affairs
Committee (AIPAC), 132

American Justice Center, 204

AMFI. *See* American Federation of
Muslims of Indian Origin

Anderson, Benedict, 155

Andolan, 140, 145–47, 213

anti-miscegenation laws, 24

Appiah, Kwame Anthony, 77

APPNA. *See* Association of Physicians
of Pakistani Descent of North
America

APSE-NA. *See* Association of
Pakistani Scientists and Engineers
of North America

Asian American Hotel Owners Association (AAHOA), 30, 136, 187, 200, 201
Asian American Legal Defense and Educational Fund (AALDEF), 145–46
*Asian American Literary Review* (journal), 100
Asian Americans, 38–48; census categories, 38, 227n29; demographics, 39–40; ethnic enclaves, 58; income levels, 39–40; perceived as foreign, 62; political participation data, 161; voting patterns, 45–46. *See also* South Asian Americans (Desis); specific ethnicities; specific religious groups
Asian Indian census category, 227n27
Asiatic Barred Zone Act (1917), 23
Asiatic Exclusion League, 20–21
assimilation: framework, 57, 165, 176, 228–29n4; pluralist model, 9, 56–60, 64, 66; political incorporation and, 9, 49–52, 59; segmented assimilation theory, 50–52
Association for Indian Americans of North America (AIANA), 201
Association of Indian Muslims of America, 199
Association of Pakistani Scientists and Engineers of North America (APSE-NA), 136
Association of Physicians of Pakistani Descent of North America (APPNA), 11, 135–36
Associations of Indians in America (AIA), 138, 227n29
Atwal, Gurmej, 71
Awaaz. *See* Workers' Awaaz

AWACKS. *See* Airborne Early Warning Surveillance Systems
Ayodhya Temple Movement, 192, 194

Bajrang Dal, 193
Bakhna, Sohan Singh, 23
Bald, Vivek, 22
Bangladeshi Americans, 21–22, 33–34, 34–38, 47, 79, 166, 169–70
Baretto, Matt, 124
belonging, 165–71
Beltran, Cristina, 67, 208–9
Bera, Ami, 41, 123
"Beyond Bollywood" (Smithsonian exhibition), 2–3
Bharadwaj, Ram Chandra, 207
Bharatiya Janata Party (BJP), 192–93, 198–99, 200, 201, 216
Bhojwani, Sayu, 234n11
Bhuyian, Rais, 81
*bindi*, 97
BJP. *See* Bharatiya Janata Party
Booker, Cory, 1
BPO. *See* Business Processing Outsourcing
Browning, Rufus P., 53–54, 59
Bush, George W., 123, 184, 187
Business Processing Outsourcing (BPO), 177

CAAV. *See* Coalition Against Anti-Asian Violence
CAG. *See* Coalition Against Genocide
CAIR. *See* Council of American Islamic Relations
California Alien Land Law (1913), 24
campaign contributions, 125–33, 210, 211–12
Campaign to Stop Funding Hate (CSFH), 195–96

caste: Brahmin, 72; business networks, 30; Dalit, 31, 175, 198, 226n19; divisions, 8, 31; identity, 226n18, 235n28
CDC. *See* Chhaya
Center for Responsive Politics, 128
Chadha, J. B., 146
Chadha, Manjit, 146
Chawla, Amrik Singh, 90
Chhaya (CDC), 140
Chin, Vincent, 75, 95
Chinese Americans, 41–42
Chinese Exclusion Act (1882), 21
Cho, Wendy K. Tam, 127–28
Chopra, Aneesh, 105
Christianity, 1, 5, 45–46, 78, 125, 192, 193, 198
citizenship: eligibility for, 25, 182, 224nn6–7; exclusions, 2, 20, 23–24, 62, 230n10; flexible, 181; by national origin, 110; political participation and, 39, 57, 160
civil rights movement, U.S., 27, 52
Clinton, Bill, 2
Clinton, Hillary, 126, 202
Coalition Against Anti-Asian Violence (CAAV), 141
Coalition Against Genocide (CAG), 198–99, 201–2
Cohen, Cathy, 67–68, 208
Communist Party of India, 190
Coney Island Avenue Project, 99
Congressional Pakistan Caucus, 139
Council of American Islamic Relations (CAIR), 5
Council of Peoples Organization (COPO), 99
Crenshaw, Kimberlé, 68, 208
CSFH. *See* Campaign to Stop Funding Hate

Dahl, Robert, 57–58, 63
Dalits, 31, 175, 198, 226n19
Das, Taraknath, 23
Das Gupta, Monisha, 29
Dayal, Har, 23
Department of Justice, U.S. (DOJ), 85–86
Desai, Bhairavi, 4, 141
*Desis,* use of term, 6. *See also* South Asian Americans (Desis)
Desis Rising Up and Moving (DRUM), 99, 140, 147–48, 213
diaspora: economic liberalization and, 177–78; foreign investment and, 181–83; queerness and, 175; transnationalism and, 173, 174–76, 195
Diversity Visa (1990), 6, 28, 32–33, 35, 226n22
*Diwali* festival, 101
Domestic Workers' Committee (DWC), 145
Domestic Workers United (DWU), 11, 146–49
Donnelly, Joe, 1
Draper International, 180
DRUM. *See* Desis Rising Up and Moving
DWC. *See* Domestic Workers' Committee
DWU. *See* Domestic Workers United

Ellison, Keith, 202
Espiritu, Yen Le, 75
ethnoracial mobilization, 9–12, 56, 59–60, 63, 66, 69–70, 106–7, 116–17, 209–10; elite, 117–35, 139, 152–53, 183–84, 188–91, 210–12; lobbying and, 133–34; nation-of-origin organizations, 138–40; occupational ethnic organizations, 135–38, 209;

47–48, 78, 229n4; organizations, 101–2, 233n40; political party affiliation, 46; political representation, 215; post-9/11 targeting, 72, 80–83, 89, 96–98, 214; racialization of, 81–82; stereotypical representations, 101–3

Hindu Education Foundation, 101–2

Hinduism, 101–2

Hindu Student Council (HSC), 194

Hindu Swayamsewak Sangh (HSS), 194

*Hindutva* (nationalist politics), 173, 175; countermobilization to, 195–205; emergence of, 191–95, 205, 215–16, 232n30

Hing, Bill Ong, 19

HLC. *See* High Level Committee (HLC) on Indian Diaspora

Hochschild, Jennifer, 55

Honda, Mike, 123, 215–16

H-1B visas, 28, 179

hotel ownership, 29–30, 241n29

House Congressional Caucus on India and Indian Americans, 138

HSC. *See* Hindu Student Council

HSS. *See* Hindu Swayamsewak Sangh

IAFPE. *See* Indian American Forum for Political Education

IAMC. *See* Indian American Muslim Council

IASLC. *See* Indian American Security Leadership Council

ICE. *See* Immigration and Customs Enforcement, U.S.

identity: dual, 165–71; Indian American, 2–3; racialization and, 7–8, 73–78, 208, 214; South Asian American, 7, 79–80, 97, 99, 134, 137, 207, 209, 213, 217. *See also* panethnic identity; religious identity

IDRF. *See* India Development and Relief Fund

immigrant labor: Punjabi, 20–21; unions, 4, 140–41

Immigration Act (1990), 28

Immigration and Customs Enforcement, U.S. (ICE), 86

Immigration and National Act (1965), 26–29, 32, 200; family reunification provision, 6, 26, 29–30, 32, 33, 35, 42, 47, 228n32

immigration policy, 3–4, 6, 19, 26. *See also specific acts*

Immigration Reform and Control Act (1986), 29, 32–33, 35; agricultural worker provision, 6, 27, 29, 32–33, 47

INA. *See* Immigration and National Act (1965)

inclusion, 29–30; diversity and, 8; elite mobilization, 211–12; identity-based, 60, 207; political, 3–4, 5, 8–9, 38–39, 48, 49, 50, 59, 63, 217, 228n3; racial hierarchy and, 122. *See also* political incorporation

India Development and Relief Fund (IDRF), 196, 240n18

Indian American Community Foundation, 203

Indian American Forum for Political Education (IAFPE), 138

Indian American Muslim Council (IAMC), 199, 202

Indian Americans: campaign contributions, 127–32, 211–12; caste divisions, 31; census categories, 38; citizenship rates, 110; diversity, 28–29; host county/home country impact, 167, 206; hotel ownership, 29–30, 241n29; identity, 2–3; immigration waves, 28–32;

Malhotra, Rajiv, 97
Maloney, Carolyn B., 122
Manavi, 140, 143–44
Marshall, Dale Rogers, 53–54, 59
Masouka, Natalie, 75–76
Mathur, Rakesh, 179
Mendendez, Bob, 1
*Mississippi Masala* (Nair film), 31
model minority discourse, 6, 65–66, 143
Modi, Narendra Bhai, 1, 192, 193, 195, 200–204
Mollenkopf, John, 55
Motwani, Jagat, 186
Mukhi, Sunita, 100
multiculturalism: authenticity and, 101–4; concept of, 76–78; panethnic mobilization and, 100–101; vs. racism, 77, 103, 104
Murthy, Vivek, 105
Muslim Americans: African American, 78; Bangladeshi immigrants, 47, 79; Bengali immigrants, 22, 26; doctors, profiling of, 135–36; Indian immigrants, 47; Pakistani immigrants, 21, 47, 79; phenotype, 81; political party affiliation, 46; population statistics, 78; post-9/11 targeting, 7–8, 10, 11, 33–34, 48, 69, 71–73, 80–84, 87–88, 89, 91, 97–100, 135–36; racialization and law enforcement, 86–89; surveillance of, 33–34, 86–89; violence against, 1, 193, 200
Muslim Peace Coalition, 202

Nair, Mira, 31
National Alliance for Domestic Workers, 213
National Asian American Survey (NAAS), 13, 109–11, 156–59, 171

National Coalition of South Asian Organizations (NCSAO), 213
National Employment Labor Project (NELP), 145–46
National Federation of Indian Americans (NFIA), 138, 186
National Security Entry-Exit Registration System (NSEERS), 33–34, 86–87
National Taxi Workers Alliance, 142
naturalization rates, 24, 25–26, 39, 44, 47, 62, 110, 111, 160, 163–65, 171
NCSAO. *See* National Coalition of South Asian Organizations
Nee, Victor, 58–59
NELP. *See* National Employment Labor Project
Newhouse, John, 139
New York City Human Rights Commission, 93
New York Construction Workers United (NYCWU), 148
New York Police Department (NYPD), 87, 93
New York State Domestic Bill of Rights, 213
New York Taxi Workers Alliance (NYTWA), 11, 44, 99, 140, 141–42, 212–13, 214
*New York Times* (newspaper), 121–22, 123
New York University Immigrant Law Clinic, 145–46
NFIA. *See* National Federation of Indian Americans
Non-Resident (External) Rupee Account, 178
Non-Resident Indian (NRI) investment, 180
NSEERS. *See* National Security Entry-Exit Registration System

Nuclear Nonproliferation Treaty
(NPT), 183
NYCWU. *See* New York Construction
Workers United
NYPD. *See* New York Police
Department
NYTWA. *See* New York Taxi Workers
Alliance

Obama, Barack, 45, 101, 105, 126,
128–29, 130–31, 203, 212
OCI card. *See* Overseas Citizens of
India (OCI) card
Okamoto, Dina G., 76
Ong, Aihwa, 181
Operation Front Line, 86
outsourcing, 176–77
Overseas Citizens of India (OCI) card,
182

Pacific Coast Hindi Association
(PCHA), 23
Pacific Islanders, 2, 36, 38, 227n29
Pakistani American Public Affairs
Committee (PAKPAC), 129, 138,
139, 216–17
Pakistani Americans, 21, 32–34, 72,
127, 135–36, 139
panethnicity: identity, 7, 19, 37, 43,
72–80, 95, 98–100, 204, 213, 214;
mobilization, 10, 75, 78, 100, 103–4,
214
Park, Jerry, 101
*Part, Yet Apart, A* (Shankar/Srikanth,
eds.), 38
Patel, Vasudev, 80–81
PATRIOT Act (2001), 85
PBD. *See* Pravasi Bharatiya Divas
PCHA. *See* Pacific Coast Hindi
Association
Pen, Kal, 105

Pentagon Twin Tower Bombing
Investigation (PENTTBOM), 85
Person of Indian Origin (PIO) card,
182
Pew Research Center, 31, 46, 47–48
Pilot Study of the National Asian
American Political Survey
(PNAAPS), 13, 109–10, 156–57,
159–64, 171
Pinderhughes, Diane, 60
PIO card. *See* Person of Indian Origin
(PIO) card
Pitts, Joe, 202
pluralism: model of political incorporation, 9, 56–60, 62–63, 64, 66, 170;
two-tiered, 61
Pluralism Project (Harvard University), 91
PNAAPS. *See* Pilot Study of the
National Asian American Political
Survey
political fund-raising. *See* campaign
contributions
political incorporation: of African
Americans, 9, 52, 53, 58–59, 60–61,
67–68, 208; assimilation and, 9,
49–52, 59; concept of, 8–9, 49–51,
53, 69; economic strength and,
125–33; elements of, 55; elite
mobilization in, 117–35, 183–84,
188–91, 211–12; ethnoracial
mobilization, 9–12, 56, 59–60,
63, 66, 69–70, 106–7, 116–17, 209;
group identity and, 54; of Jewish
Americans, 133–34; of Latinos,
53, 54–55, 59, 61–62, 107, 115, 208;
models, 9, 55–70, 207–8, 228n2;
pluralist model, 9, 56–60, 62–63,
64, 66, 170; political parties and,
63–64, 112–13; racialization model,
9, 60–63; skin color and, 59; of

South Asian Americans, 4, 5, 9–12,
15, 65, 106, 112–13, 117–25, 152–53,
170–71, 209–10, 217; transnationalism and, 55, 64–65, 164; trends in,
106; urban politics and, 53–55
political participation: citizenship
and, 39, 57, 160; ethnic group
distribution, 109–10; ethnoracial
identity and, 10, 63; home country
attachment and, 155–56, 167, 169,
171, 188, 189, 206; impacts on, 41,
47, 60, 66, 105–6, 171; political
parties and, 112–17; racial hierarchy
and, 3; of South Asian Americans,
10, 66, 105–13, 115, 125, 129, 156–65,
171; transnationalism and, 39, 47,
64, 155, 156–57, 159–65
political parties: ethnic organizations
and, 170–71; Hindu American
affiliation, 46; Indian American
affiliation, 45; Muslim American
affiliation, 46; political incorporation and, 63–64, 112–13; political
participation and, 112–17
political representation, 4–5, 41, 45,
105, 106, 117–25, 211, 212, 215
Portes, Alejandro, 58
postracial, use of term, 234n17
Prashad, Vijay, 97, 176
Pravasi Bharatiya Divas (PBD),
182–83
Punjabi migrants, 20–21
Puri, Sanjay, 188

racialization: identity and, 7–8, 73–78,
208, 214; mobilization against
targeting, 60–63, 95; model of
political incorporation, 9;
multiculturalism and, 100–101;
Muslim, and law enforcement,
85–89; of South Asian Americans,

81–82. *See also* South Asian
Americans: post-9/11 targeting
racism, 20, 23; following 9/11, 7–8, 10,
13, 65, 81, 103; homogenization
through, 67; in immigration
policies, 27; institutionalized, 93;
mobilization against, 20, 95, 99;
multiculturalism vs., 77, 103, 104;
in political incorporation, 60
Ramakrishnan, Karthick, 50, 52, 107
Ramirez, Ricardo, 54
Ramnath, Maia, 23
Randhawa, Nikki Haley. *See* Haley,
Nikki
Rashtriya Swayamsewak Sangh (RSS),
192, 196
refugee visas, 6
religious identity: antiracism and, 103;
diversity in, 7, 43, 48, 76, 208;
mobilization patterns and, 11, 66,
215–16; multiculturalism and,
101–4; post-9/11 targeting, 7–8, 10,
11, 33–34, 48, 69, 71–73, 80, 81–82,
98–100, 103, 104, 214; racialization
and, 214; transnationalism and, 48,
96. *See also specific religious groups*
Restaurant Opportunities Centers
(ROC), 11, 214
Rice, Condoleezza, 187
ROC. *See* Restaurant Opportunities
Centers
Rodgers, Cathy, 202
Rogers, Reuel, 54, 155–56
Rove, Karl, 187
RSS. *See* Rashtriya Swayamsewak
Sangh
Rumbaut, Ruben G., 58

SAALT. *See* South Asian Americans
Leading Together
SABA. *See* South Asian Bar Association

SAJA. *See* South Asian Journalist
  Association
Sakhi, 140, 143–44
SALDEF. *See* Sikh American Legal
  Defense Fund
SALGA. *See* South Asian Lesbian and
  Gay Association
SAN. *See* South Asian Network
SAPHA. *See* South Asian Public
  Health Association
Satrang, 140
Saund, Dalip Singh, 25–26, 123
Sawant, Kshama, 4
Saxenian, AnnaLee, 179
SAYA. *See* South Asian Youth
  Association
Schock, Aaron, 202
Schumer, Chuck, 1
Senate India Caucus, 138
September 11, 2001 terrorist attacks,
  86–89. *See also* South Asian
  Americans: post-9/11 targeting
sexual orientation, 8, 140, 148
Shah, Rajiv, 105
Shah, Svati, 203
Sikh American Legal Defense Fund
  (SALDEF), 5, 91–92
Sikh Americans: immigrants, 20–21,
  47; intermarriage, 26; mobilization
  and, 11; post-9/11 targeting of, 65,
  71, 89–95, 97–98, 214–15
Sikh Coalition, 5
Singh, Attar, 90
Singh, J. J., 25
Singh, Sher, 90
Singh, Sonny, 92
Singh, Surinder, 71
Skerry, Peter, 58
Smithsonian Institution, 2
social justice, politics of, 140–51, 212
Sodhi, Balbir Singh, 65, 80, 90

Soundarrajan, Thenmozhi, 175
South Asian Americans (Desis):
  campaign contributions, 125–33;
  diversity, 7, 8, 19, 28–29, 43, 48,
  78–80; early migrants, attacks on,
  20; ethnic categories, 38, 223n1,
  233n1; family visas, 29; group
  distinctions, 10, 19–20; as honorary
  whites, 65; identity formation, 7,
  79–80, 99, 134, 137, 207, 209, 213,
  217; immigration waves, 3–5, 14,
  20–26, 28, 224n9; invisibility of, 2,
  4; model minority discourse, 6,
  65–66, 143; naturalization rates, 39,
  110, 111, 171; panethnic identity, 7,
  19, 37, 43, 72–80, 95, 98–100, 204,
  213, 214; political incorporation of,
  4, 5, 9–12, 15, 65, 106, 112–13, 117–25,
  152–53, 170–71, 209–10, 217; political
  participation of, 10, 66, 105–13, 115,
  125, 129, 156–65, 171; political
  representation, 4–5, 41, 45, 105,
  106, 117–25, 133, 211; population
  statistics, 4, 6, 13–15, 25, 35–37, 40;
  post-9/11 targeting, 7–8, 10, 11, 13,
  33–34, 46, 48, 65–66, 69, 72–74, 78,
  80–84, 89, 95, 98–100, 103, 104,
  214–15; racialization of, 81–82;
  socioeconomic diversity, 6–7, 9–10;
  stereotypical representations, 101–2;
  use of term, 6, 38; voting patterns,
  5, 45–46; women, 8, 102, 143–45,
  224n9. *See also specific ethnicities;
  specific religious groups*
South Asian Americans Leading
  Together (SAALT), 5, 80, 91–92,
  99–100, 149, 213, 214, 216–17
South Asian Bar Association (SABA),
  79–80, 137
South Asian Journalist Association
  (SAJA), 79–80, 137

**Sangay K. Mishra** is assistant professor of political science at Drew University.